Field Guide to

PRODUCE

How to Identify, Select, and Prepare Virtually Every Fruit and Vegetable at the Market

By Aliza Green

QUIRK BOOKS

PHILADELPHIA

DISCLAIMER

There are thousands of varieties of produce, and addressing all possible types is difficult. While we have taken care to represent a wide variety of those available, the author and publisher cannot be held responsible for not including them all.

Library of Congress Cataloging in Publication Number: 2003095961

ISBN: 1-931686-80-7

Printed in Singapore

Typeset in Adobe Garamond, Franklin Gothic, and Impact

Designed by Andrea Stephany and Karen Onorato
Edited by Erin Slonaker
Photography by Andrea Stephany

All photographs copyright © 2004 by Quirk Productions, Inc.

Distributed in North America by Chronicle Books
85 Second Street
San Francisco, CA 94105

10 9 8 7 6 5 4 3 2 1

Quirk Books
215 Church Street
Philadelphia, PA 19106
www.quirkbooks.com

Contents

viii *Introduction*

Field Guide to Produce

FRUITS

1   Apple
6   Apricot
8   Asian Pear
10 Banana and Plantain
13 Blackberry
16 Blueberry
18 Cactus Pear
20 Cherimoya
23 Cherry
25 Citron
27 Coconut
29 Cranberry
31 Currant
33 Date
35 Durian
36 Fig
38 Grape
40 Grapefruit and Pomelo
43 Guava
45 Kiwano
46 Kiwifruit

48	Kumquat
49	Lemon
52	Lime
54	Loquat
56	Lychee
58	Mango
60	Medlar
61	Melon (including American Cantaloupe, Honeydew Melon, and Watermelon)
	Nectarine (see Peach and Nectarine)
65	Orange
69	Papaya
71	Passion Fruit
73	Peach and Nectarine
77	Pear
81	Persimmon
84	Pineapple
	Plantain (see Banana and Plantain)
87	Plum
90	Pomegranate
	Pomelo (see Grapefruit and Pomelo)
93	Quince
95	Raspberry
97	Star Fruit
99	Strawberry
102	Tamarillo
104	Tamarind
106	Tangerine, Tangelo, and Tangor
	Watermelon (see Melon)

109   Yuzu

VEGETABLES

111   Amaranth
113   Artichoke and Cardoon
116   Arugula
119   Asparagus
121   Avocado
124   Bamboo Shoots
126   Beans, Green
128   Beans, Shell
132   Beet
136   Bok Choy
138   Broccoli
142   Burdock
        Brussels Sprouts (see Cabbage)
144   Cabbage
        Cardoon (see Artichoke and Cardoon)
147   Carrot
149   Cauliflower
152   Celery
155   Chayote
157   Chestnut
160   Chicory
163   Corn
166   Crosnes
168   Cucumber
171   Edamame
173   Eggplant

176   Endive
178   Fennel
181   Fiddlehead Fern
182   Garlic
185   Ginger
187   Greens, Cooking (including Collard, Dandelion, Kale, and Mustard Greens)
190   Horseradish
192   Jicama
194   Kohlrabi
196   Leek
198   Lettuce
201   Lotus Root
204   Mâche
205   Mushroom
212   Napa Cabbage
214   Nopales
216   Okra
218   Onion
222   Parsley Root
224   Parsnip
226   Peas
229   Pepper, Chile (including Anaheim, Cubanelle, Habanero, Jalapeño, Pasilla, Poblano, and Serrano Peppers)
235   Pepper, Sweet Bell
237   Potato
242   Radicchio
245   Radish
248   Ramp

250 Rhubarb
     Rutabaga (see Turnip and Rutabaga)
251 Salsify and Scorzonera
254 Samphire
256 Shallot
258 Spinach
260 Sprouts (including alfalfa and mung bean sprouts)
     Summer Squash (see Zucchini, Summer Squash, and
     Squash Blossoms)
262 Sunchoke
264 Sweet Potato
267 Swiss Chard
269 Taro and Yautia
272 Tomatillo and Ground Cherry
274 Tomato
278 Turnip and Rutabaga
280 Wasabi
282 Water Chestnut
285 Watercress
287 Winged Bean
288 Winter Squash (including Acorn, Buttercup, Butternut,
     Calabaza, Hubbard, Pumpkin, and Spaghetti Squashes)
293 Yard-Long Bean
295 Yuca
297 Zucchini, Summer Squash, and Squash Blossoms

301 *Sources*
302 *Index*
313 *Photo Credits*

Introduction

There's a whole world of wonderful produce in our food markets to discover and enjoy. Every year, the selection grows larger, the origins more exotic, and the choices more difficult. Here's a small, easy-to-carry book to guide you through the overwhelming array of available produce, whether common, exotic, heirloom, or ethnic. You will learn all about durian (a Southeast Asian fruit with a potent aroma that you will either adore or detest), yuca (a tasty Brazilian root vegetable), cardoon (a Mediterranean cousin of the artichoke), and many more.

Each entry gives the Latin name (important to help sort out the confusion), a little history, and alternate names. You'll learn when the produce is in season, how to identify the different varieties, how to choose the best, and storage and ripening tips. When describing the peak months for each produce item, I've indicated either the season in the primary growing region or the respective season in the Northern Hemisphere. Detailed preparation instructions, simple recipe ideas, and flavor affinities make it easy to buy and serve lots more vegetables and fruits. Turn to the photo section to help identify any unfamiliar produce or those that are not labeled.

I've combined my many years of hands-on experience as restaurant chef, mother (and home cook), caterer, food writer, and teacher with extensive research in order to cram as much information possible into this little book. While it would take a book the size of a grocery cart to describe all the produce sold in today's ever-changing, global food market, I have included as many fruits and vegetables as possible, along with accompanying accurate information.

Aliza Green

Fruits

APPLE

General
Description:

The apple (Malus pumila) *is a small round fruit with crunchy flesh.* This is one of the earliest fruits to have been cultivated, originating in Kazakhstan and carried by traders on the Silk Road. As early as the second century B.C., people were producing apples of a consistent variety by taking cuttings of a tree and grafting them onto suitable rootstock. This must be done because the exact same type of apple won't grow from a planted seed.

Immigrants to America brought apple seeds, which gave rise to entirely new varieties further diversified by breeding with native American crabapples. The spread of American apples was encouraged by the aptly monikered folk hero Johnny Appleseed, born John Chapman in Massachusetts in 1774, who collected large amounts of seeds from cider mills and planted them on his travels.

About 2,500 known varieties of apple are grown in the U.S. and more than 7,500 are grown worldwide—all of which must be picked by hand. Apple varieties are categorized as eating (or dessert), cooking (or baking), cider, and crab.

The **Braeburn** apple's color varies from orange to red over a yellow background. This New Zealand apple is aromatic, juicy, and crisp with a very firm texture. Braeburns are best for snacking and baking.

Cortland apples have very white flesh and are an excellent dessert apple. Their flavor is sweet, and their skin has a flush of crimson against a pale yellow background sprinkled with short, dark red stripes and gray-green dots.

Crabapples are quite tart, but they are excellent for making jellies because of their high pectin content. Apples qualify as crabapples only if the fruit size is 2 inches (5 cm) or less in diameter. Native American crabapples remain green even when ripe, but some hybrids and Asian varieties turn red, yellow, or purple when ripe.

Crispin, developed in the 1930s, doubles as a fresh apple and a processing apple. It is typically green outside and creamy white inside with firm-textured juicy flesh and moderately sweet flavor.

Empire combines the mild tartness of McIntosh with Red Delicious sweetness. It is redder and firmer than McIntosh, and because it stores longer it provides the marketplace with a McIntosh-type apple well into the spring. Some claim that storing improves Empire's flavor. It is excellent for eating out of hand and for use in baking and cooking.

The **Fuji** apple was introduced to the U.S. from Japan in the 1980s. The Fuji holds its texture well when baked, and it is known for its firm, crisp texture and tart-edged sweetness. Cool weather in the late fall helps develop its reddish-pink color and outstanding flavor.

The **Gala** apple has pinkish orange stripes over a yellow background and crisp, sweet, aromatic flesh.

with thin, tender, smooth greenish yellow skin.

Shinseiki have skin that is light greenish yellow and smooth. **Tsu Li** is an old and famous cultivar in China that is egg- to pear-shaped with skin that is light green to yellowish green and slightly bitter. **Ya Li** is another old cultivar and is pear-shaped with light greenish yellow, smooth skin.

Season: Asian pears are available July to late October from California, Washington, Oregon, Japan, and New Zealand. 20th century are in season from mid-August to early September; Hosui and Shinseiki from late July to mid-August.

Purchase: Look for hard Asian pears with a mild pear fragrance.

Avoid: Wrinkled or soft Asian pears are undesirable.

Storage: Store Asian pears for up to 4 weeks in a plastic bag in the refrigerator. Store at room temperature for up to 2 weeks.

Preparation:

1. **Wash under cool running water.**

2. **Peel, if desired, using a vegetable peeler or a knife.**

3. **Cut into wedges, cutting out and discarding the seeds and any hard flesh surrounding them.**

Serving
Suggestions:
Combine diced sweet onions, chopped watercress, and peeled, cut-up Asian pears with chicken stock, simmer till the pears are tender, then blend and season, adding cream prior to serving to make a soup. • Dress diced, cooked chicken with diced celery, sliced scallions, diced unpeeled Asian pears, and chopped cilantro with mayonnaise and curry powder to make a curried chicken salad. • Serve Asian pear wedges with a dip made from sesame paste, lemon juice, grated ginger, and honey.

Flavor
Affinities:
Almonds, Chinese five-spice powder, ginger, honey, lemon, pine nuts, sesame seeds, star anise.

4a–d.

BANANA AND PLANTAIN

General
Description:
Bananas (Musa paradisiaca *and* Musa sapientum) *are long, thin tropical fruits with pliable skin and soft, creamy flesh.* Bananas originated in Southeast Asia, where wild bananas were known as monkey bananas. They reached China, Africa, and the Pacific Islands about 2,000 years ago. The Arabs cultivated bananas but they remained unknown to Europeans until around 1400, when Portuguese sailors brought them from West Africa to the Canary Islands, where they are still an important crop. The Spanish brought banana roots to the New World in 1516 and they spread quickly throughout Latin America.

Modern bananas fall into two main categories: "sweet" or eating bananas, and cooking bananas, also called plantains. They grow in large bunches or "hands," which are formed from the double rows of female flowers on each plant. Each flower spike produces 50 to 300 individual fruits or "fingers."

Plantains start out starchy and hard and ripen to soft and sweet. In Spanish, green or starchy plantains are known as *plátanos*, partially ripe plantains are known as *pintos* (painted), and fully ripened black-spotted yellow plantains are known as *maduros* (mature). There are two groups of plantains, which probably have a common origin: the horn plantain and the French plantain.

There are hundreds of varieties of bananas, including the **burro** banana, which is 3 to 5 inches (8–13 cm) long with squared sides and a lemon flavor when ripe; the **Cavendish** banana, the most common in the U.S., with sweet smooth fruit and yellow skin; the **Guinea Verde**, a yellow Cavendish used as a starch much like plantains; the **Ice Cream** banana, with blue skin and a creamy texture; the **Macabu** banana, which turns black when fully ripe, with firm sweet pulp and a creamy texture; the **Manzano**, a short, chubby banana that is black when ripe and whose dry flesh has the flavors of strawberries, apples, and bananas; the **Niño** banana, a mild, sweet, finger-sized banana; and the **red** banana, 4 to 6 inches (10–15 cm) long with maroon to dark purple skin and sweet, sticky, orange-tinted flesh.

Season:

Bananas and plantains are available year-round.

Purchase:	Choose plump bananas with no green at their tips but flecked with tiny brown specks (a sign of ripeness). Choose plump, unshriveled plantains at any stage from green to black. When the plantain is ripe it will be dark brown or black, soft, and deep in color, with transparent rather than opaque flesh.
Avoid:	Mushy or damaged bananas and damaged plantains will be unappetizing.
Storage:	Store bananas at cool room temperature for 4 to 5 days, during which time they will continue to ripen. To hasten ripening, enclose bananas in a brown paper bag. Do not refrigerate, or they will turn black. Store plantains at room temperature for 4 to 5 days.
Preparation:	**Bananas:**

1. **Snap back the stem end and pull the peel away from the banana; a strip of the thick skin will come away easily. Pull off the remaining skin.**

2. **Remove the dark nub at the bottom end.**

3. **Cut away any mushy brown areas, if desired.**

Note: Cut bananas just before using, because they discolor quickly. Dip in a mixture of lemon juice and water to prevent darkening.

Plantains:

Peel as for bananas, above. If it is difficult to snap back the neck, slice off the stem and cut lengthwise slits in the skin through to the flesh to facilitate peeling.

Serving Suggestions:
Mash ripe bananas or plantains and add to bread pudding, pancake batter, muffin batter, or banana bread. • Deep-fry or broil Niño bananas and top with sour cream and caviar. • Add sliced bananas to cereal or fruit salads. • Purée bananas into smoothies with other tropical fruits. • Toss cut lengths of starchy plantains with oil or butter and roast in a hot oven. • Slice *pintos* diagonally into thick sections and pan-fry till golden brown, seasoning with spices such as sugar and cinnamon, or curry and lime.

Flavor Affinities:
Bananas and **ripe plantains:** Allspice, butter, cinnamon, cloves, coconut, ice cream, rum, sugar. **Starchy plantains:** bacon, chile peppers, cilantro, cumin, curry, garlic, lime, pork cracklings, salsa, sour orange.

5. **BLACKBERRY**

Other Names:
Bramble.

General Description:
Blackberries (Rubus fruticosus) *are large blue to purplish black multiple fruits.* The blackberry is the

largest of the wild berries and, like their close relatives raspberries (see page 95) and strawberries (see page 99), are actually clumps of individual fruits. They are oblong in shape and can grow up to 1½ inches (4 cm) long. They are tart in flavor and contain prominent seeds. Blackberries are excellent for both cooking and out-of-hand eating.

The **evergreen** blackberry is native to England, where it is known as the cutleaf or parsley-leafed blackberry. After a thornless evergreen was found and propagated in the 1920s, it became the most productive of all the commercially grown blackberries. The fruit is black, firm, and sweet. The seeds are quite large—its least desirable quality.

The **boysenberry** is probably a blackberry crossed with a loganberry (see below) and a red raspberry (see page 95). It was developed in the 1920s by Rudolph Boysen. This very large, reddish purple berry is quite tart and has prominent seeds.

Loganberries date from the 1880s, when James H. Logan of California inadvertently (but fortuitously) crossed two varieties of blackberry with an old variety of red raspberry. The loganberry, now grown mainly for juice, pies, and wine, also makes excellent jams and preserves. They are juicy and sweetly tart and turn purplish red when very ripe.

The **marionberry** is named after Marion County, Oregon, where it was tested extensively. The fruit is dark red to black, medium to large, and somewhat longer than wide, with medium seeds. Marionberries have excellent flavor with the taste of wild blackberries.

The **tayberry** is a cross of a blackberry, raspberry, and loganberry. It has large, sweet red fruit and was first grown at Tayside, Scotland.

Season: Blackberries are in peak season from June through September, though because of importation from areas south of the equator, they are available nearly year-round. Loganberries are in season in June and July. The short season of boysenberries and marionberries lasts from mid-July to mid-August.

Purchase: Look for plump berries with full, deep color, a bright, clean appearance, and firm, not hard, texture.

Avoid: Overripe berries are soft and may be moldy or leaky. If the hulls are still attached, the berries are immature and were picked too early; the flavor will be tart.

Storage: Blackberries are very perishable and are best used immediately. Refrigerate lightly covered and preferably in a single layer; use within 1 or 2 days. Do not wash until ready to use. Berries don't ripen after picking.

Preparation:

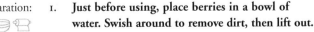

1. **Just before using, place berries in a bowl of water. Swish around to remove dirt, then lift out.**

2. **Gently pat dry with a paper towel.**

Serving
Suggestions:

Purée blackberries with a little sugar and serve raw as a dessert sauce for fruit tarts or ice cream. • Top blackberries with fresh cream, yogurt, or sour cream and brown sugar. • Make blackberry jams and preserves, adding tart apples to increase the pectin content.

Flavor
Affinities:

Cream, custard, lemon, lime, mint, pork, rose, sour cream, sugar, turkey, walnuts, white chocolate, yogurt.

6a–b.

BLUEBERRY

General
Description:

Blueberries are round, smooth-skinned, small individual fruits with juicy, sweet flesh. Blueberries and huckleberries are native to North America and have been used extensively since Colonial times.

Lowbush blueberries (*Vaccinium angustifolium*) grow only about 1 foot (30 cm) high and thrive in eastern Canada and Maine. These small, intensely flavored blueberries are often marketed as wild blueberries or huckleberries. More common **highbush blueberries** (*Vaccinium corymbosum*) grow up to 5 feet (1.5 m) tall with berries that are large and mild.

Huckleberries (*Gaylussacia baccata*) and blueberries grow in the same regions and are used in the same ways, but huckleberries are not commercially grown and must be picked in the wild. Blueberries are generally blue and have a large number of tiny soft seeds; huckleberries are generally black or purplish and have 10 larger, hard seeds.

European blueberries *(Vaccinium myrtillus)* originated in Eurasia. These tiny, dark bluish purple summer
berries are similar to small blueberries and are known as
whortleberries in North America and bilberries in Europe.

Season: Blueberries are in season locally in spring and summer;
due to imports they can be available year-round.

Purchase: Look for firm, large, plump, full-colored blueberries free
of moisture with few stems in dry, unstained containers.
Blueberries should be a deep, purple-blue to blue-black
color with a silver frost. Reddish berries are not ripe, but
may be used in cooking.

Avoid: Color is the best indicator of blueberry maturity and
flavor, so avoid blueberries that are green. Avoid dull,
lifeless, or mushy blueberries or berries with any mold.

Storage: Blueberries store in the refrigerator for 5 or 6 days, as
long as they are kept dry.

Preparation:

1. **Remove the blueberries from their container,
   spread out onto a shallow tray, and pick out any
   rotted or unformed berries as well as tiny stems.**

2. **Place the berries in a bowl of water, swish
   around to remove dirt, then lift out.**

3. **Blot the berries dry with a paper towel.**

Serving Suggestions:	Use blueberries in fresh fruit tarts, fruit salads, muffins, pies, and jams. • Combine washed blueberries with sugar and strained apricot jam or apple jelly, bring to a boil, and cook until thick, about 10 minutes, then cool to room temperature and spread onto a cold cheesecake.
Flavor Affinities:	Cinnamon, crème fraîche, ginger, lemon, mace, melons, nutmeg, orange, sour cream, walnuts, yogurt.

7. 📷   **CACTUS PEAR**

Other Names:	Barbary pear (Britain), Indian fig, Indian pear, nopal, prickly pear, sabra or Sharon fruit (Israel), tuna fig (Mexico).
General Description:	*Cactus pears are the egg-shaped fruits of numerous cacti of the genus* Opuntia. The prickly pear cactus is native to semiarid parts of the United States, Mexico, and Central and South America. Some of the earliest Spanish explorers took plants back to Spain, from where they spread throughout Sicily and North Africa. Cactus pears come in various colors corresponding to the colors of the plant's blossoms. The fruit has a stiff, spine-covered rind and is generally eaten fresh and raw. The flavor of a ripe cactus fruit depends on the variety but may resemble strawberry, watermelon, honeydew melon, fig, or banana. The best American varieties are the large purplish red **Cardona** and the yellow

Amarilla, which have relatively few spikes, pulpy flesh, and hard but edible seeds. In the Mediterranean region, the best cactus pears are pale yellow.

Season: In general, cactus pears ripen from early spring through late fall, depending on the variety.

Purchase: The perfect stage of ripeness of each fruit lasts only about 1 week. Choose firm, not hard, fruit.

Avoid: Avoid overly hard, mushy, or shriveled fruits.

Storage: Refrigerate cactus pears in plastic for up to 3 days.

Preparation: 1. **If necessary, remove the glochids (cactus spines) by passing the fruit through an open flame and pulling them out. Or, cut them away with a knife or carefully peel off the skin, preferably using gloves.**

2. **Slice off both ends of the fruit.**

3. **Make a shallow slit in the skin down the length of the pear and peel back, or cut the pear in half lengthwise and peel back the skin.**

Note: Because the fruit has no acidity, it tastes best when sprinkled with lemon or lime juice.

Serving Suggestions:	Simmer slices with water and sugar for 15 minutes or until tender, blend, strain, then chill—add a little lemon or lime juice to accent the cactus pear juice. • Combine 1 part each tequila, triple sec, cactus pear purée, and lime juice to make a margarita. • Combine cactus pear purée with vegetable oil, a little sugar, and white wine vinegar or cider vinegar to make a salad dressing.
Flavor Affinities:	Banana, honeydew melon, lemon, lime, orange, tequila, watermelon.

8.   **CHERIMOYA**

Other Names:	*Anone* (France), *chirimolla* (Venezuela), custard apple (Britain), *poox* (Mexico).
General Description:	*Cherimoya* (Annona cherimola) *is a large tropical fruit that tastes like a combination of pineapple, papaya, and banana.* Irregularly oval in shape, the cherimoya has a leathery green skin covered with a scaly pattern marked with overlapping indentations that resemble thumbprints. The flesh, peppered with large, shiny black seeds, is cream-colored and has the texture of firm custard.

The cherimoya is classified as an *Annona*, a genus of tropical fruit tree native to the Andean valleys of Ecuador, Peru, and Chile. Cherimoyas have been introduced to subtropical regions around the world. Because of their scarcity and the fact that the fruits must be individually harvested as they ripen, cherimoyas command high prices. Spain is the largest commercial producer of cherimoyas in the world.

The Annona family includes other, similar, fruits. The **sweetsop** *(Annona squamosa)* is egg-shaped with thick, coarse yellow-green skin that is sometimes tinged with purple, and yellow flesh with dark seeds. Its flesh is divided into citruslike segments. The **atemoya** *(Annona x atemoya)*, a cross between the cherimoya and sweetsop, is about the size of a large mango with tough dusty green skin that is covered with a scaly pattern. Its cream-colored custardlike pulp, which is full of large black seeds, has a delicate, sweet, mango-vanilla flavor. The **soursop** *(Annona muricata)*, which can weigh up to 15 pounds (5 kg), has spiky rather than knobby skin. Its flesh is whiter than the cherimoya and consists of numerous segments that are mostly seedless. When ripe, its flesh is soft with a rich aroma similar to pineapple. It is often extremely juicy and has more acid than its relations.

Season:

Cherimoyas are available late November through May from their chief growing regions, with peak season March through April. Atemoyas are in season from August to November. Sweetsops are grown in Florida and California and are available midsummer to midwinter, mostly locally. Soursops are available year-round.

Purchase:

Choose fruits that are firm, heavy for their size, and without skin blemishes. Buy atemoya when it's not quite ripe with pale green, unbroken skin. Ripe fruits will often split slightly at their stem end.

Avoid: Do not buy fruits with brown splotches or that have a fermented aroma.

Storage: To ripen, leave at room temperature to soften (they will give slightly with soft pressure). The skin may turn brown as the fruit ripens, which doesn't affect the flesh. Once ripe, the fruit can be refrigerated for up to 4 days, wrapped in a paper towel.

Preparation: **Note: Serve all these fruits well chilled.**

1. **Cut the fruit in half lengthwise and spoon out the flesh, discarding any big black seeds.**

2. **Dip cut fruit into lemon or orange juice to prevent darkening.**

Serving Suggestions: Freeze the fruit's flesh and eat like ice cream (sprinkle soursop with sugar to sweeten). • Combine soursop juice with milk or water and sugar, add ice, and serve chilled. • Make atemoya, cherimoya, or sweetsop sorbet by puréeing the flesh in a blender, combining with lime juice and honey, and freezing in an ice-cream maker.

Flavor Affinities: Heavy cream, kiwi, lemon, lime, mango, orange, passion fruit, pineapple, sour cream.

9a–b.

CHERRY

General
Description:

Cherries, both sweet (Prunus avium) *and sour* (Prunus cerasus), *are marble-sized stone fruits.* Cherries are native to the area near the Caspian Sea and the Balkans. First cultivated in the Middle East, both sweet and sour cherries have been cultivated in the Mediterranean for more than 2,000 years. The Anglo-Saxon word for cherry, *ciris*, was replaced in the 14th century by *cherise*, borrowed from the French. English speakers misinterpreted *cherise* as plural, and so the new singular "cherry" was coined.

Cherries grow wherever winter temperatures are not too severe and summer temperatures moderate. They require winter cold in order to blossom in early spring. The U.S. is the leading cherry producer, with Germany, Italy, France, and Switzerland the leaders in Europe. The three main types of cherries are sweet (red and white), sour, and sweet-sour (including **Dukes** or **Royales**, which are crosses of sweet and sour cherries).

The **Bing** cherry is the leading commercial sweet cherry in North America. Its fruit is firm, juicy, and a deep mahogany red when ripe. Bings are exceptionally large fruits with an intensely sweet vibrant flavor. **Oxhearts** are any of several varieties of cultivated large, heart-shaped, soft-fleshed sweet cherries. **Rainiers** have golden skin with a pink to red blush, clear flesh, very sweet, delicate flavor, and fine texture. **Sour** cherries are small, bright, and uniformly red with thin skins and are most often used for cooking, preserves, and pies.

Season:	Cherry season corresponds to warm months, depending on location. Generally, they are available from June to September.
Purchase:	Choose freshly picked cherries that have plump, crisp, green stems. Fresh red sweet cherries should be firm, plump, bright, and glossy, with a full red or purple color. (The deeper the color, the sweeter the taste.) When buying white cherries (like Rainiers) choose firm, unblemished ones with a blush of color. Look for firm, though not hard, sour cherries with even color.
Avoid:	Overmature cherries will be soft, dull, seeping, shriveled, or have brown bruised spots. Avoid cherries with dark and brittle stems.
Storage:	Cherries are highly perishable and should be sorted and refrigerated as soon as possible for 1 or 2 days. Wash cherries just before using.
Preparation:	1. **Rinse under cool water.**
	2. **To pit cherries, invest in a simple cherry pitter or slice the cherry from the stem all the way around to the stem again, then twist the two halves apart and remove the pit.**
Serving Suggestions:	Steep cherry pits in scalded milk overnight, then use the strained milk to make a cooked custard ice-cream base,

folding in pitted cherries near the end of freezing. • Add browned pitted sour cherries to demi-glace and pour over seared sliced duck breast. • Simmer sour cherries with red wine, sugar, cinnamon, and lemon zest, then strain and chill to make a syrup for topping ice cream or waffles.

Flavor Affinities: Almonds, chocolate, cinnamon, custard, duck, goose, kirsch, pork, red wine, sour cream, yogurt.

10a–b.

CITRON

General Description: *The citron* (Citrus medica) *looks like a large, rough-skinned lemon and is used mostly for preserves and candying.* The citron is native to India, where it was used from early times as a perfume and medicine. Before 600 B.C. the citron had spread to Persia and then Babylonia. In the 4th century A.D. the citron reached China, where a mutant form developed with lobes like fingers. This fragrant **Buddha's hand** citron was placed on household altars—with little flesh, juice, or seeds, it is rarely consumed.

The main citron-producing areas are Sicily, Corsica, Crete, and other islands of the Mediterranean. Most of a citron consists of thick, dense rind; inside, the flesh is dry and may be sour or sweet with a weak lemon flavor. The rind, which has a powerful fragrance, is the most useful part. Citrons are used almost exclusively for the manufacture of candied peel.

In Jewish practice, the **etrog** is a citron used during the Feast of Tabernacles. Perfect etrogs are in heavy demand in Jewish communities during this fall holiday. The etrog has a semirough, bumpy yellow peel that is faintly ribbed. This Israeli cultivar, which is the official citron for ritual use, has crisp, firm flesh with little acidic juice and many seeds.

Season: Citron is in season in the fall months.

Purchase: Buy firm, fragrant, unblemished fruit.

Avoid: Steer clear of soft or moldy citrons.

Storage: Leave citrons at room temperature to perfume the room—they will keep for several days.

Preparation: 1. **Scrub with soap and rinse under hot water.**

2. **Cut in half, scoop out and discard the flesh.**

Serving Suggestions: Use citron peel when making candied citrus peel. • Substitute etrog citron for oranges in marmalade. • Infuse vodka with citron peel.

Flavor Affinities: Almonds, chocolate, cinnamon, coriander, cream, grapefruit, hazelnut, honey, lemon, lime, pinenuts, ricotta.

11.

COCONUT

General
Description:

The fruit of the coconut palm tree (Cocos nucifera) *has a hard brown shell and creamy white flesh.* Coconuts originated in southern Asia, but because they float, they easily spread to islands and coastlines throughout the world. In the 16th century, the Spanish introduced the coconut to Puerto Rico and the Portuguese introduced it to Brazil.

The coconut common in markets is a mature fruit that has had its outer husk removed. The outer husk is smooth and very tough, green to reddish brown, becoming gray as the fruit matures. Between this outer husk and the inner nut is the familiar hard, woody brown shell covered with coarse brown fibers. The shell has three "eyes" at one end, one of which is soft. Inside the shell, a thin brown skin adheres firmly to the kernel, which is hollow and contains liquid.

In a young coconut, the kernel is soft and the liquid abundant but unpleasant. As the fruit ripens to what is called "green coconut," the kernel gradually hardens to a creamy texture and the liquid becomes sweet, called coconut juice or coconut water. Products called coconut milk or coconut cream, however, are extracted from the meat of the coconut. In mature coconuts there is a small amount of liquid, which is generally discarded, while the kernel is solid and slightly fibrous.

Season:	Mature coconuts are available year-round, with peak season September through April.
Purchase:	Coconuts have a shelf life of about 2 months. It can take longer than 2 months to reach the market, because coconuts are shipped by boat, so inspect before buying. The coconut should feel heavy and the juice should audibly slosh inside. Its three eyes should be dry.
Avoid:	Old nuts look gray instead of brown. Avoid coconuts with moldy or wet spots or with a fermented aroma. Avoid coconuts with patchy staining, which indicates a fracture in the shell that allowed liquid to escape.
Storage:	Coconuts can keep up to 1 month in the refrigerator. Store coconut chunks or grated coconut in an airtight container in the refrigerator for 2 weeks or freeze.
Preparation:	1. **Locate the softest of the three eyes. Using an awl or sharpening steel, poke open this eye.**
	2. **Drain and discard the coconut liquid.**
	3. **Bake the coconut at 350°F (180°C) for 25 minutes, then cool. (The flesh will shrink away from the shell.)**
	4. **Tap the shell several times with a hammer until**

it cracks apart. The shell pieces will pop away, leaving a thin layer of dark skin on the flesh.

5. Insert a thin, flexible icing spatula between the shell and the meat to separate them.

6. Peel the dark skin from the kernel if desired. Peeling is easiest when the coconut is warm.

7. Cut coconut meat into desired sizes with a sharp knife or shred using a box grater.

Serving Suggestions:
Serve chunks of fresh coconut as a snack or dessert. • Top desserts, pies, frosted cakes, cupcakes, or brownies with shredded coconut. • Combine peeled, sliced oranges, bananas, pineapple, and grated coconut with whipped cream and/or marshmallows, then chill to make ambrosia.

Flavor Affinities:
Banana, cherimoya, chocolate, custard, kiwi, mango, orange, papaya, passion fruit, pineapple, rum, tangerine.

12. **CRANBERRY**

Other Names: Atoca, bearberry, bounceberry, craneberry.

General Description:
Cranberries (Vaccinium macrocarpon) *are small, tart, bright red berries.* Cranberries belong to a family of low, scrubby, woody plants that thrive on moors and moun-

tainsides and in bogs and other places with acidic soil. The Pilgrims named the fruit "craneberry" due to the pink blossom's resemblance to the head and bill of a sandhill crane.

Cranberries, along with blueberries (see page 16) and Concord grapes (see page 38), are the only commercially grown native North American fruits. Because their waxy skin contains a natural preservative, they are especially long-keeping. American whalers and mariners carried cranberries on their voyages to prevent scurvy.

In winter, growers flood the bogs with water to freeze and insulate the vines from frost. The bogs are drained in spring and then flooded again to float the cranberries for harvest in September and October. Cranberry vines can survive indefinitely; some vines on Cape Cod are more than 150 years old.

Season: Cranberry season is in the fall.

Purchase: Buy cranberries at the peak of their season in November; they will be deeper in color and less bitter. Look for brightly colored cranberries. Cranberries are nearly always sold packed in plastic bags.

Avoid: Early-picked cranberries, light in color, tend to be pale and supersour. Avoid mushy or wet cranberries.

Storage: Store cranberries in the refrigerator for up to 1 month.

Preparation:	**Cranberries can be used directly from the bag, with no further preparation.**
	Note: The more sugar you use in cooking cranberries, the tougher their skins will be. Cook only till they pop, otherwise they become bitter.
Serving Suggestions:	Add cranberries to buttermilk corn muffins. • Use half cranberries when making apple cake or apple pie. • Cook down cranberries with water and sugar to make a simple cranberry sauce.
Flavor Affinities:	Apple, brown sugar, corn, cream, maple syrup, orange, pork, poultry, sugar, tangerine, walnuts.

13a–b.

CURRANT

General Description:	*Currants* (Ribes *genus*) *are small fresh berries that may be red, white, gold, or black; the gooseberry is a popular variant.* The English word "currant," taken from their resemblance to the dried currants (actually small grapes) of Greece, has been used for this fruit only since 1550. The much older English name "ribes" is of ancient Indo-European origin.
	Red currants are especially sought after for making jellies and glazes, which take advantage of their high pectin content and ruby-red color. White currants are albino forms of red currants. They are fine for cooking,

but because of their lower acidity, they may also be eaten fresh. Black currants are astringent and are generally cooked before eating. Black currants are best known as the main ingredient in crème de cassis.

The European gooseberry (*Ribes grossularia)* is the main cultivated gooseberry species. Gooseberries look like small, long green grapes covered with stripes. These light green, gold, or red berries are quite tart. They may have gotten their name because they go well with fatty meats like goose. The popularity of gooseberries in England has led cultivators to breed larger and sweeter varieties.

Season:

Currants are in season during summer. Gooseberries are available from New Zealand from October through December and from Oregon in July and August.

Purchase:
Choose currants and gooseberries that are firm and brightly colored with green stems.

Avoid:
Do not buy currants or gooseberries with brown stems, shriveling, or leakage.

Storage:
Refrigerate the fruit in a plastic bag for 1 to 2 days.

Preparation:

1. **Wash currants and gooseberries by swishing them around in a bowl of water. Lift out.**

2. **Pick off and discard any small stems.**

Serving Suggestions:	Boil currants with water to cover and sugar to taste till soft and the mixture is thick, then purée, strain, and chill before serving over ice cream, fruit salad, or cake. • Purée cooked gooseberries, mix in one beaten egg, then reheat gently, and serve as a sauce for grilled mackerel.
Flavor Affinities:	Cream, custard, duck, ginger, goose, lamb, lemon, melon, mustard, oily fish, orange, pork, sour cream, sugar, sweet spices, venison.

---

14. **DATE**

General Description:	*Dates are the small oblong fruits of the date palm* (Phoenix dactylifera). While the origin of the date palm is lost in antiquity, date gardens were well established throughout the region once known as Mesopotamia. About 2,000 years ago, nomadic tribes spread the date palm from the Middle East through the Sahara Desert, planting palms in oases. Moors from Arabia eventually brought date palms across North Africa to Spain. Spanish padres brought the palms with them to the New World. According to an Arabic proverb, the date palm grows best "with its head in fire and its feet in water."
	Dates fall into three types: soft, semidry, and dry. Soft dates have a soft flesh, high moisture content, and low sugar content. Semidry dates have firm flesh, moderate moisture content, and high sugar content. Dry dates (known as "bread dates") have dry, hard flesh and

high sugar content. The two most popular varieties are the **Deglet Noor**, a semidry date, and the soft **Medjool** date, prized by Moroccan royalty.

Season: Dates are in season in the late fall, but may be found year-round, depending on the variety.

Purchase: Choose plump, soft dates with smooth, shiny skin.

Avoid: Avoid very shriveled dates or those with mold or sugar crystals on the skin.

Storage: Refrigerate fresh dates in a plastic bag for up to 2 weeks. Dried dates can be stored in an airtight container in a cool, dry place for up to 6 months, or up to a year in the refrigerator.

Preparation: 1.   **Make a lengthwise slit and push back the flesh.**

2.   **Pull out the pit.**

Serving
Suggestions: Stuff the date with any of the following: cheese, cream cheese mixed with marmalade, or almond paste. • Add chopped dates to curried chicken salad.

Flavor
Affinities: Almonds, brown sugar, chocolate, coconut, cream cheese, honey, orange, pistachios, walnuts.

15.   **DURIAN**

Other Names: King of the fruits.

General Description: *The durian* (Durio zibethinus) *is a large, green, spiky tropical fruit.* No other fruit smells as bad or tastes as good as the durian. Native to Malaysia and Indonesia, it is considered the "king of the fruits" throughout Southeast Asia.

The durian grows on a large forest tree in the south of Thailand, Malaysia, and Indonesia, where rain falls year-round. It gets its name from "duri," the Malay word for "spike." The large fruit is oval and covered with pointy short, stout spikes, the bases of which all touch. Within the rind are five large cells of satin-white flesh, embedded with two or three seeds about the size of chestnuts. Durian flesh has a creamy texture whose flavor, while difficult to describe, hints of vanilla, sherry, cream cheese, onion, almond, and custard. But it also has an aroma that is offensive to many (some say it smells like stinky feet).

Season: Fresh durians are in season in June and July.

Purchase: Fresh durians are available in the U.S. at Asian markets. To ensure that the durian has ripened enough, choose one that has a small split somewhere in the peel.

Avoid:	A durian full of large splits all around the peel is likely to be overripe.
Storage:	Durians don't store well. It is best to eat durian as soon as possible after purchase.
Preparation:	**1. Take advantage of any splits in the skin to facilitate cutting it open; cut in half or several pieces.** **2. Pull back the peel and discard it.**
Serving Suggestions:	Remove the flesh from the seeds, simmer in coconut milk to a smooth sauce, and serve over sweetened, coconut-flavored sticky rice, or mix the sauce with whole milk or cream, add sugar as desired, and pour the mixture into an ice-cream maker to churn into durian ice cream, a Southeast Asian favorite.
Flavor Affinities:	Banana, cream, coconut, coffee, ice cream, lime, milk, rice, sugar, vanilla.

16. 📷   **FIG**

General Description:	*Figs* (Ficus carica) *are small oval fruits with a protruding stem that are delicate in texture and flavor and filled with tiny, edible, crunchy seeds.* Figs enjoy a long and prominent place in human history. In the Old Testament, Adam and Eve covered their bodies with fig

leaves, and Cleopatra hid the poisonous asp she used to end her life in a basket of fresh figs. Native to Turkey, the dark-skinned **Smyrna** fig was introduced to Mexico by the Spanish in the mid-16th century. Franciscan monks brought figs to San Diego–area missions in the late 1700s. The crop spread to various missions along California's coast and produced the dark-purple or black Mission fig.

Figs don't ripen once picked, so they must be at their peak when harvested. The fruits are extremely fragile, and their skin bruises and tears easily. A short season plus difficulty in transporting make this delicate, highly perishable fruit a high-priced delicacy in much of the U.S.

Black Mission figs have dark purple skins with light strawberry-colored flesh. **Calimyrna** figs are yellowish green on the outside with pale pink flesh. **Kadota** figs have green skins with amber-colored flesh and are less sweet than other varieties. **Brown Turkey** figs can be medium to large in size with copper-colored skin and whitish to pink pulp with few seeds.

Season: Black Mission figs are available from May through November, Brown Turkey figs are available from May through December, Calimyrna figs are available in July and August, and Kadota figs are available from May through October.

Purchase: Look for figs that are soft and smell sweet. Handle carefully. Purchase firm, unbruised fruit with the stems intact. It's common for the base of the fig to tear slightly or become moist and the skin around the stem to be slightly shriveled. Ripe figs produce clear, sticky syrup from the blossom end.

Avoid: Avoid dry-looking, overly green (unripe), or bruised figs.

Storage: Refrigerate for up to 2 days; bring to room temperature before serving.

Preparation:

1. **Wash figs under cool water.**

2. **Eat whole, peeled or unpeeled. If you choose to peel them, do so with a paring knife.**

Serving Suggestions: Fresh figs are best simply halved or quartered. • Serve figs in a green salad with Roquefort cheese and pecans. • Make a fig pizza with gorgonzola, fig halves, prosciutto, and walnut halves.

Flavor Affinities: Almond, anise, blue cheese, chicken, cured meats (such as prosciutto and smoked duck), duck, lamb, pork, walnuts.

17a–c.

GRAPE

General Description: *Grapes, members of the genus* Vitus, *are small, sweet, tart fruits clustered in large, pendulous bunches.* The fruits of vine of the genus *Vitus* have been celebrated as both a food and the source of wine since antiquity. The grape species from which all European wines are made, *Vitus vinifera*, is indigenous to the area from the Black Sea to Afghanistan and is still found there today. The Phoenicians brought the vine to Greece not long after 100 B.C. It flourished in the Mediterranean climate and spread throughout the Roman Empire.

The leading producers of table grapes in the world are Italy, Turkey, Bulgaria, the U.S., Greece, Portugal, and South Africa. There are numerous varieties of grape; all can be categorized as green, red, or blue-black and can be seeded or seedless.

In general, green grapes are more delicately flavored, with sweet yet tart notes. The most common variety of green grape is the **Thompson seedless**, though the most flavorful are **Calmeria** and **Sugarone**. Red grapes are sweet, tempered with earthy or spicy undertones. Popular varieties include the **Flame seedless**, **Cardinal**, **Emperor**, **Red Globe**, and **Tokay**. Blue-black grapes tend to have richer flavor, with the same characteristic sweet-tartness. **Beauty seedless**, **Concord**, and **Zinfandel** are all blue-black table grapes.

Season: Grapes are available year-round. Different varieties will peak at different times of the year.

Purchase: Look for grapes that are plump, fragrant, and firmly attached to pliable stems. Full color is the best indicator for flavor.

Avoid:	Look at the area surrounding the stem end, because this is the first part to deteriorate. Avoid soft or wrinkled fruits and any with wet-looking or brownish tops.
Storage:	Store grapes, refrigerated, wrapped in a paper towel in a vented plastic bag for up to 1 week.
Preparation:	1. **Rinse under cool running water.**
	2. **Shake to remove excess water.**
Serving Suggestions:	Add halved (seeded if necessary) green and red grapes to chicken salad. • Make focaccia with Concord grape halves sprinkled with sugar pressed into the dough before baking. • Serve frozen grapes as a snack on a hot summer day.
Flavor Affinities:	Almonds, apples, blue cheese, chicken, fish, pears, pistachios, venison, walnuts.

GRAPEFRUIT AND POMELO

General Description:	*Grapefruit* (Citrus paradisi) *is one of the largest of the citrus fruits, with thick tough skin and somewhat bitter flesh.* The grapefruit family has only been cultivated for about 200 years and is descended from the even larger pomelo. Its habit of growing in clusters may be the origin of the name "grapefruit."

Grapefruits are produced in two different climatic zones. One is a low-humidity desert area and the other is a tropical area. Desert-grown grapefruit are characterized by a blemish-free exterior, a very thick peel, and an acidic flavor. Tropical-grown grapefruit are characterized by a slightly blemished exterior, thin peel, and sweet taste.

The two main varieties of grapefruit are **Duncan** and **Marsh**. In 1913 a pink Marsh appeared, the **Marsh Ruby**, which is the ancestor of all pink grapefruits grown today. **Star Ruby** grapefruit is a variety with a deep rosy flesh and tangy, sweet flavor. The **New Zealand** grapefruit is more orange in color and slightly less acidic. It can tolerate a cooler climate and ripens much earlier.

Pomelo *(Citrus grandis)*, the ancestor of the grapefruit, still thrives in Malaysia and Indonesia. Pomelos have been cultivated in China for thousands of years and are now being cultivated and imported from Israel. Much of their bulk is taken up by very thick skin, which is loose, fibrous, and easily removed. Some unpeeled pomelos are as big as basketballs. Pomelo is firmer and less juicy than grapefruit.

A cross between a pomelo and a grapefruit, the **Oro Blanco** is slightly larger than a grapefruit, with a thick rind. Its skin is green to yellow, its flesh is mostly seedless, with thicker skin around each segment, and it has a juicy, sweet grapefruit flavor without bitterness or acidity.

The tangerine-grapefruit hybrid called **uniq** (trademarked under the name Ugli) fruit can be very large, but much of it consists of a thick, baggy rind with a pulled-up appearance at the top. It is a kind of tangelo (see page 106), but is most similar to a grapefruit. It is easily peeled and the segments separate freely. It has a faintly bitter flavor touched with honey and apricot.

Season:

Duncan, Star Ruby, Marsh Ruby, and the white Marsh seedless grapefruit are in season year-round. Pomelos are in season from mid-January to mid-February. Oro Blanco are in season from December to mid-April. Uniq are in season from December through April.

Purchase:

Choose fruits that are heavy for their size; the heavier it is, the juicier it will be. Grapefruits should be firm yet resilient and have shiny skin. The more blush of pink or red on the skin of a pink or red grapefruit, the deeper the color of the flesh. In the spring, extra chlorophyll produced for the new bloom creates a tinge of green on ripened fruit that hasn't been picked. This natural process is called "regreening" and does not affect quality.

Avoid:

Grapefruits that don't give when pressed are usually dry and without much juice. Rough skin indicates dry fruit.

Storage:

Store grapefruits for up to 2 weeks in the refrigerator.

Preparation:

1. **Peel the skin of the fruit as you would an orange (see page 65) and separate the segments.**

2.   **Remove all of the bitter pith before eating.**

Serving
Suggestions:

Dice grapefruit flesh, mix with olive oil, salt, and pepper, and use to dress chicken or seafood. • Mix fresh-squeezed grapefruit juice with a few drops of fruit vinegar and grapeseed oil to make a salad dressing. • Use pomelo juice and/or sections when making fish or seafood seviche.

Flavor
Affinities:

Avocado, champagne, coconut, fish, ginger, honey, salad greens, seafood, tarragon, walnuts, watercress.

---

19.   **GUAVA**

Other Names: Guyava, kuawa.

General
Description:

Guava (Psidium guajava) *is a plum-sized tropical fruit with yellow, red, or purple-black skin and a sweet, highly aromatic flavor.* Europeans first encountered guavas when they reached Haiti. Spanish and Portuguese sailors soon spread the tree and its name from its native lands in Central America and the West Indies to other regions. By the 17th century the guava was well established in India and Southeast Asia.

Guavas are generally the size of a fist and may be round or pear shaped, with rough or smooth greenish white, yellow, or red skin. The seed-filled flesh is yellow, bright pink, or red. The best varieties are soft when ripe and have a rind that softens to be fully edible. Large, pear-shaped white fruits are considered the best. Varieties differ widely in flavor and seediness (some have edible seeds). Their aroma is sweet and flowery, yet musky. The taste is sweet to sour with an unusual taste partly due to eugenol, the essential oil found also in cloves.

Season: Guavas are in season from June to August and from November to March.

Purchase: Choose tender fruits with some yellow color that have not yet begun to show spots. They should give to gentle pressure.

Avoid: Avoid spotted, mushy, or very green guavas.

Storage: Store at room temperature till soft. Refrigerate ripe fruit in a plastic or paper bag for up to 2 days.

Preparation: 1. **Cut in half crosswise.**

2. **Scoop out the flesh with a spoon.**

Serving Suggestions: Purée guava with lime juice, orange juice, and a little honey to make a marinade or glaze for poultry. • Combine guava purée, pineapple juice, passion fruit purée, dark rum, sugar, lime juice, and a little grenadine (for color) and run in an ice-cream maker till frozen to make a mai tai sorbet. • Add diced guava to fruit salads.

Flavor Affinities:	Bananas, coconut, cream cheese, honey, lemon, lime, orange, passion fruit, pineapple, rum, strawberries, sugar.

20. 📷 **KIWANO**

Other Names:	African horned cucumber, English tomato, jelly melon, hedged gourd, horned melon.
General Description:	*Kiwano* (Cucumis metuliferus) *is a spiked oblong-shaped fruit with yellow-orange skin, lime green jellylike flesh, and large seeds.* Kiwano is the registered trademark name for horned melons grown in New Zealand. These oval melons range in length from 3 to 5 inches (7.5–11 cm) and have bright, rather tough skin studded with short thick "horns." Originating in tropical Africa, their green pulp is packed with large edible seeds similar to those in cucumbers. Kiwano is grown mostly as an ornamental because of its decorative appeal and long shelf life, but it has a mild, sweet, tart flavor reminiscent of bananas, lemons, and cucumbers.
Season:	Kiwanos are available year-round from New Zealand and California.
Purchase:	Buy firm kiwanos with deep, bright yellow-orange skin. The spikes or horns should be intact.

Avoid:	Pass up soft or pale kiwanos. Avoid those with blemishes or soft spots on the skin.

Storage:	Store in a cool, dry place for up to 3 months. Do not refrigerate.

Preparation:

1. **Halve the fruit lengthwise.**

2. **Scoop out the pulp (it can be eaten seeds and all).**

3. **Sprinkle with a little sugar, if desired.**

Serving Suggestions:	Strain the fruit pulp for juice. • Cut kiwano into slices or wedges to eat like a melon. • Spoon over ice cream.

Flavor Affinities:	Coconut, cream, kiwi, lemon, lime, mango, passion fruit, pineapple, sugar, star fruit, yogurt.

21a–b.

KIWIFRUIT

Other Names:	Chinese gooseberry, monkey peach.

| General Description: | *Kiwifruit* (Actinidia deliciosa) *is a small oblong fruit with thin hairy brown skin.* Native to China, the kiwifruit was originally called a Chinese gooseberry. Specialty produce pioneer Frieda Caplan renamed them kiwifruit in the 1960s. The vine fruit has brown fuzzy skin covering emerald green flesh that's dotted with many |

edible tiny black seeds. The flavor is like a combination of strawberries and melon. Except for the seeds, the texture is soft and creamy. The skin is edible, but not appealing to everyone.

Gold kiwifruits have a thin, smooth brown skin and bright yellow flesh. They are mild with softer texture than the green variety. **Baby** kiwifruits are also known as **hardy** kiwis. They are bite-sized (about the size of table grapes) with fuzzless, smooth skin.

Season: Kiwifruit has a long season, spanning cold months, so it is available year-round if imported.

Purchase: Choose firm fruit that's free of mold and soft spots.

Avoid: Soft or mushy kiwifruits should be avoided.

Strorage: Refrigerate ripe kiwis for a few days. To ripen, leave fruit out at room temperature or put in a paper bag until it yields slightly to gentle pressure.

Preparation: **Cut in half crosswise and scoop out the fruit with a spoon, or peel with a paring knife and cut into cubes, slices, or wedges.**

Note: Raw kiwi contains an enzyme that prevents gelatin from setting and causes milk to curdle.

Serving Suggestions:	Combine fresh kiwi purée, orange juice, and sparkling water to make a kiwifruit spritzer. • Mix fresh kiwi purée, melon liqueur, tequila, triple sec, and lime juice to make a kiwi margarita. • Combine diced, peeled kiwi with diced oranges, jicama, yellow and red peppers, chopped cilantro, fresh lime juice, and minced jalapeño to make kiwi salsa.
Flavor Affinities:	Banana, berries, coconut, honey, lemon, lime, orange, papaya, passion fruit, star fruit, tangerine.

22.   **KUMQUAT**

General Description:	*The kumquat* (Fortunella *genus*) *is a tiny orange-colored, usually oblong, citrus fruit.* Kumquats are the fruits of small evergreen trees that are native to Asia and cultivated in China, Japan, and the U.S. They were brought to Europe from China by Robert Fortune (for which the genus is named) in 1846.

Some kumquats are round, others oval. The **Nagami** kumquat *(Fortunella margarita)* is oval and has yellow skin and should be squeezed and massaged to combine the rind and flesh flavors before eating. After ripening, this small fruit gradually loses water content, and is best used for preserves. The **Meiwa**, or **sweet**, kumquat *(Fortunella crassifolia)* is round and large with a tender, sweet rind and relatively sweet juice. It is considered the best kumquat for eating out of hand, rind and all. The

Marumi kumquat *(Fortunella japonica)* is round with golden yellow skin that is thinner and somewhat sweeter than that of the oval kumquat.

Season: Kumquats are available December through June.

Purchase: Select fruit that is firm and glossy, preferably with leaves still attached. Because of their thin skin, they spoil quickly.

Avoid: Do not buy bruised, shriveled, or wet fruits.

Storage: If using the fruit within a few days, store at room temperature. Otherwise, refrigerate in a plastic bag for up to 2 weeks.

Preparation: **Wash well in cool water.**

Serving Suggestions: Add sliced kumquats to fruit salads or green salads. • Add kumquats to cranberry sauce. • Glaze roast duck or ham with kumquat and mustard seed syrup.

Flavor Affinities: Cardamom, chicken, chutney, cinnamon, citrus fruits, cranberry, duck, ginger, mustard.

23a–b.

LEMON

General Description: *The lemon* (Citrus limon) *is a small, yellow rounded fruit, pointed at its ends, with acidic juice.* The origin of the lemon is unknown, though it may be native to northwest India. Arab traders in Asia carried lemons and other citrus fruits to eastern Africa and the Middle East between A.D. 100 and 700, reaching China by 1000. Christopher Columbus brought lemon seeds to the New World in 1493.

The lemon is closely related to the lime (see page 52) and the citron (see page 25), which are "nippled" citrus fruits. Lemons are grown primarily for their acidic juice, but the oil in their yellow peel is almost as important for use as a flavoring and in the perfume industry.

Because lemons ripen naturally in autumn and winter when market demand is low, growers pick the lemons green, then cure and ripen them for sale in spring and summer. During this process, the lemons shrink a little; their skin becomes thinner and tougher and develops a silky finish.

In the U.S. the most common variety is the **Eureka**, grown from the seed of an Italian lemon (probably the **Lunario**) planted in Los Angeles in 1858. Eurekas have few seeds, juicy pulp, and high acid content. The **Fino** is a small Spanish variety that has a smooth thin rind. **Femminello Ovale**, one of the oldest Italian varieties, still accounts for three-quarters of Italy's total lemon production. It is medium sized and short, with a blunt nipple and rounded base. This highly regarded lemon is tender, juicy, and highly acidic.

Meyer lemons, which originated in China, are a cross between a regular lemon and a tangerine (see page

106). Plant researcher Frank Meyer brought these highly fragrant lemons to the U.S. in 1908 from the area near Peking. Meyers are rounder than lemons and have thin, soft, smooth rinds, which are rich yellow-orange when fully ripe. The pulp is deep yellow and low in acid.

Season: Peak season is April through July, though they are available year-round. Peak season for Meyers is November through January, though occasionally available until April.

Purchase: Look for big, plump, firm lemons that are heavy for their size. When choosing Meyer lemons, look for bright, shiny fruits with richly colored orange yellow rind, indicating that the fruit was picked when fully ripe.

Avoid: Greenish lemons won't be as juicy. Avoid lemons that are shriveled, hard-skinned, soft, or spongy. Avoid old Meyer lemons with hard dry skin or with soft spots.

Storage: Refrigerate lemons in a plastic bag for up to 2 weeks (1 week for Meyer lemons).

Preparation:
1. **Scrub with soap and water if using the zest.**

2. **Cut with a knife into wedges or slices. If juicing, cut in half crosswise.**

Serving Suggestions: Squeeze lemon wedges over fish. • Add grated lemon zest to pastry dough, cannoli filling, cheesecake, marinades, or vinaigrette. • Substitute Meyer lemons for lemons in a lemon tart.

Flavor Affinites:
Artichokes, capers, cumin, fennel, fish, garlic, marscapone, mint, poultry, raspberries, shellfish, thyme.

24a–b.

LIME

General Description:
The lime (Citrus aurantifolia) *is a small green-skinned citrus fruit that is used for its acidic green juice.* Closely related to lemons (see page 49), limes are native to Southeast Asia. They made their way to the eastern Mediterranean with the Arabs, and then on to the western Mediterranean with returning Crusaders. Columbus introduced citrus fruits to the West Indies on his second voyage, and limes quickly spread.

In the 18th century, citrus juice was discovered to prevent scurvy, a disease that had devastated the British navy. Britain imported limes cheaply from its colony of Jamaica, and they were the citrus of choice for sailors, who became known as "limeys."

The dominant lime in the world, called a **Key** lime by Americans, grows on thorny trees that are sensitive to cold weather. They are approximately 2 inches (5 cm) in diameter with a thin yellow-green rind prone to splotchy brown spots. They are aromatic and very juicy, with a strong and complex acidic flavor. Their flesh is greenish yellow and full of seeds; their juice content is high (well over 40 percent).

The most common lime in the U.S., the "lime green" **Persian** lime, is probably a hybrid of the Key lime and the citron (see page 25). Botanists believe this variety was introduced to the Mediterranean area via Persia (now Iran). It was carried to Brazil by Portuguese traders and eventually made it to California in the latter half of the 1800s via Australia and Tahiti. The Persian lime, almost always seedless, is shaped like a lemon, and is larger than a Key lime, with thicker rind and juicy, pale green pulp. Persian limes are deliberately picked slightly immature so they will be green. Both Persian and Key limes have a higher sugar and citric acid content than lemons, and Key limes are more acidic than Persian.

The **sweet** lime is thought to be another hybrid. It has somewhat lower sugar content than the other limes but almost no acidity. A juicy fruit, it is popular in the Middle East and India.

Season:

Persian limes are available year-round. Peak season for Key limes is June through August.

Purchase:

Look for brightly colored, smooth-skinned Persian limes that are heavy for their size. Small brown areas on the skin won't affect the flavor. Choose Key limes with light yellow, fine-grained skin.

Avoid:

Persian limes that feel hard when squeezed will be full of dry pulp with little juice. Avoid Persian or Key limes with hard or shriveled skin. Avoid Key limes with signs of mold or blotchy, brown spots.

Storage:	Refrigerate uncut Persian limes in a plastic bag in the refrigerator for up to 10 days. Refrigerate Key limes in a plastic bag for up to 5 days.

Preparation:	1. **Scrub with soap and water if using zest.**
	2. **Cut with a knife into wedges or slices. If juicing, cut in half crosswise.**
	Note: Never put squeezed lime shells in the garbage disposal, because they are too fibrous to grind.

Serving Suggestions:	Sprinkle lime juice on cut-up tropical fruits for a flavor accent and to prevent discoloration. • Make a frozen Key lime pie in a ground cashew and coconut crust. • Make classic margaritas with equal parts fresh-squeezed lime juice, triple sec, and tequila.

Flavor Affinities:	Banana, basil, cashews, chicken, chiles, cilantro, coconut, fish, jicama, lychee, mint, passion fruit, pineapple, pork, seafood, tequila, tomato.

---

25. **LOQUAT**

Other Names:	Japanese medlar, Japanese plum, May apple.

General Description:	*The loquat* (Eriobotrya japonica) *is a rounded fruit in the Rosaceae family with yellow-orange skin and cream-*

or orange-colored flesh. Native to China, this fruit was introduced to Japan over 1,000 years ago. It was common as a small-fruited ornamental in California in the 1870s, where it was known as Japanese plum. Japan is the leading producer of loquats, followed by Israel and Brazil.

The loquat has juicy, crisp flesh that can be either orange- or cream-colored (considered the best) with 1 to 3 rather large hard seeds in the center. Loquat tastes like a mix of apricot, plum, and pineapple, with floral overtones. People describe its flavor as a delicate balance between sweet and acid. Loquats bruise easily so they're not good travelers; fresh loquats are usually found only close to where they're grown.

Season: Loquats are available locally in July and August in growing regions of the Northern Hemisphere; warm months are their season.

Purchase: Choose large, unblemished fruit.

Avoid: Steer clear of bruised fruit.

Storage: Ripen at room temperature and then refrigerate in a plastic bag for 2 to 3 days.

Preparation:
1. **Loquats may need to be peeled depending on the amount of exterior fuzz. Peel with a vegetable peeler.**

2. **Cut the loquat in half and remove the seeds.**

Note: Do not eat, chew, or swallow the seeds—they are toxic.

Serving
Suggestions:

Add loquats to salads, fruit salads, or fruit cups. • Make loquat jam, jelly, or chutney. • Poach loquats in light sugar syrup with a cinnamon stick.

Flavor
Affinities:

Allspice, apples, Asian pears, chicken, cinnamon, cloves, duck, lemon, soy sauce, strawberries.

26. 📷   **LYCHEE**

Other Names: Lychee nut.

General
Description:

The lychee (Litchi chinensis) *is a small round fruit with a hard bumpy shell enclosing translucent flesh and a hard brown seed.* Lychees have been cultivated in southern China for more than 2,000 years. During the Ming dynasty, clubs of lychee devotees met in temples and gardens to consume hundreds of lychees at a time.

The round fruit is covered by a tough, knobby shell that is deep red when picked ripe but turns rosy brown within a few days. Inside is delicate, clear or white fruit pulp surrounding a single, large, shiny mahogany brown seed that is inedible. The soft, jellylike flesh slips from the shell like a hard-cooked egg. The flavor is like

honeyed grapes with a touch of cherry, and their
perfumed fragrance is reminiscent of musk and roses.

Season: Lychees are available during the warmest months and
can be found from June to September.

Purchase: Select heavy lychees with deep-rose-colored, thin skin.

Avoid: Pass up dried-out lychees.

Storage: Store lychees in the refrigerator for several weeks.

Preparation:
1. **Slice open the shell with a knife or gently
   squeeze until the skin pops open.**

2. **Slip out the inner fruit.**

3. **Split the fruit open on the seam and remove
   and discard the hard seed.**

Serving
Suggestions: Add lychee halves to pork, chicken, or duck dishes in
the last few minutes of cooking. • Blend together lychee
halves, chopped pineapple, vanilla ice cream, and ice to
make a tropical milk shake. • Toss fresh crabmeat and
lychee wedges with mayonnaise, a little soy sauce, sliced
green onions, and lime juice to make a lychee crab salad.

Flavor
Affinities: Cashews, coconut, crab, duck, ginger, lemon, lime,
mango, orange, pineapple, pork, scallops, water chestnuts.

27. **MANGO**

General
Description:

The mango (Mangifera indica) *is a flattened to oblong fruit with colorful skin and sweet, orange-red flesh.* The mango originated in Southeast Asia, where it has been grown for over 4,000 years. Today India produces an estimated two-thirds of the world's mangoes. More than a thousand mango species fall into two branches: the **Indian**, with regularly shaped, brightly colored fruit, and the **Philippine**, with pale green, kidney-shaped fruit.

The smallest mangoes are the size of an egg; the largest can weigh up to 5 pounds (2.2 kg). Each mango has a single flat seed, surrounded by flesh that is either yellow or orange. Mangoes can be oval, round, heart-shaped, kidney-shaped, or long and slender. The colors of ripe mango range from red to yellow-red, yellow-orange, yellow-green, or deep green.

Season:

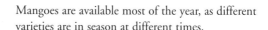

Mangoes are available most of the year, as different varieties are in season at different times.

Purchase:

Choose mangoes that are heavy for their size with firm, unblemished skin. Check the area around the stem—if it looks plump and round, the mango is ripe. With the stem end up, smell the mango. A ripe mango will have a sweet aroma and be slightly soft to the touch.

Avoid:

Because of their high sugar content, mangoes will ferment naturally. Avoid mangoes with a sour or alcohol smell. Avoid stringy-looking, shriveled, or spotted mangoes. A few brown speckles are normal.

Storage:

Most mangoes are hard when you buy them and must be fully ripened before eating. Leave at cool room temperature till the flesh is yielding, but not mushy. Most varieties will turn yellow as they ripen, though red mangoes will not become redder after harvest.

Refrigerate when ripe for up to 4 days. Green mangoes may be stored at room temperature but should be used within a few days.

Preparation:

1. **The mango has one large tongue-shaped pit in its center. The pit parallels the shape. Slice off the top and bottom of the mango.**

2. **Stand the mango up: The tip of the pit will now be exposed. Cut off the mango flesh parallel to the pit, curving slightly with the shape of the pit. Repeat on the other side.**

3. **Turn the half peel side down and cut criss-cross slices through the flesh, stopping at the skin. Turn the mango out until the center pops up—the cubes will stick out and can be removed with a fork. Or, slice the flesh into pieces.**

Serving Suggestions:

Purée mango with lime juice, ice, and rum in a blender to make a daiquiri. • Assemble sliced mango and avocado and dress with lime juice for a composed salad. • Combine diced mango, red pepper, and red onion, chopped cilantro and mint, lime juice, and minced serrano chiles to make mango salsa.

Flavor Affinities:
Apricot, avocado, chicken, chiles, cilantro, cucumber, fish, jicama, lime juice, orange, passion fruit, pineapple, rum, seafood, star fruit, sweet bell pepper, tangerine.

28.   **MEDLAR**

General Description:
The medlar (Mespilus germanica) *is a small fruit in the rose family that is related to the apple.* This Persian fruit was grown by the ancient Greeks and later by the Romans. It was popular because it is a late-ripening winter fruit and hardy enough to flourish even in Scandinavia. The medlar is a fascinating applelike fruit that is open at the bottom end, exposing the five inner seed boxes. Medlars are picked after a hard frost when the flesh is hard and green. The fruits must be kept cool until the pulp softens and mellows, turning it a light brown. This process is known as "bletting." Internal fermentation gives the fruit a lingering, slightly sweet, slightly winelike taste.

Season:
Late fall.

Purchase:
Select medlars that are anywhere from barely soft to soft and brown.

Avoid:	Pass up medlars with any blemishes.
Storage:	Store medlars in a cool, dry area.

Preparation:

1. **Wash with cool water.**

2. **Cut in half, remove the seed pockets, and scoop out the pulp.**

Serving
Suggetions:
Roast with butter and cloves as a traditional winter dessert. • Fold medlar pulp into sweetened whipped cream for a superb chilled mousse. • Make medlar jelly to serve as an accompaniment to game.

Flavor
Affinities:
Butter, cinnamon, cloves, cream, game, ginger, honey, lemon, raisins, sugar, wine.

29a–f.

MELON

General
Description:
Melons (Cucumis melo) are large, hard-skinned fruits in the gourd family with abundant sweet, juicy flesh and large seeds. Melons are native to the region stretching from Egypt to India. Melons of the *Cucumis melo* species fall into three main categories. **Cantaloupes**, including **Galia** and **Charentais**, are fragrant, small, and round with a rough surface divided into segments. **Netted** melons (or **muskmelons**) have a light netted pattern on the surface, usually orange flesh, and include

the **American "cantaloupe"** and **Persian** melons. **Winter** melons ripen slowly (even continuing to ripen in storage) and are not ready until late autumn. They are slightly elongated and their skin is finely ribbed. These include the **Cavaillon**, **honeydew**, and **casaba**.

Cantaloupes are named for the papal villa of Cantalupo, near Rome. The European cantaloupe has a warty rind and a scented, yellow flesh. In North America, the melon called "cantaloupe" is actually a **muskmelon**. It features cream-colored netting over a yellowish green rind. The soft pale orange flesh is extremely juicy and sweet.

The **casaba** is named after a town in Turkey. It has a round bottom, firm light green to yellow lightly wrinkled skin, and a pointed tip. Its smooth-textured green flesh is juicy and subtly sweet.

The **Cavaillon** has been cultivated in France since the 1400s. It is whitish green on the outside with indented ribs from the stem end to the blossom end. It is a little larger than a softball and slightly oval. Its deep orange flesh is sweet, mildly crisp, and generously perfumed.

A hybrid cross of the casaba and cantaloupe, the **Crenshaw** has dark green skin that turns yellow as it ripens. Its flesh is salmon-colored, extra sweet, and juicy, with a sweet spicy aroma.

The **Galia** melon has a beige rind and aromatic, light green flesh. If allowed to get too ripe, it can develop an unpleasant chemical taste.

A member of the muskmelon family, **honeydew** was prized by ancient Egyptians. Sweet and succulent, the honeydew has pale, greenish white skin and pale green flesh. Its flesh is honey sweet and very tender when completely ripe: the flesh turns from green to white, is very juicy, and has a melt-in-your-mouth texture.

The native Peruvian **pepino** has a waxy ivory skin with distinctive purple and greenish yellow markings. Ranging in size from a plum to a large papaya, the entire pepino is edible—skin, seeds, and yellow flesh. Sweet and firm, the flesh of the pepino is quite fragrant and tastes like a combination of pear and banana.

Persian melons are large, grayish green muskmelons with delicate netting on the rind. The rich, salmon-colored flesh is sweet, delectable, and highly aromatic.

Watermelons are in a different genus, *Citrullus lanatus*, and have a longer history of cultivation than other melons. Watermelons are native to Africa and date back as far as 2000 B.C. in Egypt. Because of their high water content, they were used as a source of liquid in areas where water was limited or tainted. They come in various shapes, sizes, and colors, including the common elongated oval-shaped with variegated green rind, black seeds (if seeded), and deep red flesh.

Season:

North American cantaloupes are available June to November. Crenshaws are available from July to October. Pepinos are available from late fall to midspring. Persian melons can be found from July through October with peak season in late summer. Watermelons are available from May through September.

Purchase: As a general rule, melons should give to gentle pressure at the blossom end and smell sweet. Precut melons, especially watermelons, sold in supermarkets must be firm and somewhat underripe so they keep their shape—a whole melon will have better flavor.

Check the stem end of a cantaloupe (or a Galia) for a clean, smooth indentation known as a "full slip." If the edge is jagged, the cantaloupe was picked before maturity. Choose cantaloupes that are heavy for their size, with a fruity aroma and thick, well-raised netting over straw-colored rind. Choose a casaba melon that has an even-colored yellow rind. A green stem end is okay.

Look for a Crenshaw with a golden yellow rind. Ripe Crenshaws give off a spicy fragrance and have springy, not mushy skin. They are softer than other melons so handle with care. Look for fragrant, firm, unblemished pepino melons. When a Persian melon is ripe, the skin turns slightly golden, the netting lightens in color, and its perfumed fragrance becomes more pronounced. Persian melons picked before they are mature never reach full flavor.

Avoid: Overripe melons will have lumps or soft spots. Avoid lopsided or rock-hard melons. Avoid watermelons with a flat side. Hard melons should sound hollow when knocked with a knuckle.

Storage: Keep uncut melons at room temperature until fully ripened, then refrigerate for up to 5 days. Cut melon easily absorbs food odors and should be tightly wrapped with plastic and then refrigerated for up to 3 days.

Preparation:

1. **Cut in half with a clean knife.**

2. **Using a large spoon, scoop the seeds out of the cavity (if the melon has a seed cavity) and discard them.**

3. **Cut away the skin, depending on how the melon will be consumed.**

4. **Cut into slices, wedges, or balls.**

Serving Suggestions:
Scoop melon into balls and add to fruit salad. • Top melon wedges with vanilla ice cream, sprinkle lightly with chopped crystallized ginger, or drizzle with hazel-nut- or orange-flavored liqueur. • Blend diced melon with lime and mint to make cold melon soup. • Add diced melon to salsa.

Flavor Affinities:
Cilantro, feta, lemon, lime, mint, orange, pecorino, prosciutto, rum, salami, smoked duck, tequila, yogurt.

ORANGE

General Description:
The sweet orange (Citrus sinensis) *has sweet, juicy, orange-colored flesh. The bitter orange* (Citrus aurantium)

has sour juice and an aromatic rind. The orange's wild ancestors are thought to have come from China and India, but today Brazil and the U.S. together produce more than two-thirds of the world's oranges. The name "orange" comes from the Sanskrit word *naranga*. The sour orange was the first to travel westward and was grown in Sicily by the 11th century. The sweet orange followed about 500 years later.

Most American oranges come from Florida and California. Due to differences in soil and climate, Florida and California oranges—even those of the same variety— vary in color, texture, and juiciness. Florida oranges are thin-skinned, very juicy, and easy to squeeze. California oranges are best for eating. They usually have full orange color (due to a drier climate with cooler nights), thicker skin, and less juice.

The mutation that produced the **blood orange**'s ruby red color arose in the 17th century in Sicily. These small to medium-sized fruits with moderate amounts of seeds have tangy juice.

The **Cara Cara orange** originated at the Hacienda de Cara Cara in Venezuela. Cara Caras are medium in size, have a bright orange peel with pink- to raspberry-colored flesh, and are usually seedless. Their taste is sweet with undertones of sweet grapefruit. They are juicy and best eaten fresh.

The **Jaffa orange** from Israel has been popular since the late 19th century. Fragrant, sweet, and juicy, Jaffas are easy to peel, have no navel, and are almost seedless.

The **navel orange** originated in Bahia, Brazil, and is now the most important eating orange variety in the world. They thrive in the Mediterranean, Australia, California, and Argentina. Each navel orange has an unmistakable "baby fruit" imbedded in its blossom end. They mature early, are typically large and seedless, and segment easily. If used for juice, they should be squeezed as needed because their juice turns bitter quickly, even when refrigerated.

The **Seville orange**, a bitter orange, has a thick, rough skin and an extremely tart, bitter flesh full of seeds. Because of its high acid content, the Seville is used for making marmalades as well as liqueurs. They are an essential seasoning in Spanish and Latin American cuisine, especially in Cuba.

Valencia oranges have a thin rind that is difficult to peel when not fully mature. They have plenty of dark juice and two to four seeds, making them good for both eating and juicing.

Season:

Oranges are available year-round, though the peak season is in colder months, starting in October and running through late March or early April.

Purchase:

Choose oranges that are firm, heavy for their size, and evenly shaped. The skin should be smooth rather than deeply pitted. Thin-skinned oranges are juicier than thick-skinned varieties, and small to medium-sized fruits are sweeter than large ones.

Skin color is not a good guide to quality: Some oranges are artificially colored with a harmless vegetable dye, while others may show traces of green although they are ripe. Through a natural process called "regreening," the skins of ripe oranges sometimes revert to green if there are blossoms on the tree at the same time as the fruit. Oranges that have "regreened" may actually be sweeter because they are extraripe.

Avoid: Superficial brown streaks will not affect the flavor or texture of the fruit, but oranges that have serious bruises or soft spots, or feel spongy, should be avoided.

Storage: Oranges keep for up to 2 weeks in the refrigerator but keep almost as well at room temperature with no wrapping. They yield more juice when at room temperature.

Preparation: 1.   **Peel the orange by hand, or slice away the skin and white pith, if desired. For juicing, simply halve the fruit with the skin on.**

2.   **To section peeled fruit for salads, cut away the outer and inner skin to expose the pulp. Run a sharp knife along the sides of the dividing membranes to release the sections. Work over a bowl to catch the juices.**

Note: For orange zest, scrub oranges with hot soapy water first. Use the fine side of a hand grater, a spe-

cial zesting tool, a sharp paring knife, or a vegetable peeler to remove the zest. Try not to scrape any of the bitter white pith.

Serving Suggestions:	Make an orange Bavarian cream surrounded by thin slices of orange simmered in sugar syrup till tender. • Add a little orange juice and zest to chocolate cake and brownie recipes. • Season scallop or fish seviche with Seville orange juice, minced chiles, salt, and cilantro.
Flavor Affinities:	Almonds, avocado, beets, black olives, chicken, chocolate, cinnamon, custards, fennel, mint, olive oil, red onion, roast pork, salad greens, seafood, sherry vinegar, sweet potatoes, vanilla, winter squash.

31. 📷 **PAPAYA**

Other Names:	*Mamao* (Brazil), papaw (Australia), tree melon.
General Description:	*The papaya* (Carica papaya) *is a large pear-shaped fruit with silky-smooth flesh, a delicate sweet flavor, and a center full of edible black seeds.* The papaya is native to Central or South America. The fruit (and leaves) of papaya contain papain, an enzyme that helps digestion and is used to tenderize meat. The edible seeds have a spicy flavor somewhat reminiscent of black pepper.

There are two types of papaya, **Hawaiian** and **Mexican**. The Hawaiian papaya is pear-shaped, generally weighs about 1 pound (.45 kg), and has yellow skin when ripe. Its flesh is bright orange or pink with small black seeds clustered in the center. The Mexican papaya, which may weigh up to 10 pounds (4.5 kg), has green skin. Its flesh ranges from salmon-red to bright orange in color, with a musky and less-sweet taste.

Season: Papayas are available year-round.

Purchase: When selecting Hawaiian-type papayas, look for plump fruit that is warm yellow in color with smooth, unblemished skin. The neck will still be somewhat green when the rest is ripe. Papayas have little aroma, even when ripe.

Mexican papayas may remain mostly green even when fully ripe. When selecting a Mexican papaya that is already cut and wrapped, choose the one that has the deepest salmon or red flesh color. When choosing a whole, uncut fruit, choose one that has the most burnt-orange skin color and an overall "give" to the fruit.

Avoid: Avoid hard or shriveled papayas or fruit that is overly soft or has a fermented aroma. Avoid papaya with dark spots because they often go beneath the skin's surface and spoil the flavor. Avoid cut Mexican papayas with pale red or pinkish color, signaling an underripe fruit.

Storage: Place papayas in a paper bag with a banana to speed

ripening. Refrigerate uncut ripe fruit in a plastic or paper bag for up to 3 days.

Preparation:

1. **Cut in half lengthwise.**

2. **Scoop out the small black seeds from the center.**

3. **Eat the flesh with a spoon or peel with a vegetable peeler and cut into slices.**

4. **Discard the seeds or save for garnish.**

Note: Unripe Mexican papayas should not be eaten raw because of the latex they contain.

Serving Suggestions: Use the black seeds as a garnish on any papaya dish. • Add diced papaya to tropical salsa. • Stuff the papaya cavity with cottage cheese, yogurt, ice cream, or chicken, turkey, or shrimp salad. • Peel, seed, and blend papaya with milk, yogurt, or orange juice for a shake.

Flavor Affinities: **Ripe papaya:** banana, coconut, lemon, lime, melon, nectarine, orange, passion fruit, pineapple. **Unripe papaya:** garlic, ginger, rice wine, scallions, soy sauce.

32. **PASSION FRUIT**

Other Names: Granadilla.

General Description: *Passion fruit* (Passiflora edulis) *is a hard-shelled fruit about the size of an egg, filled with a rich, tart pulp.*

The passion fruit is native to southern Brazil and was given its name by Portuguese colonists for whom the flower's elaborate shape symbolized Jesus on the cross. The **purple** passion fruit is subtropical and is widely grown in California. The **yellow** passion fruit is tropical and grows in Hawaii and Fiji.

The small, nearly round fruit looks like a wrinkled dented egg. Its tough shell is smooth and waxy and ranges from dark purple to light yellow. Inside, its cavity is filled with yellowish, jellylike pulp surrounding an abundance of small, black, edible seeds. The shell becomes brittle and wrinkled when ripe.

Passion fruit's distinctive pungent flavor is slightly musky and sweet-tart to extremely tart with a luscious aromatic scent. Yellow passion fruit is generally larger than purple, but the pulp of the purple is less acidic, richer in aroma and flavor, and juicier. Numerous hybrids have been made between the purple and yellow passion fruit.

Season:

Passion fruit is available year-round from Florida, February to July from New Zealand, and July to March from California.

Purchase:

Select fruit that is heavy for its size, large, and plump. When ripe, it is fragrant with a shriveled, wrinkled shell that is rich in color. Any mold on the shell does not affect quality and can be wiped off.

Avoid:	Overly hard passion fruit is underripe.

Storage: If the skin is smooth, ripen at room temperature, turning occasionally. Passion fruit is ripe when it is dented. Store ripe fruit in the refrigerator for up to 1 week.

Preparation:

1. **Slice in half.**

2. **Spoon the pulp out.**

3. **To remove the seeds, strain in a nonaluminum sieve, pressing to extract the juice.**

Serving Suggestions: Cut off the top, pour cream and sugar into the cavity, mix with the pulp, and eat with a spoon. • Add the juice to custard bases. • Add strained fruit purée to blended drinks. • Add to fruit salad.

Flavor Affinities: Cream, guava, ice cream, mango, meringue, mousse, papaya, pineapple, star fruit, sugar, yogurt.

PEACH AND NECTARINE

General Description: *The peach* (Prunus persica) *is a medium-sized round to slightly oval-shaped stone fruit with fuzzy skin. The nectarine* (Prunus persica nucipersica) *is similar to the peach but with smooth skin.* Wild peaches originated in China, where they were small, sour, and hairy. Peaches were cultivated in China over 2,500 years ago, where the fruit was revered as a symbol of longevity and immortality. The cultivated peach traveled westward to Persia, where it flourished so well people assumed it was a native Persian fruit. (Its Latin name means "Persian plum.") The Spaniards brought the peach back from the East and sent it on to the New World.

Clingstone peaches, whose flesh is firmly attached to the stone, mature early and are primarily used for canning. Since peaches survive canning better than most fruits, much of the world's production is canned.

Next in the peach season are **semi-freestone** types, including **Maycrest**, **Redhaven**, and **David Sun**. **Freestones**, with flesh that easily pulls away from the stone, ripen later in the season, about the middle of June. The top variety of freestone peach is the **Elegant Lady**. Other varieties include the **Spring Lady**, **Flavorcrest**, **Rich Lady**, **Red Top**, **Summer Lady**, **O'Henry**, **Ryan Sun**, and **Fairtime**.

A **nectarine** is a fruit all its own, thought to have originated as a mutant of the peach. Its name is derived from the Greek *nektar*, meaning "sweet liquid." Peaches and nectarines are genetically very similar but peaches have fuzz and nectarines are smooth. Many nectarine varieties have a spicy "zing" to their taste. Fuzziness is genetically dominant, but sometimes fuzzy peach trees bear a few smooth nectarines or the other way around. Clingstone varieties of nectarine include **Mayfire**, **July Red**, **May Glo**, **Summer Bright**, **Summer Fire**, and

September Red. Freestone varieties include **Spring Red**, **Summer Grand**, and **Red Diamond**.

White-fleshed peaches and nectarines are savored by connoisseurs for their sweet, luscious flavor, tantalizing fragrance, and novel color. White-fleshed fruits have been cultivated for hundreds of years and have occurred in nature for thousands. Records of white-fleshed peach varieties can be traced to the mid-1600s, and white-fleshed nectarines to the late 1700s. Varieties of white peach include **Babcock** (the most popular), **White Lady**, and **Sugar Giant**, all freestone fruits.

Flat (or **donut**) peaches, originally from China, were first grown in America in the 1800s. This freestone peach is flattened, round, and drawn in at the center. The skin is pale yellow, with a red blush and a small pit. It is sweet and juicy with lots of peach flavor.

Season:

Peaches and nectarines ripen as the weather warms, so they are in season in the spring and summer, depending on the local climate. Because they are easy to grow both above and below the equator, they are available nearly year-round.

Purchase:

Don't be put off by fuzz. The stem end of the peach should be yellow or cream-colored. Look for a well-defined crease. The peach should have a pleasingly sweet fragrance and should be soft to the touch, not mushy.

For both peaches and nectarines, crimson blush indicates variety, not maturity. For nectarines, look for smooth, unblemished skin, creamy yellow background color, plumpness, and slight softening along the seam. Ripe nectarines give to gentle pressure but will not be as soft as a ripe peach.

Avoid: For peaches, avoid "green shoulders" surrounding the stem end—a sign of a prematurely plucked peach. An immature peach will become shriveled or mushy and have tough, poorly flavored flesh. Peaches that exhibit large, flattened bruises will not ripen well. A deep red-brown color, softening of the fruit, or shriveling of the skin at the stem end indicates overripeness.

For nectarines, avoid hard, dull fruits, shriveled fruits, or soft fruits. Avoid fruits with cracked or punctured skin or other signs of decay. Russeting or staining of the skin may affect appearance but generally does not detract from internal quality.

Storage: Handle even hard unripe peaches gently, because any bruises will show later. Ripen peaches in a cool room, stem end down. When you can smell the peaches and they give just slightly, they are ready to eat.

White peaches and nectarines ripen much quicker than yellow varieties. If placed in a paper bag, they will ripen in about a day. They should be checked often. Once ripe, store in the refrigerator for 1 or 2 days.

Preparation: 1. **Wash gently.**

2. **To cut (prior to or after peeling), slice around the seam, twist, and lift or cut out the pit.**

3. **To prevent browning, squeeze fresh lemon juice over cut surfaces.**

4. **Peel, if desired, by dipping whole fruits in boiling water for 10 seconds; remove with a slotted spoon and slip off the skins. This is generally done if cooking the peaches.**

Serving
Suggestions:
Grill peach wedges and serve with pork or chicken. • Fold diced peaches into tapioca pudding just before serving. • Make peach crisp with oatmeal-almond streusel topping.

Flavor
Affinities:
Almonds, apricots, champagne, cherries, cream, ginger, honey, pistachios, plums, pork, poultry, red wine, sour cream, sugar, vanilla, walnuts, white wine.

34a–d.   **PEAR**

General
Description:
The pear (Pyrus communis) *is a firm juicy fruit in the Rosaceae family.* The pear originated in the Caucasus and was spread by Aryan tribes as they migrated into Europe and northern India. During the Middle Ages the pear was especially popular in France and Italy. The introduction of espaliered trees helped to promote the

growing of fine pears in the Paris region, and the fruit was one of the French King Louis XIV's favorites.

Because the first American pears were raised from seed, which do not breed true to variety, American pears became even more diverse than their European ancestors. Today there are nearly 1,000 varieties of pear, divided into two types: granular hard winter pears suitable for poaching and buttery soft eating pears. As pears ripen, their starch reserves convert to natural sugars, increasing their juice and sweetness. Because pears do not ripen well on the tree, they are harvested in a fully mature but unripe condition.

Anjou pears are egg-shaped, relatively hardy, sweet, and juicy with mellow flavor and pale green or red skin. They do not change color as they ripen. Anjous are firm and good for both cooking and eating.

Three-fourths of the pears grown in the United States are **Bartletts**. They are one of the finest eating pears, with smooth texture, juicy flesh, and green skin that ripens to yellow. Much of the Bartlett harvest is canned.

Boscs are winter pears with long, tapering necks that come to a point, fat bottoms, russeted yellow-brown skin, and crisp, creamy white flesh that tastes sweet and spicy. These highly aromatic pears have dense flesh that makes them ideal for baking and cooking. Boscs do not change color as they ripen.

The **Comice**, short for "Doyenné du Comice," is generally considered the best eating pear. It is a fat, blunt yellowish green French variety with a russet or red blush.

Large and exquisite, this "Queen of Pears" has buttery, smooth, sweet flesh and a fruity fragrance. Comices have almost no color change when ripe.

The **Forelle**, or **trout**, pear originated in Saxony in the early 18th century. It is the size and shape of a small Bartlett, with beautiful bright yellow skin, green and red speckles, and sweet, juicy flesh.

The **Packham** pear, originally bred in Australia in 1897, is the Australian pear of choice. A late-season pear, it has bumpy green skin. When fully ripe, it is juicy and sweet. Packham pears are excellent eaten out of hand, but are also suitable for cooking. When cooking Packhams, select slightly underripe, firm pears.

Seckels, the smallest of all commercially grown pears, have a brownish skin with a red blush and firm, sweet, spicy flesh, which makes them excellent for cooking or canning. The texture of Seckels is somewhat grainy.

Season: Anjou and Bosc pears are available in the fall, winter, and spring, while Bartlett, Comice, Forelle, and Seckel are confined to just the fall and winter. Packhams are available in spring and summer months.

Purchase: Look for firm, well-colored pears.

Avoid: Pass up bruised or blemished pears.

Storage: Ripen pears in a cool place, setting them on their bottoms. Handle pears gently: The riper they are, the more easily they bruise. When you buy a pear, the skin will be bright, shiny, and taut. As the pear slowly ripens over a period of 4 to 5 days, the skin will become matte. To hasten the ripening process, place pears in a pierced paper bag with an apple or banana. When ripe, pears are fragrant, and the flesh at the stem yields to gentle pressure and may have a few brown spots. Once ripe, store in the refrigerator for 2 or 3 days.

Preparation:

1. **Wash gently.**

2. **It's not necessary to peel pears when serving them fresh. If cooking, peel with a vegetable peeler. Pear skins darken and toughen when heated.**

3. **After peeling, place in a bowl of water with lemon juice to avoid browning.**

Serving Suggestions:

Serve sliced Bartlett or Comice pears with small chunks of Parmigiano-Reggiano or pecorino cheese. • Poach peeled Bosc or Seckel pears in flavored simple syrup. • Add diced pears to green salads. • Serve Forelle or Anjou pears at room temperature with Brie, or serve ripe pears with Gorgonzola, Roquefort, Cabrales, or Stilton cheese.

Flavor Affinities:

Allspice, bay leaf, blue cheeses, cardamom, chocolate, cinnamon, clove, duck, honey, pork, poultry, red wine, rosemary, thyme, vanilla, white wine.

35. **PERSIMMON**

Other Names: Date plum, kaki, simmon.

General Description: *The American persimmon* (Diospyros virginiana) *and the Japanese persimmon* (Diospyros kaki) *are both squat orange-colored fruits with four papery leaves on top and very sweet jellylike flesh.* The **American** persimmon was once a valuable fruit in the eastern U.S. but now is rarely eaten, partly because it has been eclipsed in popularity by the larger Asian persimmon. Early European settlers learned to eat persimmons from Native American tribes, who left the fruit on the tree well into October to ripen it thoroughly and enhance its sweetness. The colonists made persimmons into puddings, preserves, and wine and other alcoholic drinks.

The **Japanese** persimmon is a cultivated fruit whose wild ancestor grew in China. It has long been popular in China, Japan, and Korea—it is Japan's national fruit and is a traditional food for the Japanese New Year.

When ripe, these fruits are extremely sweet. Their Latin name, *diospyros*, means "food of the gods." Americans eat Japanese persimmons as a fresh fruit, while in Asia they are often dried for storage and used during the winter and early spring. The **Hachiya** and the **Fuyu** are both Japanese varieties with thin, smooth red-orange skin that can bruise easily. The entire fruit is edible except for the seed and calyx (the papery leaves). The Hachiya is heart-shaped with creamy, astringent but sweet flavor and apricot-like flesh. In California, Hachiyas are tissue-wrapped and packed in wood boxes for shipment by rail in refrigerated cars. The bright orange, tomato-shaped Fuyu is a nonastringent variety. It can be eaten like an apple and has a sweet, mildly spicy flavor.

The **Sharon fruit** is an Israeli variety bred to be edible when still firm. Though introduced to France and other Mediterranean countries in the 19th century, it is actually much older—Jewish texts dating back to the 3rd century mention the fruit. The small square-shaped fruits are orange-tan in color. They have sweet flesh even when firm and are seedless and coreless. They are named after the Sharon Valley, between Haifa and Tel Aviv, where they are cultivated.

Season:	California persimmons are available October to December, but peak season is mid-October. Sharon fruit is available from late November to mid-February.
Purchase:	Choose smooth, brightly colored persimmons that are plump and glossy.
Avoid:	Persimmons with yellow patches are unripe.
Storage:	Because Hachiyas are so delicate when ripe, they are shipped to market while still hard. An unripe Hachiya can be stored up to 1 month in the refrigerator prior to ripening at home. Ripen at home at room temperature;

they may take up to a week to reach a completely soft state. When the flesh is nearly translucent, it's ready to eat. Fuyu persimmons should be purchased when firm. Enjoy them crunchy and sweet, or soften a bit at room temperature. Once ripe, persimmons don't keep well. Eat right away or refrigerate for a day or two.

Ripen Sharon fruit at room temperature for 48 hours and then refrigerate for up to 10 days. Small brown spots may appear on the surface and inside the fruit, a sign that the sugar in the fruit has crystallized and created sweet pockets.

Preparation:

1. **Wash gently.**

2. **With a knife, cut in half.**

3. **Cut out the core and discard the seeds.**

Note: An unripe persimmon is highly astringent because of the tannin. Freeze the fruit overnight and then thaw to soften and remove astringency. Ripe persimmons can be frozen with no loss of flavor.

Serving Suggestions:

Dice Fuyu or Sharon fruit and add to fruit or vegetable salads. • Blend ripe persimmon with soy milk or soft, silken tofu and a dash of cinnamon to make a smoothie. • Add mashed Hachiyas to pancake or waffle batter. • Substitute persimmon pulp for zucchini in quick breads.

Flavor Affinities: Almonds, apple, brandy, cinnamon, ginger, grapes, hazelnuts, ice cream, kiwi, lemon, lime, orange, pine nuts, pomegranate, soft cheese, walnuts, yogurt.

36a–b.

PINEAPPLE

General Description: *The pineapple* (Ananas comosus) *is a large fruit with a crown of spiny leaves and juicy, acidic, fragrant flesh.* Pineapples are native to Brazil and were growing throughout South and Central America and the West Indies before Columbus arrived in 1493 and carried the fruit back to Spain. Spanish explorers named the fruit for its resemblance to a pinecone. Portuguese sailors who traded to and from Brazil spread the Brazilian Tuli Indian name, *anana*, meaning "excellent fruit," forms of which are used in most languages.

Because of slow transportation, a fresh pineapple was a true rarity in Europe. The search for a way to grow pineapples in England stimulated the development of the greenhouse. In colonial America, if fresh pineapple was available, it was typically displayed on an extravagantly laden banquet table. The pineapple thus became a symbol of hospitality.

The Spanish probably took the fruit to Hawaii, now the world's leading producer, early in the 16th century. Toward the end of the 19th century, James Dole, a horticulturist, arrived in Hawaii. Within 15 years, pineapple became Hawaii's second-largest industry (after sugarcane).

By the 1950s, pineapple was synonymous with Hawaii.

The cylindrical composite fruit is formed of 100 to 200 berrylike fruitlets fused together off a fibrous core. The tough, waxy rind may be dark green, yellow, orange-yellow, or reddish when the fruit is ripe. The flesh ranges from nearly white to yellow. Latin American pineapples tend to have a greener shell color, even when ripe.

There are many different varieties of pineapple. The **Baby Sugar Loaf** pineapple, native to Mexico, can be picked yellow and shipped without reducing the shelf life. In the mid-1960s, Del Monte bred its own variety of pineapple, the **Del Monte Gold**, which is twice as sweet as traditional pineapples. The **Kona Sugarloaf** pineapple is round to conical in shape, weighs 5 to 6 pounds (2.2–2.7 kg), and has flesh that is white to yellow, very sweet and juicy—it's actually too tender for shipping. The **Natal Queen** pineapple keeps well after ripening and has juicy, crisp, aromatic flesh and a small, tender core. The **Red Spanish** pineapple is the most popular cultivar in the West Indies, Venezuela, and Mexico and is well adapted for shipping to distant markets. It has spiny leaves and orange-red skin with deep eyes. Its flesh is pale yellow, fibrous, aromatic, large-cored, and flavorful. The **Smooth Cayenne**, also called **Sweet Spineless**, is the most widely planted pineapple in Hawaii. It is juicy and rich with excellent flavor that is mildly acidic and very sweet. It has an orange rind, shallow eyes, a cylindrical shape, and smooth leaves. The **South African Baby** pineapple measures just 5 by 3 inches (12.5 x 7.5 cm) and has golden-colored skin and a bright yellow interior. It is sweet, very juicy, and tender and has a crunchy edible core.

Season:
Pineapples are available year-round with peak season March to June.

Purchase:
Choose a pineapple that is plump, large, heavy for its size, and slightly soft to the touch. The stem end should have a sweet aroma. Fresh, deep green leaves are a good sign. The eyes may be flat and almost hollow. Highly colored pineapples have higher sugar content because they were picked riper. While fragrance is a sign of quality, most pineapples are kept too cold to be fragrant.

Avoid:
Pineapples that have dry brown leaves or a dull yellow appearance will have an acidic taste. Avoid pineapples that have bruises, discoloration, or soft spots. Avoid mold, an unpleasant odor, and dark, watery eyes.

Storage:
Pineapples are picked ripe because once off the tree the starch will not turn to sugar. Pineapples develop dark spots from temperature changes. If bought chilled, keep refrigerated; if bought at room temperature, keep at room temperature. Refrigerate tightly wrapped in plastic for up to 3 days or keep at room temperature for several days. Cut and tightly sealed pineapple can remain in the refrigerator for 3 days. Pineapple ferments easily, so keep it in a cool place out of direct sunlight.

Preparation:

1. **Cut a thick slice from the top and the bottom.**

2. **Pare the skin from the top downward.**

3. **Remove the eyes by cutting diagonal grooves.**

4. **Cut into wedges and cut out the core or cut into slices and remove the core with a small round cookie cutter to make rings.**

Note: When combining pineapple with gelatin, the fruit should be cooked first because an enzyme in raw pineapple will prevent gelatin from setting.

Serving Suggestions:

Broil pineapple slices with brown sugar and a few drops of rum. • Thread pineapple chunks on skewers and grill with lamb or seafood. • Blend pineapple, coconut, half-and-half, ice, dark rum, and sugar till slushy.

Flavor Affinities:

Banana, brown sugar, coconut, curry, ginger, ham, honey, lime, mango, pork, poultry, rum, shrimp, yams.

37a–c. **PLUM**

Other Names: *Prune* (France).

General Description:

The plum (Prunus domestica) is a stone fruit with green, yellow, red, blue, purple, or almost black skin and firm, juicy, tart flesh. Plums were known by the ancient Egyptians, Etruscans, Greeks, and Romans, but the earliest cultivation took place in China. They can be as small as a cherry or as large as a baseball, and round, elongated, or heart-shaped. The flavor of a good, ripe plum has a sweet-tart balance. Since medieval times the English word "prune" has meant a dried extra-sweet variety of plum. In France the fresh fruit is called *prune* and the dried fruit is *pruneau*.

European plums, including **damson, greengage, Mirabelle, Quetsche,** and **Italian prune,** are small and firm, often having yellow-gold flesh. They are generally less sweet than other plum varieties and are used frequently in jams, jellies, and liqueurs. Asian plums, including **Burbank, El Dorado, Elephant Heart, Santa Rosa, Wickson, Mariposa,** and **Satsuma,** now dominate in California. Of these, the Santa Rosa and Satsuma are the most popular varieties, the former having amber flesh tinged red and the latter having dark red flesh.

Other varieties of plum include the **Agen**, used only for prunes, the **Angelino**, with purple skin and yellow flesh, the **Black Amber**, with shiny black skin and deep red flesh, the **Casselman**, a late-season plum with bright red skin and deep amber flesh, the **Emerald Beaut**, with light green skin and greenish yellow flesh, the **Friar** plum, with black skin and amber flesh, the **Golden Nectar**, with yellow skin and amber flesh and a small pit, the heart-shaped **Kelsey**, with green-yellow skin, the **Laroda**, with dark red-purple skin and reddish flesh, the **Nubiana**, shiny black with deep amber flesh, the **Red Beauty**, with tart red-purple skin and sweet amber flesh, the **Redheart**, with maroon skin and blood-red flesh, and the **Simka**, a purple plum with amber flesh.

Season: California plums are available June through September. Chilean plums are available January through March.

Purchase: Look for plump, shapely fruit that is well colored and firm to the touch, without cracks or blemishes.

Avoid: Pass up plums that are either too soft or too hard.

Storage: Ripen at room temperature till the skin loses its shine. Once ripe, refrigerate for up to 4 or 5 days.

Preparation:

1. **Wash gently.**

2. **Slice in half around the pit and rotate the halves to separate. Discard the pit.**

Serving Suggestions: Top pastry with almond frangipane and thinly sliced plums, then bake till set and plums are juicy. • Combine thin-sliced plums, red onion, and olive oil with balsamic vinegar, arugula, and fried strips of prosciutto.

Flavor Affinities: Allspice, black pepper, brandy, cardamom, cinnamon, crème fraîche, ginger, honey, nutmeg, orange, port wine, red wine, sour cream, white wine, yogurt.

38.   **POMEGRANATE**

Other Names: Chinese apple, *granada* (Spain), *grenade* (France).

General
Description: *The pomegranate* (Punica granatum) *is a round fruit with hard red skin and many translucent crimson-colored small edible seeds.* Native to Persia (now Iran), the pomegranate is one of the seven fruits mentioned in the Old Testament. Rubylike multitudes of shiny seeds have made the pomegranate the symbol of fertility in legends around the world.

The Moors brought pomegranates to Spain around A.D. 800 and the city of Granada was named for them. The French named their hand-tossed explosive after the seed-scattering properties of the fruit. Pomegranates were brought to California by Spanish settlers in 1769 and are now grown in the drier parts of California and Arizona. Pomegranates are also grown in the Middle East, Africa, India, Malaysia, and southern Europe.

Pomegranates are nearly round, 2.5 to 5 inches (6.2–12.5 cm) in diameter, and crowned by a prominent calyx. The leathery skin is pink or rich crimson over yellow. Inside, pods of ruby red kernels, each containing a hard seed, are enclosed in a thin membrane surrounded by white, acrid, spongy pith. The many varieties of pomegranate include **Balegal**, **Early Wonderful**, **Fleshman**, **Green Globe**, **Phoenicia**, and **Wonderful**. The large, glossy, deep red or purple Wonderful is the most widely planted pomegranate in California.

Season: Pomegranates are in season from August to December.

Purchase: Choose large, brightly-colored, shiny pomegranates that are firm to the touch and heavy for their size. Pomegranates are ripe when they make a metallic sound when tapped.

Avoid: Overripe fruits tend to have cracks in their skin. Avoid bruised, shriveled, dull, or overly hard pomegranates.

Storage: Pomegranates keep well at room temperature for 2 to 3 weeks, becoming juicier and more flavorful with time. Or store pomegranates for up to 1 month in the refrigerator. Freeze pomegranate seeds for up to 3 months.

Preparation: **Note: Avoid using aluminum and carbon steel knives or pots as they can turn the juice bitter.**

1. **Cut off the crown.**

2. **Gently scoop out some of the center white core with a spoon.**

3. **Score just through the outer rind, marking the fruit into quarters.**

4. **Place your thumb in the center of the core and gently pull apart the sections.**

5.   **Peel away the white pith and discard.**

6.   **Turn the skin inside out and pop out the seeds.**

7.   **To separate the seeds from any remaining white pith, place sections of pomegranate in a bowl of cold water and gently swish around. The white pieces should float to the top while the seeds sink.**

Note: To juice a pomegranate, put the seeds through a juicer or ream the halved fruits on an orange juice squeezer. Alternatively, warm the fruit slightly and roll it between your hands to soften. Cut a hole in the stem end and place it over a glass. Let the juice run out, squeezing the fruit to extract it.

Serving Suggestions:

Add pomegranate juice to lemonade. • Use pomegranate juice to make jelly or sorbet, flavor baked apples, and instead of or in addition to citrus juice in marinades for meats and poultry. • Simmer pomegranate seeds in water to cover till soft, then press out the juice through a sieve, add an equal amount of sugar, and simmer for 10 minutes to make a syrup. (Cool and store in a bottle.) • Sprinkle pomegranate seeds on Middle Eastern dishes such as hummus, baba ghanoush, and rice pilaf.

Flavor Affinities:

Apple, cardamom, chicken, cinnamon, ginger, honey, lamb, lemon, orange, pork, port wine, red wine, tangerine, turkey, white wine.

39. **QUINCE**

Other Names:	Golden apple, *marmelo* (Portugal).
General Description:	*The quince* (Cydonia oblonga) *is a round or pear-shaped, lumpy fruit with yellow skin, sometimes covered with fuzz, that must be cooked before eating.* The quince is one of the earliest-known fruits: Many believe that Eve's forbidden fruit in the Garden of Eden was a quince. In Greek legend, Helen of Troy convinced Paris to award a quince to Aphrodite as the prize in a beauty contest, thus starting the Trojan War.

Although the quince has been cultivated for thousands of years, it has largely retained the character of a wild fruit. The fruit's unique fragrance, hinting of pineapple, guava, and pear, can easily perfume a room. Quinces weigh $1/2$ to 1 pound (.25–.5 kg), are asymmetrical and bright yellow, and look like short-necked pears. A characteristic feltlike coating wipes off easily, revealing thin waxy skin that emanates a sweet, fresh fragrance when rubbed. The hard, dry flesh of the quince turns light pink to rose red and softer and sweeter once cooked (with sugar).

Quince preserves are the ancestors of both jam and marmalade. The word "marmalade," in fact, comes from the Portuguese name for quince preserves. Quince is used for baking and preserves because of its subtle flavor and high level of pectin.

The most common variety is the **pineapple** quince,

which resembles a large, smooth, knobby pear with golden yellow skin, white flesh, and a pineapple aroma. The **perfumed** quince is oval with tapered ends, smooth yellow skin, and white flesh. The **champion** quince is a very fuzzy, pear-shaped, delicately flavored late-season quince. The rare **Portugal** quince is giant, bulbous, and football-shaped with a deep, rich flavor.

Season: Pineapple quinces are available August to November from California; perfumed quinces are available from October to February from California.

Purchase: Choose quinces that are large and firm. Although quinces bruise easily, marks on the skin do not affect quality. Once ripe, the fruit will turn from green to yellow but will still be firm.

Avoid: Steer clear of soft, shriveled, or overly bruised fruit.

Storage: Quinces may be stored at room temperature, but will deteriorate after 1 week. Refrigerate quinces for several weeks, wrapped well in paper towels to avoid bruising.

Preparation: **Note: Quince must be cooked before eating, either by baking, poaching, roasting, sautéing, or stewing.**

1. **Lightly wash the fruit. Smaller perfumed quinces tend to have fuzz on the skin that rubs off when washed.**

2. **Peel, using a vegetable peeler or knife.**

3. **To core, first halve lengthwise, then scoop out the large seed cavity using a melon baller.**

4. **Place peeled quince in water with lemon juice until ready to cook.**

Serving Suggestions: Poach peeled quince in flavored simple syrup. • Use quince in jam or marmalade. • Add quince to meat stew. • Roast quince with poultry. • Add quince to apple pie to add fragrant, spicy flavor and extra body (because of the pectin).

Flavor Affinities: Bay leaf, black pepper, cardamom, cinnamon, cloves, ginger, honey, nutmeg, vanilla.

40a–b.

RASPBERRY

General Description: *Raspberries* (Rubus *genus*) *are soft multiple fruits with tart, intensely flavored juice.* The red raspberry is indigenous to both Asia Minor and North America. Fruits were gathered from the wild by the people of Troy; later the Romans spread cultivation throughout Europe. When the colonists came to America, they brought the European cultivated raspberry *(Rubus idaeus)* with them and found Native Americans drying the American wild raspberry *(Rubus strigosus).*

Each raspberry is composed of many individual sections of fruit, each with its own seed, surrounding a central core. There are three main types: golden, black, and the more common red raspberry. Red raspberries thrive in the relatively cool, marine climate of the Pacific Northwest.

Golden raspberries are a relatively new variety. They have a luscious flavor reminiscent of softly perfumed apricots. Black raspberries are native to North America and common in the eastern U.S. and Canada. They are usually purplish black, with small seeds and a hollow core, though yellow and red forms also exist.

Season: Red raspberries are available year-round throughout the United States, especially to the restaurant trade, but peak season is June to early September. Golden raspberries are available in limited quantity from June to October. Black raspberries are in season in July.

Purchase: Raspberries are delicate. The best-tasting ones will have been handled very carefully. Look for berries that are full and round, not flattened. The walls of the berry should be full and meaty, not skimpy. Superb berries have a hazy, soft "gloss."

Avoid: Turn over the container to inspect before purchase. A stained container is a sign of overripe or decaying berries. Avoid raspberries with tiny dents or bruises or ones that are broken apart or moldy.

Storage: Raspberries are very perishable and must be refrigerated. Keep cold but not too cold: Raspberries are very sensitive to freeze damage. Moisture will hasten decay, so do not wash raspberries until just before serving. Raspberries should keep for 1 to 2 days in the refrigerator.

Preparation:

1. **Rinse gently when ready to use.**

2. **Spread onto paper towels to dry.**

Serving Suggestions: Purée raspberries for dessert sauce or beverages, adding sugar to taste and straining, as desired. • Combine sliced peaches, pears, or nectarines with raspberries and serve with chocolate sauce and sweetened whipped cream. • Blend raspberries, white balsamic vinegar, vegetable oil, honey, rosemary, salt, and black pepper to taste to make a raspberry vinaigrette for green salads or grilled chicken.

Flavor Affinities: Champagne, chocolate, cream, framboise, honey, kirsch, peaches, pears, sour cream, sugar, vanilla.

41. **STAR FRUIT**

Other Names: Carambola, Chinese star fruit, five-angled fruit.

General Description: *Star fruit* (Averrhoa carambola) *is an oval fruit with five prominent longitudinal ribs, thin, yellow, smooth waxy skin, and yellow, translucent, crisp flesh.* The carambola is believed to have originated in Ceylon and the Moluccas, but has been cultivated in Southeast Asia and Malaysia for centuries. It is grown in southern China, Taiwan, and India and is popular in the Philippines, Australia, Tahiti, and Hawaii. Star fruits were introduced to southern Florida more than 100 years ago.

Star fruit gets its name from the characteristic five-pointed stars that are formed when it is cut. The greenish yellow fruit, 2.5 to 5 inches (6.2–12.5 cm) long, ripens to a dark yellow color with brownish edges on the ribs. The flesh is translucent yellow, crisp, very juicy, and fiber free. It tastes like a cross between tart apple and grape.

There are two types of star fruit, **sweet** and **tart**—it can be difficult to tell them apart. The tart star fruit is smaller, has a strong lemony taste from oxalic acid, and is used mainly for cooking. The sweet fruit is larger with thicker, fleshier ribs. There are also several white varieties, all of which are sweet. As a general rule, the yellower it is, the sweeter the fruit. The fruit may contain up to 12 flat, thin brown seeds, or none at all.

Season: Sweet fruits are available from summer to late winter. Tart fruits are available from late summer to midwinter.

Purchase: Choose large, plump, firm, crisp fruits with shiny skin.

Avoid: Do not buy shriveled or wrinkled fruits. The skin should not be too green or have brown spots.

Storage:

Ripen at room temperature in a covered container for about 2 days, until the fruit is solid golden yellow in color. Browning along the edges is common and does not affect taste. Carambolas will keep 1 week in the refrigerator. They bruise easily, so handle with care.

Preparation:

1. **Rinse the fruit.**

2. **Slice off and discard the ends. You do not need to peel the fruit, but if the outer edges of the ribs are too brown, they will be somewhat tough and bitter and should be cut away.**

3. **Cut into crosswise slices and pick out any seeds.**

Serving Suggestions:

Grill star fruit slices with shrimp or chicken. • Blend and strain, then add pineapple juice to taste and serve over ice. • Add sliced star fruit to chicken salad. • Add slices to garnish iced tea and tropical drinks.

Flavor Affinities:

Avocado, basil, chicken, cilantro, cloves, curry, kiwi, lime, mango, mint, pineapple, rum, shrimp, tequila.

42.   **STRAWBERRY**

General Description:

Strawberries (Fragaria *genus) are small red fruits dotted with tiny yellowish achenes, often called seeds. The word "strawberry" was used as early as* A.D. *1000 in*

England. It may derive from the word "strew," because the mother plant strews or scatters new plants when it sends out runners for propagation, and the fruit itself is strewn among the leaves. The wide distribution of wild strawberries is largely due to birds. The strawberry of the Middle Ages, often portrayed in Gothic art, was the little wood strawberry *(Fragaria vesca)*, which is still much esteemed for its perfume and flavor.

Native Americans collected the North American wild strawberry *(Fragaria virginiana)*, which is larger than its wild European counterpart. They would crush the berries and mix them with cornmeal to make strawberry bread. Wild strawberries were so plentiful in America that there was no garden culture of the fruit until about 1770.

The cultivated, large-fruited strawberry originated in Europe in the 18th century when they were bred with species introduced from the New World. In 1780, the first strawberry hybrid, "Hudson," was developed in the U.S., and commercial strawberry growing began.

The strawberry fruit in the botanical sense is not a berry, but is the greatly enlarged stem end, in which are partially embedded the many true fruits, or achenes. Their flavor is sweet and luscious.

Season: Strawberries are available year-round, with peak supply

           spring through summer.

Purchase: Choose plump, bright red berries with green, fresh looking caps. The size of the strawberry is not important; all strawberries, large or small, can be sweet and juicy. Look for locally-grown strawberries in June because they will be the sweetest and juiciest.

Avoid: Pass up strawberries with limp or spoiled green caps. Avoid strawberries with white or green areas, mold, excess moisture, or damage.

Storage: Cover and refrigerate without washing for 1 or 2 days, lightly wrapped with plastic. Do not crowd or press; handle gently. Sort and remove any bruised or damaged berries as soon as possible and use in sauces, purées, or jams. To savor fresh-picked strawberries at their best, eat them right away without chilling.

Preparation:
1. **Swish them around in a bowl of cold water.**

2. **Lift out, shaking off the excess water, and lay out on paper towels to dry.**

3. **Hull strawberries with a small paring knife (cut out the core in a cone shape).**

Serving Suggestions: Dip whole strawberries in sour cream, brown sugar, or white sugar and eat raw. • Blend lemon-flavored carbonated water, fresh strawberries, lime juice, and crushed ice together, adding sugar to taste to make a strawberry slushie. • Add strawberry purée to iced tea.

Flavor
Affinities: Almonds, balsamic vinegar, blackberries, blueberries,
champagne, custards, heavy cream, kirsch, lemon,
melon, sour cream, sugar, walnuts, whipped cream.

43. 📷   **TAMARILLO**

Other Names: Tree tomato.

General
Description: *The tamarillo* (Cyphomandra betacea) *is an egg-shaped
fruit with glossy, smooth skin and soft, juicy, sweet-tart
flesh.* The tamarillo is probably native to the Andes of
Peru and is now cultivated in Argentina, Brazil,
Colombia, and Venezuela. Tamarillos are distantly
related to both tomatoes (see page 274) and tomatillos
(see page 272). They were commonly known as tree
tomatoes until 1967, when New Zealand producers
invented the new name.

Tamarillos are sold with their stem attached and
have tough, bitter skin that may be solid deep purple,
blood red, orange, yellow, or red and yellow, and may
have faint dark stripes. Most tamarillos in the market,
however, are red or yellow. Tiny edible seeds are embedded in the apricot-like flesh, which has a bitter-tart
tomato flavor.

While tamarillo skin is somewhat tough and
unpleasant in flavor, the outer layer of the flesh is firm,
succulent, and bland, and the pulp surrounding the seed
in two lengthwise compartments is sweet, soft, and tart.

Yellow tamarillos are usually sweeter. The edible seeds are thin, nearly flat circles.

Season:	Tamarillos are available from May through October in specialty produce stores and some supermarkets.
Purchase:	Choose fragrant, heavy fruit that is free of blemishes.
Avoid:	Steer clear of small, shriveled, or damaged fruit.
Storage:	Ripen at room temperature until they are fragrant and yield slightly to palm pressure. Refrigerate up to 10 days when tightly wrapped in plastic. Temperatures below 38°F (3°C) can cause the skin to discolor.
Preparation:	**Note: The fruit should not be cut on a wooden or other permeable surface, as the juice will make an indelible stain.**

1. **If eaten fresh, tamarillos need not be peeled. When cooking, remove the skin. Pour boiling water over the fruit and let it stand for 4 minutes.**

2. **Peel off the skin by hand.**

Serving Suggestions:	Cut ripe tamarillos in half lengthwise, sprinkle with sugar, and eat by scooping out the flesh and pulp.

• Combine diced, peeled tamarillos, chicken broth, diced eggplant, sliced mushrooms, diced red, yellow, or orange bell pepper, chopped garlic, basil, and oregano in a large saucepan, bring the mixture to a boil, and simmer partially covered for 30 minutes or until tender, then season, stir in a little extra virgin olive oil, and sprinkle with grated Parmesan to make tamarillo ratatouille. • Simmer tamarillos with brown sugar, water, beef stock, and Chinese five-spice powder, then blend to make a sauce for ham or pork.

Flavor Affinities:
Avocado, basil, brown sugar, cinnamon, clove, eggplant, garlic, honey, lamb, mint, olive oil, orange zest, oregano, star anise, sugar, sweet onions, sweet peppers, turkey.

44. 📷   **TAMARIND**

Other Names:
Asam koh (China), *cay me* (Vietnam), Indian date (Britain), *tamar hindi* (Middle East).

General Description:
Tamarind (Tamarindus indica) is a hard brown fruit pod filled with hard seeds surrounded by tangy edible pulp. Tamarind is the fruit pod of a large and beautiful evergreen tree native to tropical Africa. Tamarinds had already spread to India by prehistoric times, have long been established in Southeast Asia, and now grow throughout tropical and subtropical regions. The pods grow in clusters that hang on the tree long after they are mature and contain up to 10 dark brown seeds surrounded by dark brown pulp that tastes acidic and

slightly woody, with prune and orange overtones.

Its name comes from the Arabic *tamar hindi*, which means "Indian date." Its dark brown pulp reminded the nomadic Arabs, who imported tamarind from India since ancient times, of the familiar date. Tamarind is used in the Middle East, India, Indonesia, the Caribbean, and Latin America in much the same way vinegars and lemon juice are in European cuisine. It is a basic flavoring for chutneys and is made into cooling drinks. The citric, sweet-sour flavor of tamarind goes well with chiles, and it is widely used in Mexico and in India with hot foods.

Season: Fresh tamarind pods are in season in spring and early summer and may be found in Asian, Indian, and Caribbean markets and well-stocked supermarkets.

Purchase: Select clean, relatively unbroken pods.

Avoid: Do not buy old, dried-out tamarind.

Storage: Store the pods for up to 3 weeks in the refrigerator.

Preparation:

1. **Cut open the pod and remove the flesh.**

2. **Separate the tamarind flesh from the seeds by scraping with a knife or by rubbing the seeds against a bowl with a wooden spoon.**

Serving Suggestions:	Combine boiling water with tamarind pulp, add sugar or honey to taste, and cool, covered, then strain, dilute with water, and serve over ice. • Soak pitted dates and tamarind pulp in cold water to cover, then blend with the soaking liquid, strain through a sieve, stir in salt, ground coriander seed, and brown sugar to taste to make a date-tamarind chutney. • Squeeze lime juice over fresh peeled tamarind pods and then dip in a mixture of sugar, ground chile, and salt and eat raw.
Flavor Affinties:	Almonds, banana, chicken, chile peppers, cinnamon, coconut, coriander, cumin, curry, duck, eggplant, ginger, mango, pork ribs, potatoes, scallops, shrimp, star anise.

45a–d.

TANGERINE, TANGELO, AND TANGOR

Other Names:	**Tangerine**: Mandarin orange.
General Description:	*Tangerines* (Citrus reticulata) *are a group of flattened, sweet, orange-colored citrus fruits with loose, easily peeled skin and sweet-tart, juicy flesh.* Called mandarins in England and, later, tangerines in the U.S., these fruits were first cultivated in China thousands of years ago.

Their Latin name, *reticulata*, meaning "netted," refers to the fibrous strands of pith under the loose rind. Tangerines are distinguished by their zipper skin—meaning that you can easily separate the skin from the fruit. They are smaller than oranges, flattened in shape |

(except for some hybrids), easily separated into segments, and less acidic than oranges. They normally contain more water and less sugar than oranges and are often darker in color. There are many varieties of tangerine, including **Dancy**, **Fairchild**, and **Sunburst**. **Satsumas**, which were developed in Japan in the 16th century, are sometimes placed in a separate species, *Citrus unshiu*. **Tangors** *(Citrus nobilis)* are a cross between tangerines and oranges and tend to be large and similar to oranges in flavor—and include **Honey**, **Honey Murcott**, **Ortanique**, and **Temple**. **Clementines**, another member of the tangerine family, are small, thin-peeled, and usually seedless.

   Tangelos *(Citrus paradisi x Citrus reticulata)* are hybrids of grapefruits and tangerines and noted for their juiciness and mildly sweet flavor. Varieties with more tangerine qualities include **Minneloa**, **Orlando**, and **Honeybell**.

Season: Tangerines are in season from winter through early

spring. Tangelos are available in the winter, and tangors are generally in season in the winter and spring.

Purchase: When selecting tangerines, look for fruit that fills the skin. Tangerines sold with stems and leaves, found mostly in the winter holiday season, are usually of very high quality. For clementines, look at the top and the stem end and make sure it's not softened—the skin *will* seem loose.

Avoid:	Hollow-feeling fruits or fruits with soft or dented spots should be avoided.
Storage:	Store tangerines for 1 week in a plastic bag in the refrigerator. Clementines deteriorate quickly and should be eaten within 4 or 5 days.
Preparation:	1. **Peel the skin; it should come off easily.**
	2. **Separate the segments.**
	3. **To remove any seeds, cut a small slit in the inside of the segment in the center, and squeeze out the seeds through the opening.**
Serving Suggestions:	Use tangerine juice in sauces, dressings, sorbet, and marinades. • Make curd using any standard lemon curd recipe, substituting tangerine juice and zest for lemon, and spread on scones or biscuits or use to fill a fruit tart. • Add grated tangerine peel to brownie mix, cheesecake, baked custard, or pastry cream. • Dip tangerine segments (seeds removed) in chocolate sauce, caramel sauce, or flavored yogurt.
Flavor Affinties:	Apricot, banana, chicken, chocolate, crab, cream, duck, fish, hollandaise sauce, melon, passion fruit, scallops, shrimp, sugar, turkey, vinaigrette.

46. **YUZU**

Other Names: Japanese citrus.

General Description:

The yuzu (Citrus ichangensis x Citrus reticulata) *is a Japanese citrus fruit about the size of a tangerine with an intense lemon-lime flavor and rough, fragrant skin.* Yuzu, one of the most cold resistant of the citrus fruits, grows wild in Tibet and the interior of China. Bright yellow when ripe, the thick uneven skin encloses pale flesh containing many pips. It is commonly grown in Japan, where it's a prized culinary ingredient. It is stronger in flavor than lemon, with a hint of tangerine, grapefruit, and pine.

When harvested early in the season, yuzu is lime-colored, but by season's end, the fruits turn lemon yellow. Young dark green yuzu is comparable to citron or lime, the mature yellow fruit to a lemon. The surface of the yuzu is rough and uneven, and the peel's fragrance is unlike any citrus familiar in Western countries. It is an important ingredient in *ponzu,* a Japanese dipping sauce. There is a tradition in Japan to take a *yuzu-yu,* or a yuzu bath, on the evening of the winter solstice. This is a hot bath to which several whole yuzus are added; they float.

Season:

Yuzus are available November through May, in very limited quantities at specialty and Japanese markets.

Purchase:	Look for firm, rough-skinned fruit.
Avoid:	Pass up shriveled fruit or fruit with any mold.
Storage:	Store yuzu in plastic for up to 1 week in the refrigerator.
Preparation:	1. **Wash the fruit in hot, soapy water.**
	2. **Grate the zest, if desired.**
	3. **Juice the yuzu by slicing it in half and using a juicer or reamer to extract the juice.**
	Note: Yuzu juice is very fresh and tangy, though too acidic to be drunk on its own.
Serving Suggestions:	Marinate bay scallops in yuzu juice for seviche, or mix tuna tartare with mango and yuzu juice. • Add yuzu juice to iced tea. • Combine yuzu juice, soy sauce, garlic, black pepper, and grapeseed oil to make a salad dressing. • Garnish clear soups with grated yuzu rind.
Flavor Affinities:	Bitter greens, gin, mango, matsutake mushrooms, mirin, miso, olive oil, raw fish, rice wine vinegar, seviche, shellfish, soy sauce, sweet onions, tea, tofu, tuna, vodka.

Vegetables

47a–b. 📷 **AMARANTH**

Other Names: African spinach, bush greens, calailu, callaloo, Chinese spinach, hinn-choy, Indian spinach, Joseph's coat, strawberry spinach, tampala.

General
Description:

Amaranth (Amaranthus edulis and others) is a group of plants from which the edible green leaves and, in some cases, grain, is derived. Amaranth grows all around the world, mostly in the tropics. The name "amaranth" derives from the Greek *amarantos* (unfading) because of an ancient belief that it was immortal.

The Aztecs revered amaranth grain and used it in religious rituals. After Spanish conquistadors destroyed much of the amaranth, the grain fell into obscurity for the next four centuries. In the late 1990s it was rediscovered and is now touted for its healthful properties. Amaranth greens, which taste similar to spinach, are edible, as are the seeds, which can be ground into flour.

Amaranth greens can be somewhat bitter. Young amaranth and the **red micro** variety may be used raw in salads; older amaranth greens are cooked. In the Caribbean, amaranth greens are known as callaloo and are essential to the famous soup of the same name, made with taro, ham hocks, peppers, celery, okra, coconut milk, and crabmeat.

Season:	Amaranth is available in all but the coldest winter months, and it is most likely to be carried in Indian, Caribbean, and Asian markets.
Purchase:	As with most greens crops, the young succulent leaves are preferred for eating.
Avoid:	Avoid wilted or yellowed greens. Greens that are too large will be overly bitter.
Storage:	Keep amaranth greens refrigerated in a plastic bag for up to 3 days.

Preparation:

1. **Wash amaranth vigorously in a bowl of tepid water, agitating several times so that dirt falls to the bottom. Lift the greens out of the water so that the dirt stays behind.**

2. **Separate the leaves and ribs, reserving the ribs to cook separately (for a longer time).**

3. **Cook in boiling water till tender or steam to tenderize.**

Serving Suggestions: Dress boiled greens with extra virgin olive oil and a squeeze of lemon juice and serve as the Greek dish *horta* (mixed cooked field greens). • Toss steamed amaranth with Asian sesame oil, chile peppers, and soy sauce and sprinkle with sesame seeds.

Flavor
Affinities:

Bacon, coconut milk, crabmeat, garlic, lemon, olive oil, onion, smoked turkey, sweet and hot peppers.

48a–b.

ARTICHOKE AND CARDOON

General
Description:

Artichokes (Cynara scolymus) *and cardoons* (Cynara cardunculus) *are close relatives in the thistle group of the Compositae family.* Artichokes and cardoons are both edible thistles. The culinary value of artichokes is their flower buds, while the cardoon's is its leafstalks.

Large artichokes come from the end of the plant's central stem, while baby artichokes come from the lateral shoots. Baby artichokes may be trimmed, cooked, and eaten whole, while large artichokes need preparation.

The **green globe** variety accounts for nearly all artichokes grown in the U.S. They have a nutty flavor, especially the inner heart and the innermost portion of the leaves. Sharp thorns at the tips of each leaf can prick the unwary. "Thornless" artichokes have leaf ends that are split like a cloven hoof. Their flesh tends to be soft, without the nuttiness of true green globes.

All artichokes contain an acid called cynarin that makes everything taste sweet after eating it. To eat a whole steamed artichoke, pull each leaf off the choke and hold it by its pointed end. Drag the leaf across your teeth to remove the edible portion at the bottom third of the leaf. The heart, but not the choke, is entirely edible.

Cardoons are rare in the U.S. A few weeks before

harvest, the stalks of cardoon plants must be "blanched," or kept from the sunlight, in order to cut down on natural bitterness. Cardoon resembles a giant bunch of celery. Dried wild cardoon heads are used as a substitute for cheese-making rennet in parts of Spain, France, and Italy.

Season: Artichokes are available year-round, with peak season March through May and again, with a smaller crop, in October. Fresh artichokes cannot be imported into the United States. For this reason, Americans don't see many of the violet and other special artichokes sold in Europe. You are likely to find cardoons in December in areas with large Italian populations, because cardoons are a traditional part of Christmas dinner, and they are in season in the fall and winter.

Purchase: Choose artichokes that have tightly packed, crisp leaves with bright coloring. Fall and winter artichokes may be dark or bronze-tipped or have a whitish, blistered appearance due to exposure to light frost. Many consider artichokes to be the tenderest and most intensely flavored after a frost.

Avoid: Artichokes that are tough or woody or that have spread apart leaves are old. Check the cut end for freshness—avoid a black cut, which indicates the artichoke has been stored too long. Avoid artichokes that are wilting, drying out, or moldy.

Storage:

Refrigerate artichokes and cardoons for up to 1 week.

Preparation:

Whole Medium or Large Artichokes:

1. Use a small, sharp paring knife to trim off the small, tough outer leaves of the artichoke near the stem. Snip off the leaf tips, if desired.

2. Cut off and discard the stem so that the artichoke will stand upright.

3. Gently open up the leaves to expose the hairy choke inside.

4. Using a small stainless steel spoon, scrape out and discard the hairy choke and the small pointed purplish leaves covering it.

5. Place the artichokes in lemon juice and water to prevent discoloration until ready to use.

Cardoon:

1. Remove and discard the tough outer stalks.

2. Separate the individual stalks and heart and cut them up.

3. **Drop the pieces into salted boiling water and lemon juice and cook for 15 minutes.**

4. **Remove obvious strings and white skin.**

Serving Suggestions:

Artichoke: Steam whole for approximately 25 minutes and serve hot with a dipping sauce of lemon butter or hollandaise or serve cold with a flavored mayonnaise or vinaigrette. • Deep-fry whole cleaned baby artichokes until they are golden brown. • Stuff steamed artichokes with rice, ground meat, sausage, chicken, vegetables, cheese, or a combination and bake until bubbling hot. **Cardoon:** Boil whole for 30 minutes or until tender, then dip in batter and fry or bake with butter and cream, topped with cheese or breadcrumbs. • Slice raw cardoons into strips and dip into *bagna cauda*, a hot anchovy and garlic dip of Piedmont, Italy.

Flavor Affinities:

Artichoke: garlic, herbs, lemon, nuts, olive oil, white wine. **Cardoon:** cheese, cream sauces, roast meat and chicken, truffles and truffle oil, vinaigrette dressing.

49.   **ARUGULA**

Other Names:

Gharghir (Middle East), rocket or rocket salad (Britain), *roquette* (France), *rucola* or *rugola* (Italy).

General
Description:

Arugula (Eruca sativa) *is a member of the Brassica family.* Native to the Mediterranean region, arugula grows wild throughout southern Europe. A close relative of the radish, arugula has slender, multilobed leaves that resemble elongated oak leaves and have a mild bite with a mustardy tang. The young, more mild leaves can be eaten raw, while older, more spicy leaves are cooked and added to soups and sauces. Its Latin name, *Eruca*, means "caterpillar," and it describes the plant's hairy stems. The explosive hot-mustard quality of late-season arugula may be the reason it is known as "rocket salad" in Britain.

Arugula has many levels of intensity—mild if greenhouse-grown or heavily irrigated, extremely peppery if grown in a lot of sunlight. Baby arugula from California, sold cut and washed, is generally milder, though it has a tendency to turn yellow in a few days. Field-grown arugula is stronger and may be extremely sandy. Hothouse arugula picked when very young is often added to mesclun or spring mix salad greens.

Arugula from local farms is often sold in bunches with the roots attached. This arugula has thin, easily bruised leaves and may develop rot where the bunch has been rubber-banded together.

Season:

Arugula is available year-round, but is more plentiful in late summer. When grown in very hot weather, arugula will have a strong biting taste and will be extra vulnerable to spoilage.

Purchase:	Look for bright emerald green leaves that are delicately crisp, and stems that are neither withered nor slimy. Leaves that are 2 to 3 inches (5–7.5 cm) long will generally be young and tender.
Avoid:	Avoid arugula with yellowed or limp leaves. Avoid any arugula with a strong, unpleasant odor.
Storage:	Loosely wrap arugula in damp paper towels and place in a plastic bag. Refrigerate for up to 3 days.

Preparation:

1. **Cut off and discard the stems. Discard any yellowed or bruised leaves.**

2. **Place the leaves in a large bowl of cold water and swish around vigorously to release the sandy soil the arugula was grown in.**

3. **Gently lift the leaves out of the water. Drain and spread out on paper or cloth towels to dry.**

Serving Suggestions:	Purée leaves with olive oil, garlic, pine nuts, and grated hard cheese to make a pesto that can be used as a dip for crudités, a pasta sauce, or a sandwich spread. • Serve in a salad with roasted beets and baked goat cheese and a balsamic vinaigrette. • Add arugula to sandwiches.
Flavor Affinities:	Beets, goat cheese, mozzarella, nuts, olives, pancetta, pasta, roasted peppers, tomato, vinaigrette.

50a–b.

ASPARAGUS

Other Names: Sparrowgrass.

General Description:

Asparagus (Asparagus officinalis), *a perennial plant in the lily family, is the cultivated version of wild asparagus shoots* (Asparagus acutifolius) *that grow in the Mediterranean.* The ancient Egyptians and Greeks ate wild asparagus shoots as a rare spring delicacy, and asparagus has been prized by nobility for hundreds of years. In England, "sprue" is the name for extra-thin spears, called "grass asparagus" or "spaghetti grass" in America.

An underground stem (or crown) produces edible shoots for about 6 weeks each spring. If left alone, the tips (actually branches-to-be) sprout into tall, feathery, dill-like fronds. Because the shoots must be harvested by hand, asparagus is a high-priced vegetable. Asparagus is a diuretic and you may notice a distinctive odor in your urine after eating it.

Spears range in size from pencil-thin to thick jumbo stalks. Many Northern Europeans prefer white asparagus because of its delicate flavor and fiberless texture. To grow white asparagus, farmers cover the ground with a mound of loose earth to prevent exposure to sunlight, which would turn the stalks green. In asparagus season in Germany, restaurants offer a *Spargelkarte*, a special asparagus menu. Thin asparagus is popular in Italy, while Provençal cooks prize violet asparagus.

Season:	Asparagus is available year-round in American supermarkets, but for best flavor and price, buy asparagus at the end of November until early July, with peak season from March through June.
Purchase:	Pick firm, plump, straight, round spears in a medium green with purple highlights. The tips should be tight and compact and the white, woody bottoms should be less than 15 percent of the total length. The cut ends should be white or light-colored. The spears should snap easily when bent. Give the bunch a squeeze; if it squeaks, it's fresh. Because younger plants produce larger shoots, large or jumbo spears can be more tender than thin ones.
Avoid:	Do not purchase asparagus with wet, slimy, or smelly tips. Reject shriveled spears. Spears with large, white, woody stalks and only a few inches of green at the tips have been harvested too late and will be tough.
Storage:	Cut off 1 inch (2.5 cm) from the bottom, wrap the fresh-cut area in a wet paper towel, place in a plastic bag, and store in the refrigerator crisper. Asparagus will keep 2 to 3 days. To prolong shelf life, stand asparagus, cut-end down, in 1 inch (2.5 cm) of water.
Preparation:	**Peel the bottom third of the asparagus spears for maximum yield. Alternatively, break or cut off each stalk at its natural breaking point, atop the tough white part.**

Serving Suggestions:	Boil spears horizontally in 1 inch (2.5 cm) of water in a nonreactive skillet 3 to 5 minutes, turning occasionally, then remove and run under cold water to "shock" and set the color. • Toss cooked asparagus with browned butter or extra virgin olive oil, and lemon juice. • Dress steamed asparagus with vinaigrette. • Stir-fry cut spears. • Roast seasoned asparagus in a hot oven.
Flavor Affinities:	Butter, cheese, chervil, eggs, lemon, olive oil, pasta, rice or risotto, seafood, tarragon, tomato.

AVOCADO

Other Names:	Alligator pear, butter pear.
General Description:	*Avocado* (Persea americana)*, native to Central America, is in the laurel family.* The luscious avocado's pear shape and creamy flesh naturally led to its reputation as an aphrodisiac. Its Aztec name, *ahuacatl*, means "testicle," referring to both the fruit's shape and the way it hangs from the tree in pairs. Mostly eaten raw, avocados can be delicious if heated briefly. However, they become bitter when heated too long. The avocado was cultivated from Peru to the Rio Grande long before the arrival of Europeans, and it only crossed the American border into California around 1871. Avocados have been available in Europe since the early 1900s. Although they were not accepted at first,

51a–b.

avocados have made a rapid advance into the cuisines of Western Europe, with pyramids of Israeli avocados appearing on stands across Europe.

The **Hass** avocado has pebbly skin that ripens from green to purplish black. Oval-shaped with a small to medium-sized seed, it has thick but pliable skin and peels easily. Over 80 percent of California avocados are Hass. **Cocktail** or **"finger"** avocados are unpollinated fruits that resemble a thin pickle with smooth green skin, pale green flesh, and a creamy texture. **Florida** (or **Caribbean**) avocados have deep green flesh covered with a smooth, green, pliable skin and a large pit. They are light in taste and texture and are more fruitlike and less buttery than California varieties.

Season:

California avocados are available year-round. The Hass avocado is harvested from early winter through spring; other varieties fill out the year.

Purchase:

When buying an avocado for immediate use, select fruit that yields to gentle pressure; if planning to use days later, look for more firmness. The small knob at the stem end should come free easily. A ripe Hass avocado will have dark, matte purple-black skin. Other varieties may be light green in color even when ripe.

Avoid:

Don't buy bright green, rock-hard avocados because they will be difficult, if not impossible, to ripen properly. Avoid avocados that are sunken, shriveled, or mushy.

Storage:
Store avocados at a cool room temperature, feeling them daily until they reach peak ripeness. To speed ripening, place in a paper bag with an apple. Once ripe, eat immediately or refrigerate for up to 2 days.

Preparation:

1. **Cut the avocado lengthwise around the seed. Rotate the halves to separate.**

2. **Remove the seed by sliding the tip of a spoon gently underneath and lifting out.**

3. **Peel by pulling the skin back from the stem end. Or simply scoop the avocado meat out with a spoon.**

4. **Sprinkle all cut surfaces with lemon or lime juice or rub with oil to prevent discoloration until ready to use.**

Serving Suggestions:
Add sliced avocados and fried tortilla strips to chicken soup seasoned with lime and chile. • Slice avocado and add to sautéed fish or chicken dishes just before serving. • Make guacamole by crushing firm Hass avocados with lime juice, onion, tomato, chiles, salt, and cilantro. (Leave the pits in the mixture to help retain color.)

Flavor Affinities:
Chiles, cilantro, crabmeat, grapefruit, lime, shrimp, tomato, tropical fruits, tuna, vinaigrette.

52. **BAMBOO SHOOTS**

Other Names: *Chuk sun* (China), *chun sun* (spring bamboo, China), *takenoko* (Japan), *tung sun* (winter bamboo, China).

General Description:

Bamboo shoots, mainly species of the Phyllostachys *and* Bambusa *genera, are edible shoots in the grass family that resemble pointed cone-shaped animal tusks.* Cultivated in Asia, bamboo shoots are harvested as soon as the tips appear above the ground. Spring bamboo shoots are chunky and pale; winter bamboo shoots are small with an elongated shape. Once bamboo is cooked, its texture becomes dense, slightly chewy, and firm. All bamboo must be peeled and cooked before eating because it contains small amounts of toxic prussic acid. Among the many species of bamboo, *Phyllostachys dulcis* is sweet and tender and highly esteemed in China, where it is called **vegetable** bamboo. The arrival of fresh bamboo shoots each year signals the beginning of spring in Japan, where they are prized for their rich aroma and crunchy texture.

Season: Bamboo shoots are available occasionally year-round in Asian markets. They may be found at farmers' markets in spring and early summer.

Purchase: Choose solid heavy bamboo shoots that are short with a wide base.

Avoid: Steer clear of soft, moldy, or cracked bamboo shoots.

Storage: Wrap in paper towels and refrigerate for up to 2 weeks. Keep out of sunlight, which causes bitterness.

Preparation: **Note: Do not eat raw bamboo shoots, as they contain a poisonous substance.**

1. **Starting at the bottom end, slit up the side with a sharp knife.**

2. **Unwrap and discard successive layers until you reach the pale edible core.**

3. **Cut off and discard the pointed tip and the fibrous base.**

4. **Cut into thin slices and halve if desired.**

5. **Place bamboo shoots in a saucepan and cover generously with water.**

6. **Add salt and a tablespoon of rice, rice bran, or water in which rice has been rinsed to help absorb bitterness.**

7. **Boil 20 minutes uncovered to allow bitter compounds to dissipate, or until the bamboo is crunchy tender.**

8. **If the bamboo is still bitter, boil again in fresh water for 5 minutes.**

Serving Suggestions:
Cut cooked bamboo into slices, sticks, cubes, or julienne and add to tuna and chicken salad, toss with fried rice or noodles, or use to fill spring rolls or dumplings. • Dip into tempura batter and deep-fry. • Marinate cooked bamboo shoots in rice vinegar, sesame oil, and soy sauce.

Flavor Affinities:
Beef, chicken, cilantro, dashi, eggs, ginger, mirin, miso, rice, rice noodles, scallions, sesame oil, shiitake mushrooms, soy sauce, fish sauce, tofu.

---

53. 📷 **BEANS, GREEN**

Other Names:
Baby French green bean, filet, flat green bean, French bean, *haricot vert* (France), Italian green bean, pole bean, snap bean, string bean, wax bean, yellow bean.

General Description:
Green beans (Phaseolus vulgaris) *are members of the common bean family, often but not always green in color, with long tender edible pods and small, unobtrusive inner beans.* There are many types of green beans including purple, yellow, creamy white, and deep green, as well as flat and round beans. Green beans may be common, but they're hard to beat for bright color, crisp texture, and juicy vegetable flavor. Green beans used to

be called string beans because older varieties had fibrous side strings.

Almost all beans are machine picked, sometimes leaving small branchlets and unformed beans that need to be removed. Sort through them at the market so you don't pay extra for waste. The exception is expensive, slender *haricots verts*, which come neatly lined up in boxes.

Light green to white **wax** beans have a tendency to be tough. The whiter they are, the older they are. Look for slender yellow to pale green beans.

Unfortunately the beautiful streaked markings of some colorful bean varieties are lost when cooked.

Season:

All green (and other colored) beans are available year-round, with a peak in summer months. The one exception is the yellow wax bean, which is not available in hot summer months.

Purchase:

Select beans that are clean, tender, crisp, well-shaped, and smooth. Look for velvety skin on green beans, a sign that they were freshly picked. Buy pre-snipped green beans only if the cut ends are green and moist.

Avoid:

Green beans are susceptible to freezing and may become pitted, especially on the tips. Avoid beans with white mold or mushy tips. If you can see the shape of the beans in the shape of the pods, the beans are overgrown. *Haricots verts* deteriorate quickly. Inspect them carefully before purchasing, and avoid if dried out and shriveled.

Storage:

Wash beans to maintain moisture before storing in a plastic bag or container in the refrigerator for 4 to 5 days. Do not snap off the ends until ready to cook.

Preparation:

Cut off the stem ends. Don't cut off the curved tips if they are in good condition. Some snap beans may have side strings; pull these off if necessary.

Serving Suggestions:

Toss cooked beans with pared orange slices, lemon juice, olive oil, and grated orange zest. • Heat blanched beans with dill butter, made by combining finely chopped dill with an equal amount of softened butter. • Combine cooked green beans, chickpeas, tuna, and oil-cured black olives to make a salad niçoise.

Flavor Affinities:

Almonds, bacon, butter, dill, lemon, marjoram, olive oil, orange, pine nuts, tarragon, tomatoes, walnuts.

54a–d.

BEANS, SHELL

Other Names:

Shellies, shellouts, shelly beans, shuckies.

General Description:

Shell beans are any member of the legume family that are sold in their pods, ready to be shelled, or pre-shucked. All beans grow in pods of various sizes and colors but few are sold fresh like shell beans. These have a subtle flavor and tender texture, and they are easier to digest than dried beans.

Black-eyed peas *(Vigna unguiculata)* are cream-colored and kidney-shaped with a black eye on the curved inner side inside long, skinny, dark pods. Although black-eyed peas originated in Asia, Spanish explorers and African slaves brought them to the southern U.S. Mixed with rice, black-eyed peas are essential for hoppin' John, a Southern dish that must be eaten before noon on New Year's Day to ensure good luck for the year.

Cranberry beans *(Phaseolus vulgaris)* are an Italian favorite. These round, plump beans dappled with pink and wine-colored splotches have a flavor recalling that of chestnuts. They are the classic bean for *pasta e fagioli*, an Italian dish of pasta and beans. When cooked, shelled cranberry beans lose their red color.

Fava beans *(Faba vulgaris)* have large, flattened, light green pods about 8 inches (20 cm) long and 1 inch (2.5 cm) wide. Inside, the beans are protected by a white spongy material. Favas were the only bean known to Europe until the discovery of the New World. They are quite hardy and have been cultivated since ancient times around the Mediterranean and in Britain.

Lima beans *(Phaseolus lunatus)* are large, plump, pale green beans with a kidneylike curve. When young, the beans are pale green but as they ripen they develop a creamy yellow color. The name "lima" refers to their Peruvian origins, though when the name was adopted by English-speaking countries the name was incorrectly pronounced "lie-ma" rather than "lee-ma."

Season: Black-eyed peas are available year-round from central
           California. Cranberry beans are available fresh in the
           summer. Fresh fava beans are available from California
           from April through June. Lima beans are in season
           from June to September.

Purchase: Black-eyed pea pods should be firm and filled out with
           plump beans from end to end. When very fresh, cran-
           berry bean pods are firm and brilliantly colored. Look
           for shiny, bright green fava pods with evenly developed
           light green beans. Look for plump, firm, and dark-
           green lima bean pods.

Avoid: Avoid overgrown black-eyed peas. Check inside wilted
           and brown cranberry bean pods (the beans may be fine);
           avoid beans with rusty brown spots. Avoid favas that
           are yellow, an indication of age. Note that some people
           may be highly allergic to favas—this is called "favism."
           Avoid lima beans that have pale or shriveled pods.

Storage: Refrigerate unshelled beans in a plastic bag for no more
           than 1 week. Black-eyed peas, cranberry beans, and
           limas can be frozen with great success. Freeze the
           shelled beans in a double layer of plastic bags.

Preparation: ***Black-Eyed Peas and Cranberry Beans:***

              **To shell, press on the inside curve of the pod,
              split open, and pop out the beans.**

Fava Beans:

1. **Pull open along the seams and remove the beans.**

2. **Drop into boiling, salted water for 30 seconds. Drain and drop in ice water.**

3. **Slice the inner skin of each bean with a fingernail and pop out the beans.**

Lima Beans:

Snap off the stem end and unzip the pod by pulling on the string. Remove the beans.

Serving Suggestions:
Sprinkle green favas or precooked limas at the last minute into any sauté of fish, seafood, or poultry to add a colorful and tasty accent. • When cooking rice, couscous, orzo, or wheat berries, stir in favas or precooked limas just before serving. • Make Tuscan-style beans by simmering cranberry beans in chicken stock till tender, then adding with cooking liquid and chopped plum tomatoes to olive oil–sautéed garlic and sage, and simmer till beans are soft but whole—serve with grilled steak.

Flavor Affinities:
Bacon, broccoli rabe, chiles, cilantro, cumin, curry, duck, garlic, ham, mustard greens, onions, oregano, sage, shallots, smoked turkey, thyme, tomatoes, Tuscan kale.

55a–c. **BEET**

Other Names: *Barbabietola* (Italy), beetroot (Britain), *betterave* (France).

General Description:

The beet (Beta vulgaris) *is closely related to Swiss chard (see page 267) and spinach (see page 258), and grown for its root.* Beets and their cousins all descended from the sea beet, a wild seashore plant grown throughout southern Europe, which has been eaten since prehistoric times. Low in calories, beets are notable for their sweetness—they have the highest sugar content of any vegetable. **Common** beets are deep red and contain a powerful dye, betacyanin, which stains fingers, cutting boards, and tablecloths a brilliant magenta. Many colorful varieties of beet are now available including **golden beet**, **white beet**, and the **Chioggia** (or **candy cane**) **beet** (which has red and white concentric stripes).

Season:

Beets are available all year long, but their peak season, particularly for local and specialty varieties, is June through October. It's also the time of year when beet greens will be at their best.

Purchase:

Medium-sized beets—approximately 3 inches (7.5 cm) in diameter—are fine for most cooking purposes but small, young beets—about 1.5 inches (3.8 cm) in diameter—usually sold with their tops, are tender and cook relatively quickly. Beet greens should be bright, dark green, and fresh looking. Look for relatively smooth, hard, round beets with deep color. The surface should be unblemished. The taproot should be slender and whole. At least half an inch (1.3 cm) of the stems should remain, or the color will bleed from the tops.

Avoid: Very large storage beets may be extremely dense with unpalatable woody cores. They may take an extraordinarily long time to cook (up to 2 hours) but have the deepest color. Avoid beets with soft, moist spots or shriveled, flabby skin. Limp, yellowed leaves have lost their nutritional value; however, beets with wilted greens may still be acceptable, because the leaves deteriorate more quickly than the roots.

Storage: Because the greens draw moisture from the root, cut off greens before storing, leaving at least 1 inch (2.5 cm) of stem attached. Discard any damaged leaves before refrigerating the greens in a perforated plastic bag for no more than 2 days. Leaf-topped baby beets can be stored for 1 or 2 days with their tops intact. Store unwashed beet roots in the refrigerator for up to 3 weeks. Check for firmness; as they age, they will soften. Don't peel or clean the root—the skins slip off easily after cooking.

Preparation: **Beet Greens:**

   1. **Pull off and discard large ribs.**

2. If desired, roll stacked, uncleaned beet greens and cut them crosswise before cleaning.

3. Wash greens, whole or sliced, in a bowl of cool water, then scoop out.

 Beet Roots:

Note: To preserve color and nutrients, beets should never be cut or peeled before cooking in liquid; they will "bleed" and turn dull brown. Beets are almost always cooked prior to use.

1. Gently scrub the beets and rinse well, being careful not to break the thin skin. Leave at least 1 inch (2.5 cm) of stem and don't trim the root.

2. Add vinegar or lemon juice to cooking water so that red beets hold their color better.

3. Cook the beets in one of the following ways:

Roast: Place foil-wrapped beets in a baking dish and bake at 350–400°F (180–200°C) for 1 to 2 hours.

Boil: Place beets in a pot of salted boiling water, cover, and simmer until the beets are just tender, from 30 minutes to 1 1/2 hours.

Microwave: **Place 1 pound (.45 kg) trimmed beets in a microwaveable dish with ¹/₂ cup (120 ml) of water. Cover and cook until tender, about 20 minutes.**

Steam: **Place beets in vegetable steamer over boiling water. Cook until tender, about 30 to 45 minutes.**

To check for doneness, pierce with a skewer: When the skewer easily penetrates to the center, the beets are done.

4. **Peel beets while still warm, using a paper towel, plastic wrap, or gloves so your hands don't get stained.**

5. **Cut beets in wedges, slices, cubes, or julienne. If the beets are small, serve whole.**

Serving Suggestions: Add wedges to salad with green beans and goat cheese. • Toss with herb butter. • Make into borscht, a hearty Eastern European soup. • Sauté beet greens with garlic and olive oil and serve as a side dish.

Flavor Affinities: Basil, dill, goat cheese, herring, horseradish, orange, potatoes, slow-cooked beef or ham, sour cream, spinach, tarragon, vinegar, yogurt.

56. **BOK CHOY**

Other Names: Chinese white cabbage, *pak choi, pak tsoi, petsay* (Philippines), white celery mustard.

General Description: *Bok choy* (Brassica rapa, Chinensis *group*) *is a plant in the cabbage family.* Of the myriad members of the Brassica family, bok choy is the most versatile. Cultivated in China since ancient times, bok choy is popular in soups, stir-fries, appetizers, and main dishes. Bok choy was introduced to Europe in the 1800s, and it is now grown in the United States and Canada.

More than 20 varieties of bok choy are available in Asia. Bok choy may be long- or thick-stemmed, with green or pearly white stalks. It is upright in shape with tall, smooth stalks ending in green leaves. The mild-flavored crunchy stalks are juicy and almost sweet, while the leaves are more cabbagelike in flavor. Because the stalks and leaves are so different, in culinary terms, it's like getting two vegetables in one.

Shanghai choy has apple green leaves and stalks. You may also find baby Shanghai choy or baby bok choy, which are miniaturized versions. **Choy sum**, or **bok choy sum** (*choy* means "vegetable" or "cabbage," *sum* means "heart"), has light green leaves and tiny yellow flowers. Choy sum is the most tender of the bok choys and is usually expensive. **Tat soi** is a variety whose dark green leaves grow in a large, flat rosette. Baby tat soi is often added to spring mix salad greens.

Season:	Bok choy and its varieties are available year-round, with the greatest selection at Asian markets.
Purchase:	The stalks of bok choy should be thick and fleshy but firm; the leaves should be crisp and green. Select bok choy with bright-colored whole green leaves and plump, firm stalks.
Avoid:	Low-quality bok choy will have wilted, broken, or spotted leaves, limp stalks, or discoloration.
Storage:	Store unwashed bok choy in a perforated plastic bag in the refrigerator crisper. It will wilt within a couple of days.
Preparation:	1. **Trim off the heavy base.**
	2. **Discard blemished or tough leaves.**
	3. **Separate the stalks from the base and slice the leaves from the stalks.**
	4. **Wash thoroughly in cool water.**
Serving Suggestions:	Combine thin ribbons of bok choy leaves with stock, shreds of meat, ginger, and tofu for soup. • Add cooked bok choy to fried rice, or fillings for spring rolls or pot stickers. • Braise baby bok choy in a combination of chicken stock, butter, soy sauce, and sesame oil.

| Flavor Affinities: | Beef, chicken, chiles, duck, ginger, oyster sauce, pork, rice, seafood, sesame oil, shiitake mushrooms, soy sauce. |

BROCCOLI

General Description:

Broccoli (Brassica oleracea, Cymosa *group*) *is a deep emerald green vegetable that is part of the huge Brassica family.* Broccoli's name comes from the Italian for "little arms." Broccoli is harvested before its flower buds open. America still raises mostly green broccoli, while purple, green, or white flower heads may be found elsewhere. The main variety of broccoli grown in the U.S. is **Calabrese**, which goes by that name in Britain.

Broccoflower is a hybrid mix of cauliflower and broccoli. The florets are light, bright green and packed into a round head like cauliflower. Its flavor and use are somewhere between broccoli and cauliflower. **Broccoli Romanesco**, common around Rome and starting to come into the U.S. market, matures later in the year and displays distinctive yellow-green pointed spiral cones. Like broccoflower, its flavor and use are somewhere between broccoli and cauliflower.

Broccoli rabe is a nonheading broccoli-like vegetable, also known as *broccoletti di rape*, *broccoletto*, and *cima di rapa*, that resembles broccoli florets on long, thin stems. Prized in southern Italy and increasingly well-known in the United States, it has a bitter but zesty flavor and intense green color. It is similar to

rapini, but rapini has fewer florets and a flavor more similar to mustard greens.

Chinese broccoli has broad, glossy, blue-green leaves with long, crisp, thick stems and a small head. Its flavor is similar to, though juicier and more tender than, Calabrese broccoli.

Broccolini (or Asparation) is a trademarked name for baby broccoli, a new hybrid cross of broccoli and Chinese kale. Broccolini has a long, slender, juicy stem like asparagus topped with small flowering buds.

Season: Broccoli is available year-round, with peak season from October through April. Broccoli rabe is most plentiful from late fall to early spring, but is usually available year-round. Rapini from California is available August through March. Broccoli Romanesco may occasionally be found at farmers' markets in early fall. Chinese broccoli is grown year-round in California. Broccolini is occasionally available throughout the year.

Purchase: Look for broccoli with tight compact bud clusters with an even, deep green color, or green tinged with purple. The buds should be tightly closed and the leaves crisp, with thin stems that are a lighter green than the buds.

You'll usually find broccoli rabe sprinkled with ice to prevent wilting. Choose small, firm, green stems with compact heads and an abundance of florets. The flower buds should be tightly closed and dark green. Choose rapini that is firm with relatively few buds and flowers.

Avoid: In hot summer weather, all members of this family may
          spoil. As broccoli grows, the stalks become larger and
          tougher. Avoid broccoli with large, thick, whitish stalks
          because the florets will be tough, woody, and strong-
          tasting. Broccoli rabe is quite perishable and should be
          examined closely. Sniff the stalks where they are tied
          together, and avoid any with a sharp mustardy smell.
          Avoid rabe with yellowed flowers or stalks that are
          heavily split at the bottom, indicating age.

Storage: Refrigerate unwashed broccoli in an airtight bag in the
          crisper for up to 4 days. If the stalks are tough, peel
          before cooking. Broccoli rabe should be wrapped in a
          wet paper towel in a plastic bag in the crisper.

Preparation: ***Broccoli:***

          1.   **Wash under cold running water.**

          2.   **Peel or pare the tough outer skin from the
                stalks. Cut off 1 to 2 inches (2.5–5 cm) from
                the bottom or any split portions and discard.**

          3.   **Divide the broccoli into lengthwise spears, or
                cut into florets and slice the stalks.**

          Chinese Broccoli:

          1.   **Wash under cold running water.**

2. **Separate leaves and flower buds from the stems.**

3. **Peel the fibrous outer layer from the stems.**

Broccoli Rabe:

1. **Wash under cold running water.**

2. **Cut off the bottoms of the stalks, then slice across into 1- to 2-inch (2.5–5 cm) lengths for ease of cooking.**

3. **To lessen bitterness, blanch in boiling, salted water for 1 minute. Drain, rinse under cold running water to set the color, then drain and proceed with cooking.**

Serving Suggestions:
Create a broccoli slaw with peeled and shredded stalks. • Make broccoli amandine by mixing cooked broccoli with toasted almond slices, butter, and lemon. • Add Chinese broccoli to Asian soups or stir-fries. • Sauté broccoli rabe with oil and garlic. • Serve broccolini like asparagus (see page 119). • Serve broccoli Romanesco like cauli-flower (see page 149).

Flavor Affinities:
Broccoli and broccoli rabe: anchovy, balsamic vinegar, butter, cheese, chicken, chiles, garlic, lemon, pasta, sausage. **Chinese broccoli:** chiles, garlic, oyster sauce, seafood, sesame oil, soy sauce, teriyaki sauce, tofu.

58.   **BURDOCK**

Other Names: Beggar's button, gobo, Japanese burdock.

General
Description:

Burdock (Arctium lappa) *is a root esteemed in Japanese and macrobiotic cuisines for its healing nature.* There are two species of burdock: wild *(Arctium minus)* and Japanese *(Arctium lappa)*, which is cultivated. The large, dark, woody-looking burdock root has a sweet, nutty, delicate, crunchy flesh. Its bark-like skin looks thick, but is actually tissue paper thin and can be scraped away with a fingernail or light scrubbing. Burdock's flavor resembles a combination of salsify and artichoke, with a sweet, earthy flavor and tender-crisp texture.

Burdock roots, largely eaten in Japan and Hawaii, can be up to 4 feet (1.2 m) long, but 2 feet (.6 m) is more common; they are about as thick as a common carrot. The rather fibrous flesh is a grayish white that quickly oxidizes. When cooked, burdock changes color from milky white to shiny gray or brown.

In Asian markets, burdock is sometimes sold covered in sawdust to preserve it. Although burdock grows throughout Europe and North America, until recently it was cultivated only in Japan. For the Iroquois and other Native American tribes, burdock was an important winter food. They dug it in the fall, dried it, and then ate it throughout the winter.

Season: Burdock is available irregularly year-round. It usually comes from Hawaii, California, or Japan.

Purchase: Choose soil-covered roots that are firm and relatively crisp. Larger pieces can be stringy.

Avoid: Limp burdock is best avoided.

Storage: Wrap in wet paper towels and refrigerate. It will keep for a few days. For longer storage, be sure to keep moist.

Preparation:

1. **Wash burdock gently with a scrubbing brush.**

2. **Scrape off the skin with the back of a knife.**

3. **Cut into small pieces and drop immediately into cold water to prevent oxidation.**

4. **To rid burdock of a slightly bitter aftertaste, soak pieces in salted water for 5 to 10 minutes before cooking.**

5. **To tenderize the roots, cook first in a combination of 1/4 teaspoon (1 ml) baking soda per cup (240 ml) of water, bring to boil, then drain.**

Serving Suggestions: Make *kimpira*, a Japanese dish in which slices of burdock and carrot are lightly fried, then sprinkled with sesame seeds, soy sauce, and dashi. • Slice fresh roots for use in soups, stir-fries, and tea. • Sauté burdock and thinly sliced beef seasoned with mirin and sake.

Flavor
Affinities:

Beef, carrot, chicken, dashi, ginger, mirin, mushrooms, sake, sesame, soy sauce.

59a–d.

CABBAGE

General
Description:

Cabbage (Brassica oleracea, Capitata *group*) *is a common vegetable that can be white, red, or green.* Cabbage was the earliest cultivated vegetable in the Brassica family and is the ancestor of its numerous relations, such as cauliflower (see page 149) and broccoli (see page 138). Loose-leafed cabbage was valued by ancient Egyptians and Greeks. Around 2,000 years ago the first cabbages appeared in Northern Europe. The word "cabbage" is a derivation of the French *caboche*, or "head."

In the U.S., the most common cabbage has compact heads of waxy, tightly wrapped leaves. The infamous smell of cooking cabbage comes from various sulfur compounds. Coleslaw, from the Dutch *koolsla*, meaning "cool cabbage," is a salad of shredded cabbage that is ubiquitous at picnics. The German specialty sauerkraut (sour cabbage) is salted, fermented cabbage.

Red cabbage was developed in the 16th century and is especially popular in Germany and Eastern Europe. If exposed to even slightly alkaline conditions, such as hard water, it turns slate blue. To avoid this, traditional red cabbage recipes often include acid fruit, vinegar, or wine.

Savoy cabbage has a loose, full head of soft, crinkled leaves varying from dark to pale green. It was developed in Italy and probably descended from old Roman types. Mellow-flavored Savoy cabbage is considered culinarily superior, but is less readily available than common cabbage.

Portugal cabbage (also called **Braganza**, **Galician**, or **sea kale** cabbage; *couve tronchuda* in Portugal) has no head but large wide-spreading leaves and thick, white, fleshy ribs.

Brussels sprouts (*Brassica oleracea, Gemmifera* group) are miniature head buds of cabbage that grow in a spiral up around a thick central stem. Brussels sprouts became popular in Europe toward the end of the 18th century and a little later in North America.

Season:

Red, green, and white cabbages are available year-round. Savoy cabbage is predominantly sold in the fall. Peak season for Brussels sprouts is November and December.

Purchase:

Choose cabbage with firmly packed, crisp-looking, fresh leaves; the head should feel heavy for its size. In green and Savoy cabbage, opt for heads with dark leaves (as the cabbage ages, these leaves wilt and are removed, revealing light leaves). The leaves should be fairly thick and pliably crisp, not limp, and there should be no sign of browning. Choose Brussels sprouts with good green color that are firm, with compact leaves and clean ends.

Avoid:	Pass up cabbage with yellowed leaves, a strong smell, or a woody, split core. Avoid Savoy cabbage that has thin, wilted leaves or a cracked head. Avoid puffy, wilted, or yellow Brussels sprouts.

Storage: 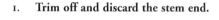	Cabbage may be refrigerated, tightly wrapped in plastic, for about a week.

Preparation:

1. **Trim off and discard the stem end.**

2. **Cut the core out in a cone shape and discard if desired. (It has a stronger taste.)**

3. **Slice or cut cabbage into thin wedges before washing. Discard any withered or stringy parts.**

4. **Rinse in cool water and drain well.**

5. **For mildest flavor and tenderness, cut out and discard the thickest ribs from the outer leaves.**

Serving Suggestions: Stuff cabbage leaves with ground beef or pork, rice, raisins, and season with vinegar or sauerkraut. • Make coleslaw with mayonnaise, vinaigrette, or other dressing. • Braise red cabbage with apples, onion, and cider vinegar or with apricots and balsamic vinegar. • Make minestrone with shredded Savoy cabbage and fresh shelled beans. • Cook Brussels sprouts with chestnuts.

Flavor
Affinities:

Green and white cabbage: bacon, butter, caraway, carrots, game birds (such as pheasant or goose), juniper berry, onions, potatoes, sausage. **Red cabbage:** apples, red wine, vinegar. **Savoy cabbage:** garlic, olive oil, polenta, potatoes, sweet onions, white beans. **Brussels sprouts:** bacon, butter, chestnuts, chicken stock, shallots.

60. 📷

CARROT

General
Description:

The carrot (Daucus carota sativus) *is a biennial plant in the Umbelliferae family.* Carrots were cultivated in Afghanistan as a food crop in the 7th century, but, with their purple exteriors and yellow flesh, they did not resemble those of today. Carrots slowly spread into the Mediterranean with the Moors, and in the 1600s, patriotic Dutch farmers bred orange carrots to honor the royal House of Orange. Carrots were brought by the colonists to the New World.

Versatile, brightly colored, and honey-sweet, carrots are loaded with beta-carotene, from which we get vitamin A. Easily paired with both savory and sweet, carrots are featured in both main courses and desserts.

Today you can find purple, white, gold, and round carrots. Most "baby carrots" are actually larger carrots that have been cut and peeled from a special variety of carrot that is grown close together, resulting in smaller, more tender carrots. More than 25 percent of carrots grown in California end up as "mini peeled carrots."

Season:	Carrots are found year-round, with peak season from October through April. Fresh young bunch carrots with their tops are found in spring.
Purchase:	Carrots should be well-shaped with smooth exteriors and closely trimmed tops. For the freshest, most tender carrots, buy bunches with bright green leaf tops. These are by necessity picked days before sale because the tops deteriorate quickly. Baby carrots should be moist and plump, not slimy, broken up, or whitish.
Avoid:	Do not purchase flabby, soft, wilted, or split carrots. The tops should not be at all dark, slimy, yellowed, or sprouting. Examine the carrots to determine brightness of color, often an indication of sweetness.
Storage:	Carrots will keep in the refrigerator in a plastic bag for up to 10 days. Remove green tops before storing as they will draw moisture from the roots. Carrots should be stored away from apples, pears, and other produce that create ethylene gas, which causes them to become bitter.
Preparation:	**1. Peel lightly, or scrub with an abrasive cleaning pad or special brush. Many of the carrot's nutrients are in the skin, but it is also where much of the bitterness lies.**
	2. Trim off the top and bottom.

3. **When cut open, large carrots may have a tough yellow, stringy core, which should be cut away.**

Note: Mini peeled carrots require no preparation. However, if they turn white from refrigerator dehydration, place them in cold water for a few minutes and they will become vivid orange again.

Serving Suggestions:
Shred raw carrot and mix with olive oil, lemon juice, and rosemary to make a salad. • Make carrot confit by slow-cooking carrots with olive oil, orange juice, cumin, lemon juice, and garlic. • Add carrots to beef stew, tomato sauce, vegetable soups, or stir-fries. • Make carrot cake, carrot torte, or carrot pudding.

Flavor Affinities:
Beef, celery, chicken, chives, cinnamon, coriander, cumin, curry, dill, dried apricots, honey, onion, orange, raisins, rosemary, shallots, tarragon, thyme, tomato.

61. **CAULIFLOWER**

Other Names:
Cabbage flower, *cavolfiore* (Italy), *chou-fleur* (France).

General Description:
Cauliflower (Brassica oleracea, Botrytis *group*) *is a head of white flower buds in the cabbage family.* Cauliflower was first grown in the Middle East—perhaps in Cyprus—although no one is sure when. By the Middle Ages, Arab growers had many highly developed cauli-

flower varieties. By the 16th century, imported cauliflower from the East had become the rage at the French court; it was featured in rich dishes with cream, sweetbreads, foie gras, and truffles. Middle Eastern and Indian dishes use bold spices to bring excitement to this mild, self-effacing vegetable.

Like its closest cousin broccoli (see page 138), cauliflower is made up of flowers that began to form but stopped growing at the bud stage. The thick stems under the buds store the nutrients that would have gone into the flowers and eventually their fruits. Cauliflower is therefore rich in vitamins and minerals; one serving can provide the entire daily requirement of vitamin C.

Growing cauliflower is very demanding. Much of the work of planting and harvesting must be done by hand because of its delicate nature. To keep the cauliflower head creamy white, it must be protected from the sun to prevent the development of chlorophyll, which would turn it green.

Season: Fresh cauliflower is available year-round, though colder months yield the best quality.

Purchase: Cauliflower should have creamy white, compact curds with bright green, firmly attached leaves. Some small leaves extending through the curds do not affect quality.

Avoid: Old cauliflower can have tiny black mold spots on the florets or yellow, wilted leaves.

Storage:
Place cauliflower in a plastic bag and refrigerate in the crisper for up to 1 week.

Preparation:

1. **Pull off and discard the green leaves, exposing the stem and core.**

2. **Using a small, sharp knife, cut around the core in a cone shape, pull it out, and discard.**

3. **Cut away any black mold spots.**

4. **Separate the florets by cutting them apart.**

Note: The pleasing flavor of cauliflower is fresher tasting and less "cabbagey" when it is cooked briefly in boiling water. To tone down the odor when cooking cauliflower, add celery seeds or celery leaves to the pot.

Serving Suggestions:
Make a creamed cauliflower soup known as crème Dubarry. • Mix cooked florets with Gruyère cheese sauce and bake into a gratin. • Serve raw cauliflower florets with curry dip.

Flavor Affinities:
Anchovy, butter, chervil, chives, cream, curry, garlic, ginger, Gruyère cheese, lemon, mustard seed, olives, Parmesan cheese, thyme, turmeric.

62a–b.

CELERY

General Description:

Celery (Apium graveolens) *is a green-stalked plant in the Umbelliferae family.* Wild celery is a common plant in Europe and Asia and has been used since ancient times. It is mentioned in Homer's *Odyssey* as *selinon*, from which we derive the modern name. Celery was used originally as a seasoning because it was quite bitter. The practice of earthing up the growing plant results in milder celery; this practice started in the 16th century, probably in Italy. Celery exists in three forms—a wild plant with thin, hollow stalks; common celery with thick, solid, pale green stems; and celeriac, an enlarged bumpy knob ranging from 2 to 6 inches (5–15 cm) in diameter.

Leaf celery *(Apium graveolens secalinum)* is dark green and closely related to wild celery. It is used in France and Italy as an aromatic to flavor soups and stews. **Pascal green celery** *(Apium grareolens dulce)* is the standard green celery variety for the fall market. "Celery hearts" are simply the inner, more mild-flavored, and almost stringless hearts of standard celery, and they are more expensive. **Blanched** celery is a regional specialty of the Pennsylvania Dutch that has a more delicate flavor and none of the bitter aftertaste of deep green celery. In Britain, special varieties of Pascal celery that have long white, pink, or red stems are grown in trenches out of sunlight.

Celeriac *(Apium graveolens rapaceum)*, also called

Color Plates

Produce Icon Key

Season	Storage	Preparation

Season	Storage	Preparation
spring	refrigerator	bowl of water
summer	no light exposure	tap water
fall	ventilation	pater towel
winter	paper bag	vegetable peeler
	plastic bag	knife
Caution	perforated plastic bag	scissors
		salt shaker

1a. **apple, braeburn**

1b. **apple, fuji**

1c. **apple, gala**

1d. **apple, golden delicious**

1e. **apple, granny smith**

1f. **apple, jonagold**

1g. **apple, mcintosh red**

1h. **apple, pink lady**

1i. **apple, red delicious**

1j. **apple, winesap**

1k. **apple, york**

1l. **crabapple**

2. **apricot**

3. **asian pear**

4a. **banana, burro**

4b. **banana, cavendish**

4c. **banana, red**

4d. **plantain**

5. **blackberry**

6a. **blueberry**

6b. **huckleberry**

7. **cactus pear**

8. **cherimoya**

9a. **cherry, bing**

9b. **cherry, rainier**

10a. **citron**

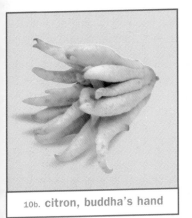

10b. **citron, buddha's hand**

11. **coconut**

12. **cranberry**

13a. **currant, pink**

13b. **currant, red**

14. **date**

15. **durian**

16. **fig**

17a. **grape, concord**

17b. **grape, flame seedless**

17c. grape, thompson

18a. grapefruit, duncan

18b. grapefruit, star ruby

18c. pomelo

19. **guava**

20. **kiwano**

21a. **kiwifruit**

21b. **gold kiwifruit**

22. **kumquat**

23a. **lemon, eureka**

23b. **lemon, meyer**

24a. **lime, key**

24b. lime, persian

25. loquat

26. lychee

27. mango

28. **medlar**

29a. **melon, cantaloupe**

29b. **melon, casaba**

29c. **melon, crenshaw**

29d. **melon, galia**

29e. **melon, honeydew**

29f. **watermelon**

30a. **orange, navel**

30b. **orange, valencia**

31. **papaya**

32. **passion fruit**

33a. **peach, babcock**

33b. **peach, elegant lady**

33c. **nectarine**

34a. **pear, anjou**

34b. **pear, bartlett**

34c. **pear, bosc**

34d. **pear, packham**

35. **persimmon**

36a. **pineapple, del monte gold**

36b. **pineapple, south african baby**

37a. **plum, black amber**

37b. **plum, red beauty**

37c. **plum, santa rosa**

38. **pomegranate**

39. **quince**

40a. **raspberry, golden**

40b. **raspberry, red**

41. **star fruit**

42. **strawberry**

43. **tamarillo**

44. **tamarind**

45a. **tangelo**

45b. **tangerine, clemetine**

45c. **tangerine, dancy**

45d. **tangerine, satsuma**

46. **yuzu**

47a. **amaranth**

47b. **amaranth, red micro**

48a. **artichoke**

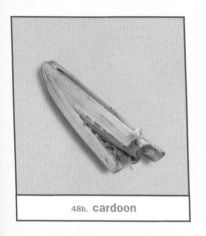

48b. **cardoon**

49. **arugula**

50a. **asparagus**

50b. **asparagus, white**

51a. **avocado, florida**

51b. **avocado, hass**

52. **bamboo shoots**

53. **beans, green**

54a. **beans, cranberry**

54b. **beans, fava**

54c **beans, lima**

54d. **black-eyed peas**

55a. **beet, common**

55b. **beet, chiogga**

55c. **beet, golden**

56. **bok choy**

57a. **broccoli, calabrese**

57b. **broccoflower**

57c. **broccoli rabe**

58. **burdock**

59a. **cabbage**

59b. **cabbage, red**

59c. **cabbage, savoy**

59d. **brussels sprouts**

60. **carrot**

61. **cauliflower**

62a. **celery**

62b. **celeriac**

63. **chayote**

64. **chestnut**

65a. **belgian endive**

65b. **red belgian endive**

65c. **chicory**

66a. **corn, baby or miniature**

66b. **corn, bi-colored**

66c. **corn, silver queen**

67. **crosnes**

68a. **cucumber**

68b. **cucumber, dutch**

68c. **gherkin**

69. **edamame**

70a. **eggplant, asian**

70b. **eggplant, black beauty**

70c. **eggplant, graffiti**

70d. **eggplant, ivory white**

71a. **endive, curly**

71b. **escarole**

72. **fennel**

73. **fiddlehead fern**

74a. **garlic, elephant**

74b. **garlic, softneck**

75. **ginger**

76a. **greens, collard**

76b. **greens, dandelion**

76c. **greens, mustard**

76d. **kale**

77. **horseradish**

78. **jicama**

79. **kohlrabi**

80. **leek**

81a. **lettuce, bibb**

81b. **lettuce, boston**

81c. **lettuce, iceberg**

81d. **lettuce, looseleaf**

81e. **lettuce, romaine**

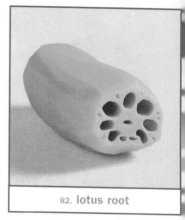

82. **lotus root**

83. **mâche**

84a. **mushroom, chanterelle**

84b. **mushroom, cremini**

84c. **mushroom, lobster**

84d. **mushroom, morel**

84e. **mushroom, oyster**

84f. **mushroom, porcini**

84g. **mushroom, portobello**

84h. **mushroom, shiitake**

84i. **mushroom, white**

85. **napa cabbage**

86. **nopales**

87. **okra**

88a. **onion, green**

88b. **onion, italian red**

88c. **onion, pearl**

88d. **onion, vidalia**

88e. **onion, white**

89. **parsley root**

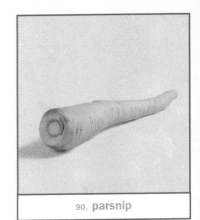

90. **parsnip**

91a. **peas, garden or english**

91b. **peas, snow**

91c. **peas, sugar snap**

92a. **pepper, anaheim**

92b. **pepper, cubanelle**

92c. **pepper, habanero**

92d. **pepper, jalapeño**

92e. **pepper, poblano**

92f. **pepper, scotch bonnet**

92g. **pepper, serrano**

93a. **sweet bell pepper, green**

93b. **sweet bell pepper, orange**

93c. **sweet bell pepper, red**

93d. **sweet bell pepper, yellow**

94a. **potato, fingerling**

94b. **potato, purple**

94c. **potato, round red**

94d. **potato, russet**

94e. **potato, yukon gold**

95. **radicchio**

96a. **radish, black**

96b. **radish, daikon**

96c. **radish, red globe**

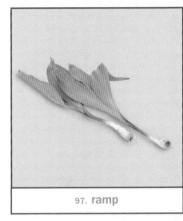

97. **ramp**

98. **rhubarb**

99a. **salsify**

99b. **scorzonera**

100. **samphire**

101. **shallot**

102a. **spinach, curly or savoy**

102b. **spinach, flat-leafed**

103a. **sprouts, alfalfa**

103b. **sprouts, mung bean**

104. **sunchoke**

105a. **sweet potato, beauregard**

105b. **sweet potato, garnet**

106a. **rainbow chard**

106b. **swiss chard, green**

106c. **swiss chard, ruby**

107a. **taro**

107b. **yautia**

108a. **tomatillo**

108b. **ground cherry**

109a. **tomato, beefsteak**

109b. **tomato, brandywine**

109c. **tomato, cherry**

109d. **tomato, mr. stripey**

109e. **tomato, sicilian plum**

110a. **turnip**

110b. **rutabaga**

111. **wasabi**

112a. **water chestnut, chinese**

112b. **water caltrop**

113. **watercress, upland**

114. winged bean

115a. squash, acorn

115b. squash, buttercup

115c. squash, butternut

115d. **squash, calabaza**

115e. **squash, hubbard**

115f. **squash, pumpkin**

115g. **squash, spaghetti**

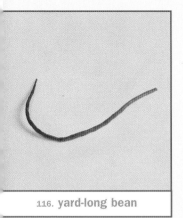

116. **yard-long bean**

117. **yuca**

118a. **zucchini**

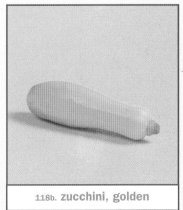

118b. **zucchini, golden**

118c. **pattypan squash**

118d. **squash blossoms**

celery root, **turnip-rooted celery**, and **knob celery**, has a long history and was used by Arabs as a delicacy by the 16th century. It has a delicate celery flavor and solid, fibrous flesh.

The Chinese, who have used wild celery since as early as the 5th century A.D., independently developed cultivated varieties of celery. **Chinese celery**, called *kintsai* or *heung kunn*, has thin, hollow, and juicy stalks with a strong flavor. It should be picked young.

Season:

Pascal celery may be found year-round. Blanched celery is a specialty that can be found in late fall in some areas. Celeriac is in season from November through April.

Purchase:

Look for celery with straight stalks and rigid ribs that snap crisply when bent. Their inside surface should be clean and smooth. The leaves should be fresh and well colored, with no sign of wilting. Opt for large, relatively smooth, and uniform celeriac knobs for less waste. The leaf tops should be lively and green, never slimy.

Avoid:

Celery that is overly large with dark green stalks may be bitter or stringy. Avoid small celeriac. With its thick peel, there won't be much left.

Storage:

Keep celery and celeriac in a perforated bag and refrigerate in the crisper for up to 1 week. Celery will freeze in a colder section of the refrigerator.

Preparation: *Celery:*

1. Cut off the base of the bunch of celery and discard, or wash it and save it for soup stock.

2. Separate the individual stalks and wash, being especially careful at the base, which collects dirt.

3. Cut off the tops below the joint, which will be tough.

4. Discard darker green leaves. You may use the mild inner yellow-green leaves.

5. To remove strings (only necessary on large outer stalks), bend back and snap a rib of celery at the point where the stalk changes color from green to white. The strings will be exposed and can be gently pulled off the stalk.

Celeriac:

1. Cut off the top and a thin slice of the base.

2. Pare away the tough outer skin with a knife.

3. Drop immediately into cold water so the bare root doesn't oxidize.

4. **Cook either whole or cut up in water with lemon juice until tender to the core when pierced.**

Serving
Suggestions:

Stuff raw celery stalks with mashed Roquefort or other blue cheese. • Combine equal amounts diced celery, unpeeled red apples, chopped walnuts, and cooked chicken or turkey (if desired), then dress with mayonnaise to make Waldorf salad. • Make celeriac mashed potatoes by mashing together 2 parts cooked potatoes to 1 part cooked celeriac.

Flavor
Affinities:

Celery: blue cheese, butter, chicken soup, fish, Gruyère and other mountain cheeses, poultry, shellfish. **Celeriac:** apples, cream, game birds, mayonnaise, mustard, potatoes, roast beef, veal, or chicken, truffles.

63. **CHAYOTE**

Other Names:

Chocho (Africa, Brazil), *christophine* (France, Trinidad), custard marrow (Britain), mango squash, mirliton (Haiti, Louisiana), vegetable pear, *xuxu* (Vietnam).

General
Description:

Chayote (Sechium edule) *is a mild-tasting, pear-shaped, firm-textured, light green vegetable in the Cucurbita family.* The chayote, whose name is Aztec, is native to Mesoamerica. It is an unusual member of the gourd family in that it has one large, edible seed. With shallow furrows running its length, its color may be cream to celadon to zucchini-green. Its taste and texture are between cucumber and apple. In the U.S., the most common chayote is light green with relatively smooth skin and weighs about half a pound (225 g), although larger, hairy, round, and knobby varieties exist.

Chayote goes by many names and is now cultivated in the subtropics worldwide, but it is especially popular in Latin America and the Caribbean. It is versatile, eaten raw or cooked, and is substituted for apples and pumpkins in pies in Latin America. The young shoots, flowers, seeds, and roots are also eaten.

Season: Chayotes are most abundant from September through May but may be found year-round, especially in Asian, Latin American, and Caribbean markets.

Purchase: Choose firm chayotes. Large chayotes are easy to stuff (a common serving method) but have tough skin; small chayotes have tender, usually edible skin.

Avoid: Do not purchase sticky or discolored chayotes.

Storage: Lightly wrap chayote in a paper towel and refrigerate for up to 3 weeks.

Preparation:
1. **If the chayote is relatively smooth, and you will be serving it raw, peel it. When peeling a raw chayote, the liquid that oozes out may irritate**

your skin. Work under running water or wear gloves. Small chayotes needn't be peeled.

2.   **If you will be baking or steaming the chayote, it does not need to be peeled raw. After cooking, the skin is generally tender enough to eat, but if not, scoop out the tender flesh and discard the skin. A simple method of cooking chayote is to microwave it: Cut the chayote into 1/2- to 1-inch (1.3–2.5-cm) cubes and place in a microwaveable dish. Add 1/4 cup (60 ml) water, cover, and cook on high for 8 to 10 minutes or until tender when pierced.**

Serving
Suggestions: Stuff chayote with fillings such as mixed seafood, ham with soffrito, pork, ginger, and scallions (or raisins, nuts, and brown sugar) and bake. • Remove the outer skin, cut up, and sauté or deep-fry. • Cut raw chayote into julienne strips and add to coleslaw-type salads.

Flavor
Affinities: Chicken, chiles, cilantro, corn, ham, lime, onions, seafood, sweet peppers, tomatoes.

64.   **CHESTNUT**

General
Description: *The chestnut* (Castanea sativa) *is a large, starchy nut inside a shiny, tough, brown shell.* "Chestnut" is a name originally and primarily given to the European cultivated

chestnut, *Castanea sativa*, but also to various Asian varieties now found in Asian markets, mostly *Castanea mollissima*. The once magnificent American chestnut trees were mostly wiped out by chestnut blight early in the 20th century. For both Native Americans and Europeans, chestnuts were an important food source.

The richly flavored cultivated chestnut called **marrone** or **marron** produces only a single, large nut inside each case. AAA is the highest grade, but it is rarely found in the retail market. **Castagne**, or **châtaignes**, come from the wild chestnut tree and have several small nuts to each case. **Asian** chestnuts have relatively thin skin and are sweeter and less starchy. Chestnuts contain more starch and less oil than most other nuts.

Season: Chestnuts are in season from October through March, peaking in December.

Purchase: Choose the biggest, freshest chestnuts from a market that sells them in quantity. If possible, cut open several chestnuts to check for plump, meaty, light tan chestnuts because it is difficult to judge unopened chestnuts by their outer appearance.

Avoid: Inside their shells, chestnuts tend to form greenish mold between the convoluted folds between the nut and its outer skin. They can also have hard, darkened areas that are inedible. Chestnuts with these qualities should be discarded.

Storage: Store chestnuts in the refrigerator for up to 1 week.

Preparation:

1. **Carefully make a crisscross cut on the domed side of each chestnut with a sharp paring knife.**

2. **Roast at 400°F (200°C) for 20 minutes, boil, or deep-fry.**

3. **Cool slightly and break away the shell. Remove the brown inner skin. It's easiest when the chestnuts are warm, so work with a few at a time, keeping the rest in the pot or oven. Work with heat-resistant gloves to make this task easier.**

4. **Roast cut chestnuts over the embers of a fire by placing them in a popcorn popper or special perforated steel chestnut roasting pan and shaking over the fire for about 15 minutes, or until all sides of the chestnuts are darkened.**

Serving Suggestions: Boil chestnuts in chicken stock, then purée into a soup. • Stir chestnuts into risotto near the end of cooking along with browned sweet sausage bits. • Add chestnuts to poultry stuffing. • Layer chocolate cake with chestnut buttercream (made by cooking chestnuts in milk with sugar and vanilla until tender, then whipping).

Flavor Affinities: Brussels sprouts, butter, chicken, chocolate, Marsala, onion, pork, rum, sweet sausage, turkey, vanilla.

65a–c.   **CHICORY**

Other Names: Asparagus chicory, Belgian endive, Catalan chicory, Catalogna, Catalonia, *chicorée* (France), dandelion chicory, French endive, witloof chicory.

General
Description: *Chicory* (Cichorium intybus), *closely related to endive, is a group of leafy vegetables in the Compositae family.* Endive (see page 176), chicory, and radicchio (see page 242) all developed from wild chicory, a common blue wildflower of Europe, western Asia, and Africa that also grows by the roadside in America. Young wild chicory was used as a vegetable in classical Greece and Rome. Chicory describes the whole family of leafy vegetables and is often used interchangeably with endive and escarole. The most common chicory is Belgian endive.

Belgian endive has an ivory-white head with pale yellow-edged, closely wrapped leaves, a mildly bitter flavor, and tender juicy texture. The complicated process of raising Belgian endive originated in France and was improved around 1850 in Belgium, which is still the major grower. In the fall, chicory plants are harvested, and their leaves are cut off and discarded. The remaining roots are replanted in deep soil or another medium in a dark cellar so that they regrow shoots of small, white leaves in a compact spear shape. This laborious planting method explains the high price of Belgian endive. **Red Belgian endive** may also occasionally be found.

In America, Belgian endive is raised hydroponically

in darkness. Because it is sensitive to light, imported Belgian endive is packed in opaque paper, usually deep blue. A cross of Belgian endive and radicchio marketed as California red endive or Endigia resembles Belgian endive with red-edged leaves.

Catalonia, another chicory variety, is of Italian origin and quite popular there, with different cultivars that have different appearances and characteristics, including *cicoria* and *barba di frate* (monk's beard) that may occasionally be found in the market. Its common form has long, relatively thick white stalks and narrow spiked leaves that resemble dandelion. Much of the "dandelion greens" raised in the U.S. are actually cultivated Catalonia.

Puntarelle, meaning "shoots," have pale white ribs and long thin leaves that can be fairly smooth or deeply notched and anywhere from light to deep green in color. They are a Roman specialty now raised in the U.S.

Season: Belgian endive is in peak season from November to March but is available almost year-round when imported. Hydroponically grown endive is available from May to December. Other chicories can be found year-round.

Purchase: Select Belgian endive and other chicories with smooth white spears that are tightly closed. Smaller heads are more delicate in flavor but don't yield as much. Select firm spears of red Belgian endive and red California endive with deep red color and no browning at the edges.

Avoid: Chicories with open, wilted, or brown-tipped leaves will be unpalatable.

Storage: All these vegetables should be stored in a plastic bag and refrigerated for up to 5 days.

Preparation: **Note: Don't cook any of these vegetables in cast iron because they have a tendency to discolor.**

Catalonia:

1. **Discard any discolored or extradark leaves.**

2. **Cut off a thin slice from the stem end.**

3. **Using a sharp paring knife, cut out and discard a cone-shaped core about $^1/_2$ inch (1.3 cm) deep from the stem end.**

4. **Separate the leaves, or cut into crosswise slices.**

5. **Wash in a large amount of cold water.**

Belgian Endive and California Red Endive:

1. **Pull off and discard any loose outer leaves. It is not usually necessary to wash these vegetables.**

2. **Cut away the whole leaves from the base, or cut**

**away a cone-shaped core and then quarter or
halve the heads.**

Serving
Suggestions:

Braise whole or quartered Belgian endive spears in a
mixture of butter, chicken or veal stock, white wine, and
a little sugar. • Add whole or sliced Belgian endive or
California red endive to winter salads with walnuts,
apples or pears, and blue cheese. • Sauté Catalonia or
puntarelle in olive oil and season with red wine
vinegar, black olives, and anchovies.

Flavor
Affinities:

Belgian Endive: apples, cheese sauce, cream, ham, walnuts. **Catalonia:** anchovies, bacon, cured black olives,
pancetta, red pepper flakes, sweet-and-sour sauces, vinegar.

66a–c. 📷

CORN

Other Names:

Maize (Britain).

General
Description:

Corn (Zea mays) *is a long husk-covered "ear" filled with
even rows of toothlike kernels surrounding a central
woody core.* Corn is the New World's most important
contribution to the world diet. Originating in Central
America, corn has been cultivated since at least 3500
B.C. and was a basic food for the Incas, Mayas, Aztecs,
and native North Americans. Sweet fresh corn on the
cob is a luxury outside the U.S.

    Bi-Colored (or **Butter and Sugar**) corn with mixed

yellow and white kernels in each ear is a favorite in New England. In the Mid-Atlantic, people prefer white corn such as **Silver Queen**. Silver Queen is a premier white corn with tight dark green husks and long ears filled to their tips with succulent white kernels. Yellow corn, like **Golden**, is sought after in the Midwest. **Red** sweet corn is uncommon but beautiful, with ruby-tipped sweet kernels that keep their color when cooked.

Baby or **miniature corn** is very young corn, about 6 inches (15 cm) long with a core tender enough to eat. Yellow high-sugar hybrids, such as **Sweetie** and **Kandy Korn**, grown extensively in Florida, slow down the conversion of sugar to starch. These corn varieties can be twice as sweet as other corn, actually get sweeter after harvest, and stay sweet up to 14 days. However, the skin tends to be tough and much of the delicate complex corn flavor is lost.

Season:

Florida corn is available October to June with peak season April to June. California corn is in season May to October with peak season June and July. New York, Pennsylvania, and New Jersey corn is sold from July to September with peak season August and September. Ohio corn is at peak season from August to October.

Purchase:

To choose corn in the husk, pull back enough of the husk to expose the kernels. You should see full rows of pearly rounded teeth. Evenly spaced rows should be plump and milky all the way to the tip of the ear; the husk should be bright green and snugly fitting. The pale to deep gold silks should be dry, not soggy. Don't be scared off if you see a corn worm at the top of the ear, more common in organic corn especially toward the end of the season. Just cut off the tip and enjoy. It has probably chosen the sweetest ear for you.

Because the sugars in corn convert so quickly to starch, buy corn as soon as possible after it's been picked. Look for a market that buys local corn in season with high volume and quick turnover. When buying tray-pack corn, look for plump rounded kernels and no shriveling.

Avoid: Prehusked tray-pack corn may be old or tough, and it's difficult to gauge quality inside the package. Avoid corn with flattened, tightly packed kernels; the corn will be starchy because it's overmature.

Storage: Refrigerate the ears in plastic for 1 to 2 days.

Preparation:

1. **Pull back and tear off the husks.**

2. **Rub off the silk using a nylon scrubber, toothbrush, or vegetable brush.**

3. **To remove the kernels, cut off the tip and bottom of the ear. Stand the cob upright, then use a firm-bladed, sharp knife to slice downward. Cut off 3 to 4 rows at a time without cutting too**

> deep, or the kernels will be woody. Scrape the
> cobs downward to extract the corn "milk."

4. **Corn on the cob is best cooked briefly by either boiling, steaming, or grilling. When boiling, don't salt the cooking water, which will toughen the skin. Cook corn until just tender; overcooking will toughen it. The sweeter and younger it is, the faster the corn will cook.**

Serving
Suggestions:
Make spoon bread with fresh corn purée added. • Make corn chowder with potatoes and salt pork or bacon. Add fish, clams, scallops, crab, or lobster. • Serve corn on the cob with spice- or herb-flavored butter or olive oil. • Cut kernels from cooked corn and add to salad, omelets, pasta, risotto, salsa, or soup.

Flavor
Affinities:
Basil, beefsteak tomatoes, butter, clams, crab, eggs, fish, lobster, red onion, shrimp, tarragon.

---

67. **CROSNES**

Other Names:
Chinese artichokes, chorogi, Japanese artichokes.

General
Description:
Crosnes (Stachys sieboldii *and* affinis) *are small, crisp, tan-skinned white tubers in the mint family with a nutty, artichoke-like flavor.* Crosnes are unusual tubers that grow like potatoes (see page 237) and resemble

sunchokes (see page 262) in flavor, texture, and use. Though rare in the U.S., they are much appreciated by the French, who first imported them from China in the late 19th century. Their name comes from the town of Crosnes, France, where they were first raised.

Crosnes are small and resemble caterpillars with marble-sized sections that are joined together, increasing in size from the ends toward the middle. Much of their flavor resides in the skin. Peeled crosnes discolor quickly when exposed to air. Chinese poets compare crosnes to jade beads.

Season: Crosnes are in season in the winter.

Purchase: Look for the palest, firmest crosnes.

Avoid: Avoid soft or spotted crosnes.

Storage: Refrigerate in an open container for up to 1 week.

Preparation:

1. **Trim the top and bottom of the crosnes.**

2. **To remove the skin, spread out on a towel and sprinkle with kosher salt. Rub the crosnes together to remove most of the skin.**

3. **Rinse under cold water.**

4. **Cut away protruding roots to even the shape.**

Serving Suggestions:	Boil in salted water or stock until crisp-tender. • Cook in a mixture of butter and water with desired seasonings until the water boils away and the crosnes begin to sizzle. • Pickle in a mixture of spices and vinegar to use as a relish. • Blanch, chill, and fry in tempura batter.
Flavor Affinities:	Butter, chervil, chives, dill, lemon, rice vinegar, scallions, shallots, wine vinegar.

68a–c.

CUCUMBER

General Description:

The cucumber (Cucumis sativus) *is commonly an oblong, dark green, seedy vegetable with flesh that is more than 90 percent water.* One of the oldest cultivated vegetables, the cucumber is believed to be native to India and has been cultivated in western Asia for 3,000 to 4,000 years. Cucumbers were brought to the New World by Columbus in 1494, first arriving in Haiti and spreading to Canada. Cucumbers were being grown by the Iroquois when the Mayflower arrived.

All cucumbers have crisp texture and mild flavor. **Common American cucumbers**, usually 8 inches (20 cm) long, are bred to have thick skin for protection during shipping and longer shelf life. Their smooth, dark green skin is often waxed. Unwaxed local cucumbers may have tiny spines that should be rubbed off.

Many slicing cucumbers are grown in greenhouses. Originally grown in Holland, they're sometimes known as **Dutch cucumbers**. They are invariably shrink-wrapped. These superlong (12 to 15 inches [30–38 cm]), smooth, lightly ridged dark green cucumbers are uniform in shape and length and are practically seedless, making them more easily digestible. Extremely thin-skinned, they taper at the tip (where they will spoil quickest) and have a mild, sweet flavor.

Pickling cucumbers, such as **gherkins**, **American dills**, and **French cornichons** are small. Gherkins and cornichons are about 2 inches (5 cm) long; American dills, about 4 inches (10 cm) long. American pickling cucumbers have knobby warts or spines, pale stripes, and skin that ranges from light to dark. They have solid crunch, evenly distributed juiciness, and sweet flavor. They are often called **Kirbys**, though this is a misnomer, because the original Kirby is no longer cultivated.

The name gherkin also refers to the **West Indian gherkin** (*Cucumis anguria*), related to the cucumber. These are 1 to 3 inches (2.5–7.5 cm) long, light green with prominent spines, and filled with tiny seeds. They are used mainly for pickling.

Middle Eastern or **Beit Alpha cucumbers** probably came from Israel in the early 1900s and are also called **Persian cucumbers**. Thin-skinned and smooth, they are slightly ridged, slim, small, and slightly curved. The pale green flesh is crunchy, juicy, and fine-textured, perfect for diced Middle Eastern cucumber and tomato salad.

Armenian cucumbers (*Cucumis melo*) are grouped botanically with melon although they look and act like a cucumber. They are long, thin-ribbed, chartreuse-colored coils with downy, almost nonexistent skin and mild flavor. The flesh is pale and very crisp.

Asian cucumbers have concentrated crispness and deep flavor. They exist in a dramatic range of lengths, colors, and flavors, from mild to bitter, and may have conspicuous dark or light spines, which are easily brushed off. Their flavor is rich, slightly earthy, and not sweet. The **Japanese cucumber** is a mild, narrow, thin-skinned variety with few seeds.

Season: Slicing cucumbers are available all year but peak season is in the summer months. Most pickling cucumbers are sold only during the summer months. Florida provides the majority of the U.S. crop and ships almost year-round except for July. Mexico ships November through May. Hothouse cucumbers are available year-round but peak March to November.

Purchase: Choose common cucumbers that are well shaped and firm with deep green color. Choose hothouse cucumbers that are firm all the way to the tip with no soft spots.

Avoid: Cucumbers are quite perishable because of their high water content. Avoid exceptionally large cucumbers or those that are yellowing, puffy, or shriveled. Examine cucumbers for any soft spots or soft ends, indicating spoilage. If the cucumber flesh is yellow rather than pale green, it has started to deteriorate.

Storage:	Refrigerate cucumbers in the crisper for up to 1 week.

Preparation:

1. **Pickling cucumbers should be scrubbed to remove loose spines. Greenhouse cucumbers do not need to be peeled or seeded. If unwaxed, outdoor varieties may be peeled and seeded or not, as desired. Waxed cucumbers should be peeled with a vegetable peeler.**

2. **To seed a cucumber, slice in half lengthwise and scrape out the seeds with a small spoon.**

Serving
Suggestions:
Slice, chop, or grate cucumber and dress with yogurt and vinegar or lemon to make Indian raita, Turkish *cacik*, or Greek tzatziki. • Slice, salt, and rinse firm cucumbers then sauté in butter and add chervil, dill, or tarragon. • Use like citrus slices to garnish mixed drinks, lemonade, or sparkling water.

Flavor
Affinities:
Buttermilk, chervil, dill, mint, salmon, scallions, tarragon, tomato, yogurt.

---

69. **EDAMAME**

Other Names:
Fresh soybean, vegetable soybean.

General
Description:
Edamame (Glycine max) *are fresh green Japanese soybeans sold in their hairy green pods.* These young green

soybeans, as bright and as sweet as green peas, have small, flattened pods. Inside the pods are smooth-skinned plump beans that resemble baby limas in both appearance and use. Edamame were specially developed in Japan to use as a fresh shell bean. They are a well-loved snack in China and Japan and often served in the U.S. at sushi restaurants. Their Japanese name, *eda-mame*, means "branch beans." They are sold as bunches of stalks with the pods attached in Asian markets and as loose pods in supermarkets.

Season: Edamame are in season in the summer although they are now greenhouse-grown in Japan year-round.

Purchase: Look for brightly colored, even-sized, plump pods.

Avoid: Do not purchase shriveled or discolored edamame.

Storage: Refrigerate in an open container for up to 1 week.

Preparation:

1. **Cut the pods from the stalks with scissors.**

2. **Place the beans pods in a bowl and sprinkle with salt. Rub until evenly coated.**

3. **Let the beans rest for 15 minutes to absorb the salt, enhancing their color and accenting their sweet flavor.**

4. **Boil 1 pound (.45 kg) edamame in 1 gallon (4 l) of water for 7 to 10 minutes. Taste and continue cooking if you prefer a softer bean. Or roast in the pod at 350°F (180°C) for about 15 minutes.**

5. **To eat, press the beans from the pod into your mouth. Eat the beans the same day they are cooked as their delicate flavor fades quickly.**

Serving Suggestions:
Serve as a snack with cocktails or beer. • Add boiled edamame to composed salads. • Use in succotash or other dishes in place of baby lima beans. • Use in pasta dishes or sautés of fish, chicken, or seafood in place of fresh fava beans or peas.

Flavor Affinities:
Corn, crab, ginger, green onion, lemon, sesame oil, soba noodles, soy sauce, sushi, tofu, tomatoes.

70a–d. **EGGPLANT**

Other Names:
Aubergine (Britain, France), *brinjal* (India), eggfruit (Australia), garden egg (Africa), *melanzana* (Italy).

General Description:
Eggplant (Solanum melongena) *is most commonly a large, pendulous, teardrop-shaped purple-black vegetable that is in the Solanaceae family.* Eggplant has been known since the 5th century in China; from there it

spread throughout Asia and the Near East. It arrived in Europe through Italian trade with the Arabs starting in the 13th century. Till the Renaissance, Italians believed eggplants to be poisonous; its name there, *melanzana*, derives from the Latin *mala insana*, "apple of madness."

Eggplant is cultivated throughout the world, but India, the Middle East, and Asia use it most. Good eggplant has a melting texture and meaty quality.

In America, the most common eggplant is the big, deep purple **Black Beauty**. **Italian** or **Sicilian** eggplants may occasionally be found in the market. These are smaller, curved, plump eggplants with deep purple skin and very firm flesh. **Ivory white** and **graffiti** eggplants may be found, especially in areas with a large Italian population. They are smooth and creamy when cooked, without the bitterness sometimes found in dark varieties. However, they do have tougher skin and larger seeds.

Asian eggplants range in color from ivory white to variegated lavender and rich purple. Smaller, rounded fruits include pale green, white, and bright orange eggplants from Thailand. Long, thin Chinese eggplants have purple calyxes; long, thin Japanese eggplants have bright green calyxes.

Season: Eggplant is available year-round, but locally grown eggplant is in season in the late summer.

Purchase: Choose eggplant that is heavy for its size, firm, and almost hard without wrinkles. Just picked, an eggplant's skin is firm and shiny. When selecting eggplants, look for solid color all the way to the stem, without any green.

Avoid: Overgrown eggplants can be bitter and spongy. Avoid soft or spotted eggplants, or eggplants with wrinkly skin.

Storage: Eggplant will keep for about 4 days in the refrigerator but will begin to shrivel as it ages.

Preparation:
1. **Trim the stem end.**

2. **Cut large eggplants into ¹/₄-inch (³/₄-cm) slices.**

3. **Peel the end slices or discard them.**

4. **Soak in cold salted water for 30 minutes, or until the eggplant releases brown juices.**

5. **Drain and proceed with the recipe.**

Note: Small Japanese and Chinese eggplants don't need salting.

Serving Suggestions: Dip sliced eggplant in flour, then beaten egg, then breadcrumbs, and pan-fry. • Make Greek moussaka with layers of cooked eggplant, ground lamb, and tomato and red wine, and top with thick cream sauce. • Mash roasted eggplant flesh with garlic, lemon, olive oil, and tahini to make Lebanese baba ghanoush. • Layer fried breaded eggplant slices with marinara sauce and mozzarella cheese and bake to make eggplant Parmesan.

Flavor
Affinities:

Capers, garlic, ginger, hot peppers, lamb, marinara sauce, melting cheeses, onions, Romano cheese, sesame oil, sesame paste, soy sauce, tomato.

71a–b.

ENDIVE

General
Description:

Endive (Cichorium endivia), *closely related to chicory, is a group of leafy vegetables in the Compositae family that share a tendency to be slightly to overtly bitter and fibrous.* **Curly** endive, which is common in American markets, is fairly tough and bitter and best cooked in soup or vegetable ragouts. It grows in bunches of long, deep green, curly edged leaves with thin white ribs. The center is yellow-white.

Blanched curly endive is more commonly marketed as **frisée**, its French name, or **riccia**, its Italian name. This smaller, lighter version of common curly endive is kept from light while growing, resulting in slim ragged-edged leaves that range from ivory to apple green. The heads have an opened, flattened shape because they are pressed down while growing. It is a common addition to spring mix salad greens. Raised in California, Italy and France, it is expensive because of its demanding growing process.

Escarole has broad, lightly ruffled leaves that form

an open, flattened head. It ranges in color from light yellow to deep green. It is also called **Batavian** endive after the ancient tribe that occupied Holland. Escarole, which is very popular in Italian cookery (especially for soups), is quite mild in flavor, with a melting texture when cooked.

Season: Endive is available year-round, with peak season from December through April.

Purchase: Select curly endive or escarole that is brightly colored with perky leaves. The best curly endive is kept on ice. Select blanched curly endive that is light in color.

Avoid: Avoid endive with brown discoloration, excessive dirt, or flabby, dry, yellowing leaves.

Storage: Store in a plastic bag in the refrigerator for up to 5 days.

Preparation: **Note: Don't cook any of these vegetables in cast iron because they have a tendency to discolor.**

Curly Endive and Escarole:

1. **Discard any discolored or extradark leaves.**

2. **Cut off a thin slice from the stem end.**

3. **Using a sharp paring knife, cut out and discard**

a cone-shaped core about 1/2 inch (1.3 cm)
deep from the stem end.

4. **Separate the leaves, or cut into slices crosswise.**

5. **Wash in a large amount of cold water.**

 Blanched Curly Endive:

It is not usually necessary to wash. Just trim
and cut up as desired.

Serving Suggestions:	Make Lyonnaise salad by tossing together warm bacon bits, cut up frisée, and vinaigrette dressing, then top with a poached egg. • Make Italian escarole soup. • Sauté escarole in olive oil with raisins and pine nuts.
Flavor Affinities:	Anchovies, bacon, cured black olives, eggs, pancetta, red pepper flakes, sweet-and-sour sauces, vinegar.

72. **FENNEL**

Other Names:	Florence fennel, sweet anise.
General Description:	*Fennel* (Foeniculum vulgare) *is a pale green bulbous member of the Umbelliferae family.* Although fennel is a rather odd-looking vegetable with spiky stalks and an enlarged bulb-shaped base, it's easy to love. The bulb,

which can be as large as a fist, is made up of onionlike layers culminating in stringy celery-like stalks, all enclosing a sweet-tasting dense heart.

Fennel is easy to prepare and can be eaten raw or cooked. Raw fennel has a cleansing flavor akin to licorice and anise, though lighter and less persistent. The fennel bulb's crisp texture lends itself to crunching just like an apple. Its distinctive flavor becomes delicate when cooked. When slow-cooked, fennel acquires a luscious melt-in-your-mouth quality. Large-bulbed sweet Florence fennel probably originated in Italy, where it is still eaten extensively, especially as *pinzimonio*, raw wedges dipped in olive oil and sea salt.

Season:

Fennel is available year-round, though the quality varies greatly according to availability. Commercially grown California fat-bulbed fennel with much or all of its green stalks and feathery fronds is sold much of the year. During the coldest winter months you'll occasionally find pale bulbs of greenhouse-grown fennel from Holland.

Purchase:

Opt for large, squat, white bulbs with a pale green tint, fluffy green fronds, and a pearly sheen. The larger the bulb, the less waste. The decorative fronds have little flavor but make a lovely garnish.

Avoid:

Split, shriveled, dried-out, stringy bulbs with brown or soft spots should be avoided. If the stalks have been cut away, the fennel has most likely been on the shelf too long, as the stalks deteriorate first.

Storage:

Wrap fennel in plastic and refrigerate for up to 3 days.

Preparation:

1. **If your fennel has stalks, cut them off at the top of the bulb.**

2. **Trim off a thin slice from the darkened bottom end of the bulb. Pull away the outer layer, which is likely to be stringy and tough. Discard (or add to chicken, fish, or vegetable stock).**

3. **Separate the dark green outer and upper stalks from the light-colored, more-tender inner portions, throwing out all the tough stuff.**

4. **To prevent oxidation, immediately place cut fennel in a bowl of cold water with a little lemon juice until cooking or eating.**

Serving Suggestions:

Serve raw sticks or wedges with dip or olive oil and lemon. • Shave the bulb paper thin and soak in ice water with a little lemon juice till curled, then add to a salad. • Sauté wedges in olive oil over high heat until caramelized. • Boil diced bulb and add to rice, pasta, or polenta. • Chop light green stalks and add to meatballs, crabcakes, red sauce for seafood, or soup.

| Flavor Affinities: | Black olives, chicken, fish, lemon, olive oil, oranges, shellfish, tomatoes. |

FIDDLEHEAD FERN

73.

| Other Names: | Crosier, ostrich fern. |

| General Description: | *Fiddlehead ferns are new-growth fronds, usually of the ostrich fern* (Matteuccia struthiopteris). The name "fiddlehead" refers to any unfurled fern, not to a particular variety, because of their resemblance to the scroll of a violin (or fiddle) head. In the U.S., Maine and Vermont are the main sources of this seasonal wild food. Fiddleheads taste like asparagus combined with artichoke. Note that fiddlehead ferns should be consumed very young and in limited quantities, because of risks that they are carcinogenic. They must be cooked before eating to remove bitterness and minimize gastric problems. |

| Season: | The fiddlehead fern season lasts about 2 weeks in any locale, starting in early April in the South through late July in Canada. |

| Purchase: | Choose fiddleheads that are bright jade green, springy, and firm. |

| Avoid: | Avoid fiddleheads with excessive fuzzy brown scales. Any scales should not be at all blackened. |

Storage:	Fiddleheads do not keep well. They should be wrapped in plastic, refrigerated, and eaten within 2 days.

Preparation:	1. **Trim the base of each fiddlehead, leaving only a small tail protruding beyond the curled section.**
	2. **Rub off any brown scales with your hands.**
	3. **Rinse well.**
	4. **Boil in salted water 3 to 5 minutes. If desired, add a pinch of baking soda to the cooking water to soften them and brighten their color.**

Serving Suggestions:	Toss with butter and chopped herbs. • Cool and toss at the last minute with mild vinaigrette. • Treat like asparagus: drizzle with lemon butter, cheese sauce, or hollandaise. • Toss with soy sauce and sesame seeds.

Flavor Affinities:	Asparagus, butter, lemon, morel mushrooms, new potatoes, salmon, watercress.

GARLIC

General Description:	*Garlic* (Allium sativum) *is a bulb covered with papery skin enclosing individual cloves of the most potent member of the Allium family.* Garlic is thought to have originated in the deserts of Central Asia. This "stinking

rose" is indispensable in nearly all the world's cuisines, but because people who eat garlic give off a strong garlic smell, it has not always been socially acceptable. Known in China since antiquity, garlic was important to ancient Egypt, Greece, and Rome.

A mature head of garlic contains anywhere from 6 to 24 individual cloves that release a notoriously strong aroma when crushed. There are two main types of garlic bulbs: softneck and hardneck (or rocambole). **Softneck** has a fibrous stem that dries into a grasslike top that can be braided. Pleasingly fragrant **hardneck** garlic has a long hard central stem surrounded by firm, easy-to-peel cloves with an intense flavor.

Elephant garlic is more closely related to a leek, though it looks like an extralarge garlic bulb. It is quite mild with potato-like flesh. **Green garlic** is pulled from the ground before the bulb forms, when the plant resembles a leek stalk about $1/2$ inch (1.3 cm) in diameter. Its mild, fresh, sharp flavor is fleeting and herblike rather than oily and lastingly pungent.

Season:

Garlic is in season year-round, though new crop garlic is the best choice when it can be found.

Purchase:

Choose bulbs that are large, plump, and firm with a tight and unbroken sheath. Garlic bulbs from the current year's crop will have plump hard cloves that fill their skins. Look for pink-skinned rocambole in markets with a large Latino or Mediterranean population.

Peeled garlic cloves are also available. This garlic has had its skin removed by blowing air. When buying peeled garlic, look for pearly white, firm cloves with no shriveling and no mold or soft stickiness.

Avoid: As garlic ages, it starts to shrivel and begins to sprout, which turns the flavor bitter. Avoid soft, spongy, or shriveled bulbs.

Storage: Store best-quality garlic bulbs for up to 3 weeks in the refrigerator. Keep dry; moisture will make garlic spoil. As it ages, garlic begins to lose its plumpness. Store peeled garlic in its container for up to 2 weeks in the refrigerator. Store green garlic and garlic chives for up to 5 days in the refrigerator.

Preparation:

1. **Rub off the loose outer skin of the head of garlic, exposing the individual cloves. Pull the cloves away from the core.**

2. **Using the side of a heavy knife, smash down each garlic clove to break open its skin. Remove skin from individual cloves.**

3. **Use garlic whole, smashed, sliced, slivered, chopped, or pressed through a garlic press.**

Serving Suggestions: Use as the base for nearly all savory dishes, sautéing briefly prior to adding other ingredients. • Make garlic

and potato cream soup with mature or green garlic. •
Caramelize garlic cloves by frying in olive oil till golden
brown, then use the garlic or oil separately in cooking.

Flavor
Affinities:

Basil, broccoli, chicken, crab, mushrooms, potato,
shrimp, spinach, steak, tomatoes, tomato sauces.

75. **GINGER**

General
Description:

Ginger (Zingiber officinale) *is a plant grown for its
spicy, aromatic, gnarled, and bumpy root.* Ginger is a
rhizome that probably originated in Southeast Asia.
Ginger's name comes from the Sanskrit word for "horn
root." In the 13th century, Marco Polo reported seeing
vast ginger plantations in Cathay (China). Ancient
Hindu and Chinese cultures valued ginger's medicinal
qualities. Ginger was probably introduced to Japan more
than 2,000 years ago from China. The Chinese and
Japanese consider ginger a *yang*, or hot, food, which bal-
ances cooling *yin* foods to create harmony.

Babylonians, ancient Egyptians, and Persians used
ginger in cooking. Ancient Mediterranean and Middle
Eastern cuisines utilized dried ginger, as it was the only
form that arrived unspoiled after the voyage from East
Asia and India. Cooks in those areas still make use of
dried ginger. Most likely, ginger was brought to Britain
by Roman soldiers. The Spaniards brought ginger to
Jamaica to cultivate it there and avoid the long voyage

from the Far East. Portuguese slaves cultivated ginger in West Africa and Brazil, where it is a basic seasoning.

Ginger ranges in color from pale green-yellow to ivory and has a peppery, slightly sweet flavor and pungent, spicy aroma. It may contain inconspicuous to prominent fibers, depending on age and variety. Fresh ginger sold in the "hands" that it resembles is basic to Asian and Indian cooking. Other members of the ginger family are turmeric, galangal, cardamom, and the mild mioga ginger, *Zingiber mioga*, whose shoots the Japanese pickle and dye pink to serve with sushi.

Season: Fresh ginger is available year-round with peak season March through September.

Purchase: Look for roots that have a firm, smooth skin with a light sheen and fresh, spicy fragrance. Hawaiian ginger has very thin skin and fiber-free flesh.

Avoid: Avoid knobby, shriveled, or moldy ginger.

Storage: Refrigerate ginger wrapped in paper towels and then plastic up to 2 weeks. For longer storage, freeze (slice off as much as you need and return the rest to the freezer).

Preparation:

1. **Trim off as small a knob as needed.**

2. **Peel using a vegetable peeler or the edge of a spoon.**

3. **Grate or slice across the grain, or chop finely as needed.**

Serving
Suggestions:
Chop or grate ginger with garlic as a base for Asian stir-fries or Indian or Southeast Asian curries. • Steep slices in boiling water for ginger tea, then add sugar or honey. • Add to steak marinades with soy sauce, molasses, toasted sesame oil, chopped garlic, dry mustard, hot red pepper flakes, and scallions.

Flavor
Affinities:
Beef, chicken, curry, duck, fish, honey, pork, puddings, salad, saté, seafood, sesame oil, soy sauce, sugar.

76a–d.

GREENS, COOKING

General
Description:
Cooking greens is a category of dark, leafy vegetables in the Brassica family with strong, assertive flavors and often tough, fibrous leaves. Cooking greens are some of the oldest members of the cabbage family, closest to their original wild ancestor. Many of these greens are at their best in winter months and all are high in vitamin A. The older the green, the tougher and more strongly flavored it will be. These greens are cooked to break down their fibrous texture and mellow their bitterness, resulting in tender, succulent leaves with a flavorful bite.

Collard greens are very popular in the American South, where most of the American crop is grown. They resemble flat cabbage leaves.

Dandelion's name comes from the French *dent de lion*, meaning "lion's tooth," a reference to its jagged edges. When young, the bright green leaves have a bitter, tangy flavor that adds interest to salads. When older, dandelion should be cooked.

Flowering kale resembles a giant, ruffled flower ranging in color from white to pink to purple surrounded by curly green leaves. It is used more often as a garnish because of its lovely appearance but tough texture. **Kale** has deep green, long, thin leaves with ruffled edges, tough central ribs, mild flavor, and semicrisp texture.

Mustard greens are a rich, dark green and have a sharp mustard flavor. They are a popular soul food in America and are also common in Indian cooking. **Turnip greens** are similar to mustard greens but with a purplish tint and mellower turnip flavor when young.

Tuscan kale is an heirloom green from Italy that is a winter staple in Tuscany. Distinctive looking, it has very dark blue-green, almost black leaves, about 1 foot (30 cm) long that are heavily curled. Its flavor is sweet and mild, particularly after frost.

Season:

Collards are available year-round with peak season from December through April. Dandelion greens are available year-round, with peak season in April and May and limited from December through February. They are most tender in early spring, before the plant begins to flower. Flowering kale and kale are most abundant December through February. Mustard greens can be found on a regular basis, with peak season December through April and least in July and August. Turnip greens are at their peak October through March. Tuscan kale is in season in winter months.

Purchase: Because they're mostly water, greens shrink greatly when cooked. Two large bunches will serve as a side dish for four people. Look for fresh, plump, crisp leaves. It's normal for mustard greens to show a slight bronze tint.

Avoid: Reject greens with yellow, flabby, or pitted leaves or thick, fibrous stems. Sniff the bunch and avoid greens with any overly strong odor from deteriorating leaves.

Storage: Refrigerate in a plastic bag for up to 5 days. Or trim and wash, wrap in paper towels, place in a plastic bag, and store away from any direct airflow in the refrigerator.

Preparation:

1. **Cut off and discard the stems. If they are thick even up into the leaf, remove them by folding the leaves in half and ripping the stems out.**

2. **Wash in a large bowl of lukewarm water, swishing to dislodge sand or dirt. Lift the greens from the water, allowing the dirt to remain on the bottom.**

3. **Don't dry the greens, as the residual water will help them wilt as they cook.**

Serving Suggestions:	Cook diced bacon until crispy, sauté onion in the bacon fat, then add shredded mustard greens, dandelions, kale, or Tuscan kale, cook until wilted, then toss with pasta and freshly grated Parmesan cheese. • Simmer collard, mustard, or turnip greens with salt pork or ham hocks and accompany with wedges of cornbread to soak up the juices. • Add Tuscan kale to Italian vegetable and bean soups.
Flavor Affinities:	Aged grating cheese, bacon, corn, cornbread, curry, garlic, ham, hot sauce, lemon, onion, salt pork, smoked turkey, vinegar.

77. 📷

HORSERADISH

General Description:	*Horseradish* (Armoracia rusticana)*, a member of the vast Brassica family, has a long, knobby, dusty, pungent root used as a condiment.* Horseradish is believed to have originated in central Europe, the area where it is still most used. The word "horse" denotes large size and coarseness; "radish" comes from the Latin *radix*, meaning "root." During the Renaissance, horseradish consumption rapidly spread from central Europe northward to Scandinavia and westward to England. By the late 1600s, horseradish was the standard accompaniment for beef and oysters for Englishmen. Commercial cultivation in America began in the mid-1850s, when immigrants started horseradish farms in the Midwest.

Horseradish roots are usually from 6 inches to 1 foot (15–30 cm) long with several rounded knobs at the root end. The skin is the color and texture of a scruffy, wrinkly, gnarled parsnip. It may have a green top. Horseradish has a hot, spicy, sinus-clearing bite that is almost absent until it is grated or ground. As the root cells are crushed, volatile oils are released. Vinegar stops this reaction and helps stabilize the flavor. Horseradish quickly loses its pungency after grinding. Fresh horseradish also loses flavor as it cooks, so it is best added toward the end of cooking.

Season:

Horseradish is harvested in the early spring and late fall but is occasionally available year-round. Many American markets carry fresh horseradish root especially for the Jewish community, which uses it to make the "bitter herb" consumed as part of the ritual Seder plate for the Passover holiday in early spring.

Purchase:

Look for a root that is exceptionally hard and free of spongy or soft spots.

Avoid:

Sprouting, green-tinged horseradish may be bitter. Very large horseradish roots may be quite fibrous.

Storage:

Wrap horseradish root in a slightly dampened towel and then a dry one. Keep in the refrigerator for up to 2 weeks. Cut away any soft or moldy spots as they develop.

Preparation: 	1. **Cut off as big a piece as needed.**
	2. **Pare off the outer skin.**
	3. **Grind or grate horseradish in a well-ventilated room, keeping your nose away from the fumes. You may want to wear gloves. Use a blender or food processor for grinding to make the process less tearful than hand grating, cutting into smaller pieces first.**
	4. **Either place immediately in cold water to cover or mix with vinegar or lemon juice to prevent discoloration.**

Serving Suggestions: Add grated horseradish, salt, and lemon juice or vinegar to sour cream and serve with cold roast beef or asparagus. • Serve with cold cuts sandwiches, or with gefilte fish. • Make homemade cocktail sauce with ketchup or chili sauce and grated horseradish.

Flavor Affinities: Cream, gefilte fish, lemon, potatoes, raw seafood on the half shell, roast beef (cold or hot), vinegar.

---

78. **JICAMA**

Other Names: Mexican potato, Mexican water chestnut, Mexican yam bean, potato bean, yam bean root.

General
Description:

Jicama (Pachyrhizus erosus) *is a tropical legume that produces an edible, light brown, round, fleshy taproot.* Native to Central America, this cousin of the sweet potato is widely cultivated there and in Southeast Asia. The underground tuber comes in two types: agua (watery juice) and leche (milky juice). Jicamas range in weight from a few ounces (100 g) to 6 pounds (2.7 kg), with the most common weighing about half a pound (220 g). The jicama's crisp white flesh is hidden under a fibrous dust-brown skin, which must be completely stripped off. Jicama is also called a Mexican potato because it is a root vegetable with a potato-like texture when cooked. Raw jicama is very crunchy, with an apple-like, nutty flavor reminiscent of fresh water chestnut.

Season:

Most jicamas on the market are imported from Mexico and South America and are available year-round.

Purchase:

Look for well-formed plump tubers. Choose medium-sized jicamas with smooth, unblemished skins. Scratch the skin; it should be thin and the creamy flesh should be juicy.

Avoid:

Avoid shriveled or sticky jicamas with cracks or bruises.

Storage:

Store in a cool, dry place, uncovered, for up to 3 weeks. Too much moisture will cause mold. If mold develops, cut it away. Refrigerate after cutting, wrapped in plastic, for up to 1 week.

Preparation:	**Remove the skin and the fibrous flesh directly under the skin using a knife or vegetable peeler.**

Serving Suggestions: Cut into squares and add to fruit salad. • Sauté with carrots or green beans. • Stir-fry with chicken or shrimp. • Simmer in savory stews as if it were a potato. • Serve cut sticks of jicama with a squeeze of lime and a shake of fiery chili powder, as is done in Yucatán and other places.

Flavor Affinities: Chili powder, cilantro, ginger, grilled fish, lemon, lime, oranges, red onion, salsa, sesame oil, soy sauce.

79. **KOHLRABI**

General Description: *Kohlrabi* (Brassica oleracea) *resembles a turnip with protruding stalks topped by broccoli-like leaves.* Kohlrabi, whose German-derived name translates to "cabbage turnip," is either a lovely shade of deep violet or light green. In Italy, the same vegetable is known as *cavolo-rapa* (cabbage-turnip), describing its flavor perfectly. Under its tough outer skin, both the violet and green varieties have whitish green, firm, crunchy flesh.

Kohlrabi is two vegetables in one: The root and the leaves are both delicious but completely different in flavor and texture. Kohlrabi root is reminiscent of celery root, broccoli stem, and cabbage, with a bit of the hotness of radish and the sweetness of turnip. Its leaves are like turnip greens. Though not very well-known, kohlrabi is among the most versatile of vegetables.

Season: Kohlrabi is available year-round with supply peaking in early summer.

Purchase: Choose small to medium-sized kohlrabi with small, smooth bulb-stems and firm green leaves.

Avoid: Overly large kohlrabi will be tough and strong tasting.

Storage: Kohlrabi will keep in the refrigerator for several weeks, but first separate the leaves, which will not keep more than a few days. The leaves will draw moisture away from the root, which will lose its crispness.

Preparation:

1. **Remove the leaves, discarding the stems and any tough center ribs, and then shred them. Use the leaves for slow-cooked greens.**

2. **Steam kohlrabi bulb to loosen its skin, or pare away the tough outer skin before cooking.**

Serving Suggestions: Cut into slices or wedges and add to Chinese stir-fry or Indian curry. • Combine peeled kohlrabi with potato when making scalloped potatoes. • Dip kohlrabi slices or sticks into tempura batter and deep-fry. • Add shredded kohlrabi to coleslaw for extra crunch. • Roast chunks of kohlrabi in the pan with meats or poultry.

Flavor Affinities:	Cheese, curry, Dijon mustard, garlic, ginger, potatoes, rice wine, roasted meats, sesame oil, soy sauce.

80.   **LEEK**

Other Names: Poor man's asparagus.

General Description:

Leeks (Allium porrum) *are large sweet stalks in the onion family that range in color from creamy white through deep greenish blue.* Native to the broad region stretching from Israel to India, leeks have been cultivated since at least 3000 B.C. Phoenician traders introduced leeks to Wales while trading for tin. Legend has it that in A.D. 640, the Welsh wore leeks in their hats to distinguish themselves from the invading Saxons and won a great victory over their enemies.

In France, Belgium, and the Netherlands—the world's leading producers—leeks are considered indispensable to cooking. The deep sandy soil of Flanders is ideal for the cultivation of special large leeks with long, white stems. The leeks are transplanted into drilled holes to keep them away from sunlight. These leeks are tender and delicate and fetch a high price. Tender baby leeks, about 1/2 inch (1.3 cm) in diameter, may also be found. To blanch their stems, leeks are grown either in trenches or with soil mounded around each plant. Some of this soil inevitably winds up between the layers, so you must take special care to wash out the grit.

Season: Leeks are at peak season from October through May, though they can be found year-round.

Purchase: Good-quality leeks are firm and smooth, free of blemishes, with crisp, brightly colored leaves and flexible stems. Baby leeks with thin stalks, similar to a large asparagus, will be tender and sweet.

Avoid: Do not purchase leeks with rounded rather than flattened bottoms, an indication of age. Avoid those with withered, yellowed, or slimy leaves. Unfortunately, in the U.S. leeks are sometimes overgrown until they're dark, tough, and fibrous. The center stalk may have a hard woody core that must be discarded.

Storage: Cut off and discard the tough dark green tops. Store leeks wrapped in damp paper towels inside a closed plastic bag in the refrigerator for up to 1 week. Leeks produce odors that will be absorbed by soft fruits.

Preparation:

1. **Cut leeks into matchsticks, squares, or rings.**

2. **Fill a large bowl with tepid water. Place cut leeks into the bowl and swish around vigorously to encourage the sand to wash away and drop to the bottom of the bowl.**

3. **Scoop out the leeks and transfer to a colander to drain. If the bowl of water has a lot of grit**

on the bottom, repeat the process. Leeks will be especially gritty if they have been harvested in wet weather.

4. **If you will not be using the leeks immediately, drain and roll in paper towels before storing in a plastic bag in the refrigerator for several days.**

Serving Suggestions:

Deep-fry matchstick-sized pieces until crunchy and serve sprinkled with salt. • Make chilled leek and potato soup enriched with cream and garnished with chives (called crème vichyssoise). • Substitute leeks for asparagus (see page 119) in dishes featuring that vegetable.

Flavor Affinities:

Butter, chicken, cream, fish, mussels, mustard, potatoes, tarragon, thyme, vinaigrette, white wine.

81a-e.

LETTUCE

General Description:

Lettuce (Lactuca sativa) *is the most popular of the leafy salad vegetables in the Compositae family and includes many different types.* Lettuce gets its Latin name from the word for milk, *lac*, because of the white sap that oozes from cut stems. In wild lettuce this sap has a mildly soporific effect. There are hundreds of varieties of lettuce and, because they peak at different times of year, there's always a plenitude of this universal salad favorite. The five general classifications of lettuce are butterhead, crisphead, looseleaf, celtuce, and romaine.

Butterhead lettuces have small, round, loosely formed heads with soft, buttery-textured leaves ranging from pale green on the outer leaves to pale yellow-green on the inner leaves. Their flavor is sweet and succulent. Popular varieties include **Boston**, **Bibb** (or **limestone**), and **Merveille des Quatre Saisons**, all of which have rounded heads and delicate flavor.

Crisphead lettuce has a solid head of tightly wrapped leaves. Crisp, succulent, and wilt-resistant, it has a rather neutral watery flavor. **Iceberg** lettuce got its name from the fact that California growers shipped it covered with heaps of crushed ice in the 1920s. It had previously simply been called "crisphead" lettuce. **Batavian** lettuce, a French type, is very crisp like iceberg, but sweet and juicy without bitterness. The plants are at first open like looseleaf lettuce, becoming densely packed at full maturity.

Looseleaf lettuces have leaves that branch from a single stalk in a loose bunch rather than forming a tight head. The leaves are crisper and more full-flavored than head lettuce types, though more perishable. Some varieties include **Black Seeded Simpson**, **green oak leaf**, **red oak leaf**, **Red Sails**, **Lolla Rosa**, and **Valeria**. They range in color from green to red.

Celtuce is the name given to a Chinese lettuce raised for its thickened soft stem. The young leaves are used in salads, while the succulent stem is pared, sliced, and eaten raw or pickled.

Romaine lettuce is America's second-most-popular lettuce (especially in Caesar salad). It is an elongated head of dark green, narrow, stiff leaves with a distinctive rib reaching almost to the tip of the leaf. Called **cos** lettuce in Britain, it is said to have originated on the Greek island of Kos (Cos), off the coast of Turkey. Romaine has been cultivated and eaten cooked or raw for almost 5,000 years and may very well be the oldest form of cultivated lettuce. Red romaine is also grown.

Season:

Different types of lettuce are available intermittently throughout the year with the most common varieties available every day.

Purchase:

Choose head lettuce that is crisp and free of blemishes with a head that gives a little. The leaves should be an even green with little russeting. For looseleaf varieties, look for whole unbroken leaves with no wilting or spoilage of the leaves either at the tips or at the base.

Avoid:

Avoid heads of iceberg that lack green color or are irregular in shape. For romaine, avoid heads with signs of rust; avoid oversized butts; avoid older plants with large, strong milky ribs. Choose heads that are cut close to leaf stems and are free from decay and browning.

Storage:

Store unwashed, whole heads of lettuce in plastic bags to retain nutrients and natural moisture and to maintain crispness. Romaine and iceberg will keep for up to

1 week; young or more tender varieties like Boston and red leaf lettuce will keep for 3 to 4 days. Keep lettuce away from apples, bananas, and pears, as the ethylene gas they give off will turn lettuce brown.

Preparation:

1. **Wash thoroughly. Never allow lettuce to soak, as the water tends to soften some leaves.**

2. **Drain completely or blot with a paper towel to remove any excess moisture. Bibb lettuce is extremely sandy and must be washed with care.**

Serving Suggestions:

Add whole lettuce leaves to sandwiches or burgers. • Use red leaf lettuce leaves for Vietnamese spring rolls, combining cooked shrimp (or beef), softened rice noodles, grated carrot, mung bean sprouts, cucumber, mint, and cilantro leaves and rolling them up inside.

Flavor Affinities:

Anchovies, cucumber, fresh herbs, lemon, mustard, raw onion, tart fruits, tomato, vinaigrette.

82. **LOTUS ROOT**

Other Names:

Chinese lotus, *leen ngau* (China), lily root, pink lotus, *renkon* (Japan).

General Description:

The lotus (Nelumbo nucifera) *root is the enlarged underwater stem (rhizome) of a water lily.* Lotus root has been raised in ponds in Southeast Asia for more than 3,000 years. Both the leaves and seeds can be used, but the root is most common. The lotus was undoubtedly known in classical antiquity—it appears clearly in a mosaic at Pompeii. The lotus has special significance for Buddhists: It is a symbol of purity because it is undefiled despite its muddy origin. Buddha is often depicted holding or sitting on a lotus blossom.

Lotus root resembles sausage links about 6 to 8 inches (15–20 cm) long and about 3 inches (7.5 cm) in diameter. The interior has five to seven tunnels running through it that form lacy patterns when it is sliced crosswise. Lotus root has crispy white flesh with a mild flavor reminiscent of water chestnut or jicama. There is also a wild American lotus, called water, chinquapin, or duck acorn, that was valued by Native Americans, who baked it. However, the lotus for sale in markets is the Asian type, usually imported from China.

Season:

Fresh lotus root is available year-round, especially in Asian markets, but its natural harvest cycle is from mid-summer to late winter.

Purchase:

Select firm, pinkish or grayish lotus root with smooth, unblemished skin and no soft spots. In Asian markets, the roots are boxed and wrapped in newspapers or straw and kept in a cool place. It's considered bad form by Asian grocers to break up the hands of roots.

Avoid: Pass up whole lotus root with dark or soft spots. When sliced, the channels should not be ringed with a dark brown or black lining, a sign that the root is old.

Storage: Store whole lotus root in the refrigerator for 2 to 3 weeks. Store cut lotus root covered in lemon juice and cold water in the refrigerator for up to 5 days.

Preparation:

1. **Wash lotus root under running water, scrubbing gently to remove the mud that is often caked on the outside.**

2. **Remove any small patches of mold and cut out any dark spots.**

3. **Cut off both ends and discard. Pare off the tough outer skin. Slice if desired.**

4. **Soak immediately in lemon juice and water.**

Serving Suggestions: Lightly fry root slices with a little red chile pepper, then sprinkle with soy sauce, sake, sugar, and water and simmer until syrupy. • Cook lotus root slices in sugar syrup and add to fruit salad. • Add cooked lotus root slices to a composed salad or float in clear soup.

Flavor Affinities: Ginger, lemon, lime, rice wine, rice wine vinegar, soy sauce, sweet-and-sour sauce, tempura.

83. **MÂCHE**

Other Names:	Corn salad, field salad, lamb's lettuce, nut lettuce, valerianella.

General
Description:

Mâche (Valerianella locusta) *is a tender winter salad green with soft rounded green leaves.* This salad green has been cultivated since at least the 16th century in France, Italy, Germany, Britain, and Belgium. Cultivated from a wild Eurasian plant, mâche has tender, velvety, spoon-shaped leaves that grow in rosettes and have a gentle flavor reminiscent of sweet hazelnuts.

Mâche is known as lamb's lettuce for several reasons: its resemblance to a lamb's tongue, its harvest at the lambing season, and its status as a favorite food of lambs. European-grown mâche has a complex flavor. In Europe, mâche is usually field grown, although export mâche is mostly greenhouse grown in Holland.

Season:

Greenhouse-grown mâche is available year-round. Field-grown mâche is occasionally found in specialty markets.

Purchase:

Look for bright, lively green leaves. Most American mâche is greenhouse grown and comes with its root-ball attached, meaning that it is still alive and growing.

Avoid:

Pass up mâche with wilted, yellow, or broken leaves.

Storage:

Store mâche in a plastic bag in the refrigerator for 1 to 2 days, using it as soon as possible.

Preparation:

Note: Mâche bruises easily, so handle it gently.

1. **Trim away the rootlets.**

2. **Swish the leaves in a bowl of tepid water and then lift out.**

3. **Pat dry on paper towels.**

Serving Suggestions:

Make a salad of winter greens, including Belgian endive or Treviso radicchio, mâche, and frisée. • Dress delicate mâche with walnut, hazelnut, or grapeseed oil dressing.

Flavor Affinities:

Beets, champagne vinegar, chives, lemon, nuts, shallots, sherry vinegar, tarragon, winter greens.

MUSHROOM

General Description:

Mushrooms are a huge group of edible fungi that are grown, picked, and eaten around the world. The finest and rarest mushrooms, including the truffle, were highly esteemed in classical Greece and Rome. Scientists use the term mushroom to denote only the fruiting body of either agarics (white mushrooms or brown field mushrooms) or boletes (cèpes or porcini). There are more than 300 types of cultivated mushrooms, not including the myriad varieties of edible wild mushrooms.

Mushrooms are mysterious things: They seem to lack roots, some have hallucinogenic properties, and others are deadly poisonous. Wild mushrooms grow and are eagerly gathered in most parts of the world. The most desirable mushrooms grow in wooded areas. Mushrooms tend to have a wide distribution because their spores are easily carried on unsuspecting travelers.

Every year, more varieties of cultivated mushroom come to market. These mushrooms are raised on pasteurized compost in conditions that replicate damp mornings; they take about 6 weeks to grow before being picked by hand. The Chinese and Japanese have been raising shiitakes on rotting logs for thousands of years.

As a rule, if a mushroom is large, dark, and has open gills, it will have a deeper and more profound flavor. The smaller, paler, and less open the mushroom, the more delicate and subtle the flavor. While white mushrooms, cremini, portobellos, and enoki are frequently used raw, some people may not digest raw mushrooms well. The flavors of specialty mushrooms are enhanced by cooking and almost all wild mushrooms should be cooked.

Cultivated **beech**, or *hon-shimeji*, mushrooms *(Hypsizygus tessulatus)* are petite with either white or light brown button caps joined in a clump at the base. They have small thin caps with sharply defined ivory gills and thick, tender stems. Beech mushrooms are crunchy with mild flavor that can be slightly bitter.

Black trumpets *(Craterellus fallax)*, called "trumpets of death," are gray-brown to dark brown-black and distinctively aromatic with a buttery flavor. Their flesh is thin and brittle, their caps wavy-edged, and their outer surface can be smooth or wrinkled. Black trumpets grow wild under deciduous trees throughout North America in the summer and fall.

Chanterelle refers both to the golden chanterelle *(Cantharellus cibarius)* and to close relatives such as red, trumpet (or funnel), and white chanterelles. Depending on the variety, the cap can be yellow, orange, white, brown-gray, or black. The caps are wavy, cup shaped, and firm, with wrinkles, not gills, on the underside. Chanterelles, noted for their soft flesh and apricot-like fragrance, are both cultivated and wild.

Cremini *(Agaricus bisporus)* are similar to common whites. They have naturally light tan to rich brown caps and deeper flavor than white mushrooms. Reasonably priced, cultivated cremini are firm and have good keeping qualities. Substitute cremini for white mushrooms if more flavor is desired.

Enoki mushrooms *(Flammulina velutipes)* are a cultivated Japanese variety that grow in small fragile clusters of white stems topped by tiny caps. They have a mild, light flavor with a slight crunch. They are usually eaten raw in salads or used as a garnish.

Hedgehog mushrooms *(Dentinum repandum)* have buff- to tawny-colored caps with pale stems. Tiny spine-like teeth fill the undersides of the caps instead of gills.

They have mild, sweet flavor and firm, chewy texture. Hedgehogs are picked wild, not cultivated, and should be cooked before eating.

Lobster mushrooms *(Hypomyces lactifluorum)* get their name from their knobby appearance and bright color. They have a minutely pimpled surface and fishy aroma. With their crisp white flesh and bright color, they are a spectacular wild mushroom.

Maitake mushrooms *(Grifola frondosa)* have a cluster of dark fronds with supple, firm texture at the base and brittle, crumbly texture at the edges. They have a distinctive aroma with a rich, woodsy taste enhanced by cooking. They are indigenous to the northeastern part of Japan and are both cultivated and wild. Sometimes maitakes grow to over 50 pounds (22.5 kg), which is why they are called the "king of mushrooms."

Matsutake mushrooms *(Tricholoma matsutake)* are a dark brown Japanese wild mushroom with a dense, meaty texture and nutty flavor prized by Japanese and Koreans. They have firm flesh and an intoxicatingly potent, spicy aroma that is somewhat fruity, but stinky.

Morels *(Morchella esculenta* and others) may be tan, yellow, or black with short, thick, hollow stems topped with spongelike pointed caps. Morels have a rich, nutlike flavor and woodsy fragrance. Their honeycomb whorling texture combines softness with crunchiness. Wild morels flourish in temperate parts of the world. Cultivated morels are available year-round though they are not as flavorful.

Pleurotte, or **oyster** mushrooms *(Pleurotus ostreatus)* have fluted soft brown caps 1 to 3 inches (2.5–7.5 cm) in diameter. They have a delicate, mild flavor and velvety texture. These cultivated mushrooms are best when cooked. The stems are tough; only the furled cap should be eaten. The stems may be chopped or ground for stuffings or used for stock.

Porcini mushrooms *(Boletus edulis)* are rich, meaty, and amazingly versatile—delicate enough for a sauce, yet vigorous enough to stand up to grilled steak. The legendary porcini (also called **cèpes**) have fat, firm, curved white stalks and broad, dark brown caps with a spongy layer of long miniscule tubes beneath the cap. They are one of the few wild mushrooms that can be eaten raw.

Portobello mushrooms *(Agaricus bisporus)* are large, hardy fully mature cremini with caps that can reach 6 inches (15 cm) in diameter. Portobellos have a long growing cycle resulting in a solid, meatlike texture and flavor. These incredibly popular mushrooms are available whole, caps only, and sliced.

Shiitakes *(Lentinus edodes)* originated in Japan and are still most popular in Japanese and Chinese cooking. They range in color from tan to dark brown with broad, umbrella-shaped caps with wide open veils and tan gills. The caps are soft and spongy with a meaty, slightly chewy texture when cooked. They have a distinctive smoky aroma. Their stems are too woody to eat as is, though flavorful if ground finely or used for stock.

White mushrooms *(Agaricus bisporus)* are the most

well-known mushroom in Europe and America. They range from creamy white to beige and are good raw or cooked; their flavor intensifies when cooked. Freshly picked white mushrooms have closed veils (caps that fit closely to the stem) and delicate flavor; mature whites, with open veils and darkened caps, develop a richer, deeper taste. Whole white mushrooms range in size from small buttons suitable for slicing raw in salads to jumbos suitable for stuffing and baking.

Season:

All cultivated mushrooms are available year-round. Black trumpet mushrooms are in season in late summer to late autumn in Europe and late autumn to late winter in America. Chanterelles are in season in spring, summer, and fall. Hedgehog mushrooms are available December through March from California and Oregon. Lobster mushrooms are found from August through October. Porcini mushrooms are available in May and June and again in October. Matsutake mushrooms are in season from late fall to midwinter, especially in Japanese markets or specialty produce stores. Wild morels are in season in earliest spring and are abundant in the American Midwest.

Purchase: Select mushrooms with spongy, firm, and fleshy caps.

Avoid: Do not purchase mushrooms with black spots, worms, an unhealthy shriveled appearance, or discoloration. Wet or slippery mushrooms are past their prime.

Storage:

Most mushrooms are very perishable, but nearly all mushrooms will remain fresh for 5 to 7 days when stored properly. When stored whole, they will last much longer than if sliced, no matter the variety. Handle mushrooms with care as they bruise easily. If you buy them in a prepack, take off the cling film and put the mushrooms into a paper bag or wrap them in absorbent paper towels for up to 3 days. The exception is some of the dry, firm types such as shiitake and cremini. Any vacuum-sealed mushrooms (such as enoki) will keep for up to 14 days if refrigerated.

Preparation:

1. **Clean the mushrooms. You may either rub or brush mushrooms if they are relatively clean. If the mushrooms are very dirty, quickly rinse them under cold running water just before use. Many people peel mushrooms, though this is not necessary, especially for cultivated mushrooms.**

2. **Dry washed mushrooms on paper towels.**

Note: To prepare fresh porcini, scrape dirt off the stalks and wipe the mushrooms clean with a damp cloth—only wash if you absolutely must, and never in hot water. Use as soon as possible. If you must wait, stand the mushrooms on their caps to prevent any of the tiny worms sometimes inhabiting the stalks from traveling into the cap.

Note: Before using fresh chanterelles, rinse them quickly though carefully, especially inside the wrinkles. Drain immediately, and dry them with a cloth or paper towel.

Serving
Suggestions:
Marinate small white mushrooms in vinaigrette. • Stuff large white mushrooms with sausage, breadcrumbs, or spinach. • Grill whole portobello caps instead of meat and serve burger-style. • Use shiitakes in Chinese and Japanese dishes, pasta, or soups. • Use lobster mushrooms in terrines or other seafood dishes. • Broil matsutake for a few minutes on each side, adding a bit of rice wine and soy sauce just before serving. • Add any mushroom to soup, chicken, seafood, or other dishes.

Flavor
Affinities:
Beef, chicken, cream, fish and seafood, game, garlic, herbs, onion, pasta, pork, rice, wine.

85. **NAPA CABBAGE**

Other Names:
Celery cabbage, Chinese cabbage, *hakusai*, Peking cabbage, *pe-tsai*, Tientsin cabbage, *wong bok*.

General
Description:
Napa cabbage (Brassica rapa, Pekinensis group) is a Chinese cabbage with an oblong head and tightly packed pale green to white crinkled leaves. A close cousin to bok choy (see page 136), this cabbage has crinkly, thickly veined fibrous leaves, which is why it is

called "celery cabbage." Napa is mild and sweet, like a cross between cabbage, iceberg lettuce, and celery. A versatile cabbage, it can be eaten raw or cooked and is used in stir-fry and soups. The leaves are cream colored with celadon green tips. Unlike the strong-flavored waxy leaves on round heads of cabbage, these are thin, crisp, and delicately mild. In Korea, it is fermented with salt and chiles to make the hot and spicy relish *kimchi*.

Season: Napa cabbage is available year-round.

Purchase: Look for a compact head with tightly closed, crisp, green-tipped, moist leaves.

Avoid: Steer clear of heads with wilted, yellowed, or brown leaves.

Storage: Refrigerate napa cabbage in a plastic bag, as it readily absorbs nearby odors. Keep away from ethylene-producing fruits, such as apples. Napa will keep for 1 week or more.

Preparation:

1. **Cut out the core.**

2. **Wash the leaves under running water.**

3. **If the leaves look wilted, soak in cool water to crisp.**

4. **Remove from the water and shake dry.**

Serving Suggestions:	Sauté garlic and ginger in hot oil, then add sliced napa and sauté until crisp-tender, about 5 minutes. • Drop shredded napa into soup during the final 3 minutes of cooking. • Slice napa and steam 3 to 5 minutes until crisp-tender. • Shred raw cabbage for an Asian seasoned coleslaw. • Use whole leaves to cover the bottom of a bamboo steamer basket.
Flavor Affinities:	Chicken, coleslaw, duck, fish, garlic, ginger, pork, rice wine, seafood, sesame oil, soup.

86. **NOPALES**

Other Names:	Cactus leaves, cactus paddles, nopalitos.
General Description:	*Nopales* (Nopalea cochenillifera) *are the edible thick, green fleshy branches of the prickly pear cactus.* The nopal's pads, or "paddles," are flat, hand-size vegetables, either green or purple, covered with spines that must be removed before eating. Long popular in Mexico, the fleshy oval pads are gaining popularity in the U.S. They contain a mucilaginous liquid that is cooked out in most recipes. Nopales have a slightly tart green bean–like flavor and chewy texture. Wild nopale plants have more spines than cultivated nopales. Almost all those sold commercially have the spines already removed. In many cases, the pads have also been cut up into small squares or strips called nopalitos.

Season: Though fresh nopales are available year-round in Mexican markets and some supermarkets, they're at their most tender and juicy in the spring.

Purchase: Buy small, firm, pale green nopales with a glossy sheen.

Avoid: When the leaves have grown thick and lost their sheen the nopales will be pithy inside. Avoid wrinkled nopales.

Storage: Refrigerate for 1 week lightly wrapped in plastic.

Preparation:

1. **Use a vegetable peeler or brush to remove the skin, which will remove any protruding nodes—the beginnings of new spines.**

2. **Trim any rough edges with a paring knife or vegetable peeler.**

3. **Pat with paper towels if desired to remove sticky secretions.**

Serving Suggestions: Add grilled or boiled nopalitos to salad or cut into small dice and add to salsa. • Sauté nopalitos with scrambled eggs and diced onion, chiles, and tomato for a traditional Mexican Lenten breakfast. • Marinate cooked nopalitos with carrots, jalapeños, and onions escabeche-style for a Latin American pickled side dish. • Cut nopales into strips, batter, and fry like French fries.

| Flavor Affinities: | Chiles, cilantro, corn, eggs, lemon, lime, onions, sweet bell peppers, tomato, tortillas, tropical fruits. |

87. **OKRA**

| Other Names: | *Bamia* (Middle East), *bhindi* (India), *gombo* (Africa), lady's finger. |

General Description:

Okra pods (Abelmoschus esculentus) *are fuzzy and deeply ridged, 2 to 4 inches (5–10 cm) in length, commonly olive greenish in color, and contain crunchy round seeds and mucilaginous juices.* Okra is the fruit of a plant native to tropical Africa and Asia related to hibiscus and mallow. It has been cultivated by Egyptians since the 12th century. From there it traveled to central Africa, the Mediterranean, and India. Okra was brought to the U.S. three centuries ago by African slaves. The word "gombo" used for okra came from West Africa and was in use in the U.S. by the late 1700s.

Okra blossoms, which resemble their cousin, hibiscus, are beautiful and edible. Red, white, and purple okra may be found in specialty markets.

Season:

Okra is often available fresh year-round in the American South and from May to October in many other areas. Peak season is June through August.

Purchase:	Okra is highly perishable, so make sure the okra is as fresh as possible. Look for young pods free of bruises, uniform in color, tender but not soft, and no more than 4 inches (10 cm) long. The younger the pod, the less glutinous it will be.
Avoid:	Soft, shriveled, or very large okra will be tough and fibrous. Dried-out, stringy, or flabby okra may be ropy.
Storage:	Refrigerate okra in a paper bag or wrapped in a paper towel in a perforated plastic bag for 2 to 3 days.
Preparation:	**Note: Don't use iron or copper pans to cook okra, because the chemical reaction will blacken the okra.**
	Rinse in cool water. Okra does not need to be peeled or trimmed prior to consumption.
Serving Suggestions:	Dip whole small okra pods in flour, egg, and cornmeal, then deep-fry until golden brown and serve with lemon and hot sauce. • Add diced okra to traditional gumbo, Brunswick stew, or rice pilaf. • Substitute okra for zucchini in ratatouille. • Add okra pods toward the end of braising lamb with Middle Eastern seasonings.
Flavor Affinities:	Chiles, corn, cornmeal, lemon, onion, rice, sweet peppers, tomato, vinegar.

88a–e. **ONION**

General
Description:

The mature onion (Allium cepa) *is a white, yellow, or red bulb that is pungent when raw and sweet when cooked.* The diverse onion family probably originated in central Asia, although onions now grow throughout the world. Onions have been eaten and cultivated since prehistoric times, when they were raised in ancient Mesopotamian gardens and appeared in Egyptian tomb paintings.

Fleshy layers attached at the root end are covered with layers of thin paper skin that develop as the onion matures. The bite of raw onions is due to sulfur compounds. When an onion is cut, the crushing of the cells and contact with air releases allicin—which in turn causes one's eyes to water.

Onions are of two general categories: spring/summer fresh bulb onions and storage onions. Fresh onions can be yellow, white, or red, with varied shapes—flat, top-shaped, round, and long. These mild, juicy onions have thin, light-colored skin and are often used raw. Storage onions are yellow, white, or red but almost always round. These moderate to strong, full-flavored onions are noted for their storing, shipping, and cooking qualities. Several layers of thick, dark skin protect them. Storage onions are typically much harsher when eaten raw, though they may be the sweetest when cooked. Picklers, pearls, creamers, boilers, standards, and jumbos are simply size names for the same variety of onion, planted differently and picked at different times.

Most sweet onions are hybrids. With a sugar content that is actually lower than other onions, they are not truly sweeter than common onions. However, they are milder, having less pyruvic acid, which imparts "heat" to onions. They are also exceptionally juicy with large thick rings and thin skins separating the layers. The sweet onion's delicate nature requires that it be harvested by hand, thoroughly dried, and treated gently during grading and packaging.

There are many different kinds of onions. **Apaz** onions are wild onions that resemble pearl onions topped with a green stalk. **Bermuda** onions come in red, white, and yellow and all are mild. The Bermuda onion may actually be of Italian origin. **Boiling** onions are thin-skinned, small onions meant for cooking whole in stews. **Cipollini** are distinct, flattened flying saucer–shaped onions from Italy. They are unusually rich and sweet but more perishable than round pearls. **Green** onions (also called **scallions**) are pulled while the tops are still green and before a large bulb has formed.

Italian red onions are flattened with definite ridges and thick layers. The inner skin layers are deep purple. They don't store well but have sweeter flavor and crunchier texture than other red onions. **Pearl** onions are small because they are planted tightly together and are picked early. They are as pungent and storable as larger onions. **Spanish** onions are a large category of generally mild globe onions. They are the most common onion at the market and may be found in very large sizes. **Spring** onions have formed bulbs but their tops are still green. They are sweet and sharp and must be used quickly.

Vidalia onions are Georgia-grown and known for their sweet, mild flavor, which is partly due to the unique combination of soils and climate in their production area. Maui, Hawaii, is the home of the famous sweet **Maui** onion. **Walla Walla** sweets were brought to Walla Walla, Washington, from Corsica at the beginning of the 20th century. These "French" onions were developed over several generations to be exceptionally sweet, jumbo-sized, and round.

Tropea in Calabria, Italy, is famous for its pungent, football-shaped, **red torpedo** onion. The history of the **Tropea** onion in Italy can be traced back to its introduction by the Phoenicians around 2,000 years ago. **White** onions are mild in flavor with papery white skins. They can be quite large and round and are good both raw and cooked.

Season:

Many onions are available year-round. Apaz onions from Oregon peak in June. Italian red onions are in season April through August. Pearl onions are in season beginning with whites in July and followed by the red and gold pearls. Availability typically continues through March. Spanish sweets will be found January through March and August through December. Vidalia onions are harvested from late April through mid-June. Retailers usually have fresh Vidalia onions available through mid-July, although with modified atmosphere long-term storage, they are now available much of the year. Walla Walla onions are best in June and July.

Purchase: Look for onions that are dry, firm, and shiny with a thin skin. The necks should be tightly closed with no sprouts. The outer skins should be papery and can be loose. Good-quality pearl onions will be a uniform size and have firm, clear skin with no bruises or blemishes.

Choose scallions with medium-sized necks that are well blanched 2 to 3 inches (5–7.5 cm) above the root.

Avoid: Onions with green sprouts will taste bitter. Avoid onions with dark patches and soft spots. Examine the sprout end of Italian red onions: It is often sunken and this is where the first signs of spoilage begin. Avoid any onions with soft, deeply sunken or yellow tops and any black mold. Avoid pearl onions that are too big or blemished, or have soft or moldy spots.

Storage: Onions should be stored in a loosely woven bag—not plastic—in a cool, dark, dry, and well-ventilated area. For long-term storage wrap each onion separately in foil and refrigerate. Do not store onions under the sink or with potatoes because potatoes give off moisture that can cause onions to spoil. Pearl onions should be kept away from fluorescent lighting, which turns them green.

Preparation:

1. **To lessen crying, chill an onion before chopping and use a very sharp knife.**

2. **Peel away the papery outer skin and any blemished layers. If the onion will be chopped, trim off the top and peel the outer layers while leaving the root end whole. (The root end contains the most sulfuric compounds.)**

Note: To cut down on sharpness when serving raw onions, place in a bowl of ice water for 30 minutes and then drain.

Serving Suggestions:

Marinate pearl or cipollini onions and thread on kebabs for grilling. • Roast whole small onions at high heat till they are caramelized (peel before or after roasting). • Top sandwiches, salads, or burgers with slices of red, white, or yellow sweet onion. • Make pink onion pickles by soaking sliced red onions in ice water and vinegar until the onions turn pink, then drain and serve.

Flavor Affinities:

Onions complement any savory food.

---

89. **PARSLEY ROOT**

Other Names:

Dutch parsley, German parsley, Hamburg parsley, turnip-rooted parsley.

General Description:

Parsley root (Petroselinum crispum radicosum) *is a beige, carrotlike root with a flavor somewhat like celery, turnips, and parsley.* Parsley root has a long history of use as a winter vegetable in Holland, Germany, and Poland, as is indicated by such names as Hamburg parsley and Dutch parsley. It is often double-rooted and can easily be confused visually with parsnip, its sweet cousin (see page 224). Parsley root is much used in northern Europe in soups, stews, and as a cooked vegetable. In the U.S., it is most likely to be found in markets with a large Jewish, German, or Polish clientele. The leaves, which may be sold as "soup greens," are broader than those of curly leaf parsley and can be used for garnishing or chopped as an herb.

Season:

Parsley root is in season August through April with heaviest supply at the beginning of January.

Purchase:

Buy parsley root with the feathery, bright green leaves attached. The roots should be creamy white and unblemished. Buy parsley roots of the same size, preferably small to medium.

Avoid:

Pass up parsley root with wilted greens or withered roots. The leaves should look fresh, not limp.

Storage:

Refrigerate for up to 2 days. For longer storage, store the roots in paper towels in a plastic bag for 1 week; use the leaves within 1 or 2 days.

Preparation:

1. **Trim the greens off the root.**

2. **Wash and dry the greens and reserve for use like regular parsley.**

3. **Scrub the roots with a vegetable brush, or peel.**

Serving
Suggestions:

Cook 1 part parsley roots to 3 parts potatoes and mash together. • Add parsley root to hearty soups or stews. • Make a shredded parsley root and celery root salad.

Flavor
Affinities:

Barley, beets, cabbage, chicken soup, horseradish, oxtail, root vegetables, shallots, sweet potatoes, thyme.

90. **PARSNIP**

General
Description:

Parsnips (Pastinaca sativa) *are root vegetables in the Umbelliferae family that resemble ivory-colored carrots.* Parsnips have been cultivated in Europe since ancient times, but they became less important over the centuries as other sources of (once rare) sweetness became available. Europeans brought the parsnip to America in the early 1600s. Parsnips are complex, combining sweetness with earthy herbal notes. Parsnips and parsley root are similar in appearance, though only the parsnip is sweet.

Season:

After the first frost of the year, the parsnip's starch is coverted to sugar, and they are ready to be harvested.

Purchase:	Look for small to medium, well-shaped roots free of pitting. It is the age rather than the size of the parsnip that determines tenderness, so choose large squat parsnips for ease of preparation.
Avoid:	Parsnips that have been stored too long may be tough and even woody. Avoid limp, shriveled, or spotted parsnips. The tops should show no signs of sprouting. Avoid parsnips that are thin and long because they are apt to be stringy.
Storage:	Wrap parsnips in paper towels, place inside a plastic bag, and refrigerate in the coldest, moistest part of the refrigerator for up to 1 month.
Preparation:	**Note: Parsnips are usually eaten cooked, as they tend to be fibrous, particularly their cores. If the cores seem overly tough or stringy, cut them out and save them for soup stock.**

1. **Trim off the ends and knobs.**

2. **Peel with a peeler before cooking if cutting into chunks for stew or roasting; peel after cooking if mashing them (this helps preserve their color and flavor and saves nutrients). The outer layer of raw parsnip may be shredded and added to coleslaw.**

3. **Boil, steam, or roast. Don't overcook. Their flavor is sweeter when just tender.**

Serving
Suggestions:

Toss cooked parsnips with butter and herbs such as tarragon, thyme, chervil, or chives. • Season cooked parsnips with nutmeg, ginger, cinnamon, or allspice and a little brown sugar or maple syrup. • Cook parsnips with potatoes and mash together. • Roast chunks of parsnip tossed with olive oil and sage or rosemary in a hot oven till soft inside and caramelized outside.

Flavor
Affinities:

Apples, brown butter, brown sugar, cream, curry, leeks, oranges, root vegetables, stews and ragouts, truffles.

91a–c.

PEAS

Other Names:

English peas, garden peas, *pease* (Old English), *petit pois* (France), *piselli* (Italy), sweet peas.

General
Description:

Peas (Pisum sativum) *are members of the legume family that contain up to eight small green seeds lined up inside pods.* Peas are one of the world's oldest vegetables, but early varieties were starchy even when young. Both the Greeks and Romans cultivated shelling peas for drying. The word "pea" itself is a very old term; Greek, Italian, old Irish, French, and English share variations on the same word. Pease, the old English name for the pea, is actually a singular, not a plural form. Italian

Renaissance gardeners first cultivated the sweet green pea. The people of Italy and France still celebrate spring by eating sweet young peas.

Garden or **English** peas are the familiar "peas in a pod." Their parchmentlike pods are too stringy to eat, though they may be added to a soup broth for flavor. They are at their best when as small as possible, usually early in spring.

Sugar snap and **snow** peas are both types of sugar peas: peas with tender, edible pods. Sugar snap peas resemble English peas but have smaller, smooth, curved pods, and they are eaten whole. The common assumption is that snow peas are an Asian vegetable, but they were probably first cultivated in Holland and were originally known as Dutch peas.

Pea tendrils are the furling, tender leaves and shoots of young pea plants. They are sweet and tender with a strong pea taste.

Season:

Sweet young peas are at their best in May, though they are available from February through September. Sugar snap and snow peas are found year-round. Pea tendrils are best in the spring.

Purchase:

Choose garden peas with pods that are bright green and velvety to the touch, filled with pearl-shaped peas that barely fill their pod. Look for barely discernible miniature peas inside snow peas. Snow peas should be light green in color. Snap peas should be brilliant green in color and

smooth with no breaks or cuts and have the same
smooth, firm skin as snow peas.

Avoid: Stay away from overgrown, starchy peas that are flattened against each other, resembling teeth. Avoid
immature peas that are flat, dark green, and wilted or
overgrown peas that are swollen and flecked with gray
specks. A yellowish color indicates age or damage.
Avoid water-soaked pods or any that show mildew.

Inspect snow peas for small circles of rot, a sign that
they are deteriorating. Avoid overgrown sugar snap peas
with visible peas bulging out, or pods with breakage,
white patches, or soft or moldy tips.

Storage: For the ultimate in sweet succulence, eat peas just after
they're picked. But don't despair if this isn't possible;
peas will maintain almost all of their sweetness for 3 to
4 days if they're placed in a closed plastic bag and
refrigerated. Store sugar snaps, snow peas, and pea tendrils in plastic bags in the refrigerator for up to 2 days.

Preparation: ***Shell Peas:***

Pop open the pods and remove the peas.

Sugar Snaps and Snow Peas:

**Hold the pod just below the stem, between the
thumb and forefinger, and break back the stem**

end. Grasp the tip of the stem and pull it down parallel to the pod to remove the stem and strings on either side of the pod.

Pea Tendrils:

Trim away any large stems and rinse.

Serving Suggestions:

Cook peas for just a few minutes with sliced spring onions and shredded butter lettuce for a traditional French spring dish. • Add snow peas to Chinese stir-fry. • Add sugar snap peas to a crudités platter. • Stir-fry pea tendrils in hot oil with salt, garlic, and a splash of sherry or rice wine until they are wilted.

Flavor Affinities:

Artichokes, chervil, chives, crabmeat, lettuce, mint, salmon, scallions, scallops, shad, shrimp, sorrel, tarragon.

92a–g.

PEPPER, CHILE

Other Names:

Chilli (Britain), *aji* (South America).

General Description:

Chiles (Capsicum annuum, chinense, *or* frutescens) *are a huge family of peppers that contain capsaicin.* There are hundreds, if not thousands, of chile varieties used throughout the world to impart fiery flavor to foods. Wild chiles were gathered in Mexico as long ago as 7000 B.C. and were cultivated before 3500 B.C. The Spaniards and Portuguese brought chiles to India and Southeast Asia; they reached Europe by the mid-16th century.

Chiles get their heat from capsaicin, an alkaloid found mainly in the spongy white tissue to which the seeds cling. Individual chiles from the same plant can vary greatly in their hotness quotient, which in the U.S. is measured by the Scoville scale. Anaheims score 1,000, jalapeños 2,500 to 4,000, and habaneros 200,000 to 300,000. The general rule is, the smaller the chile, the hotter it will be. Each type of chile has subtle flavors in addition to its heat.

Capsaicin can also irritate or even burn human skin and inner tissues. People develop a tolerance for the hotness, so that those who are accustomed to eating chiles can eat much hotter food than novices. Chiles may also be mildly addictive; people who eat a lot of chiles miss them quite badly if deprived. All chiles change color as they mature from green to white, yellow, orange, red, purple, or brown (depending on variety).

Anaheim peppers are long, round-tipped green or red peppers, developed in California in about 1900 for use in a new cannery. They are considered mild.

Cherry hots are very meaty, bright red, and cherry-shaped. Often found pickled, they are medium hot.

Cubanelle, or **Italian frying** peppers, are large, blocky, and light green maturing to light red. The thin walls of this mild pepper make it excellent for frying.

Habaneros are famed for their intense heat and underlying sweet apple-tomato flavor. Distinctive in shape, habaneros are squat, orange, lantern-shaped pods 1 to 2 inches (2.5–5 cm) in diameter. They may have originated in Cuba as their name means "from Havana." Close relatives of the habanero, **Scotch bonnet** peppers come from the Caribbean and are light green, yellow, or red. Take real care when handling and eating both of these types of chiles because their heat level makes them extremely potent, and cooks can burn their fingers without realizing it.

Hungarian wax peppers range from mild to medium hot. They are waxy yellow in color maturing to light red, with small, elongated, pointed tips.

Jalapeños have blunt, almost oval pods about 2 inches (5 cm) long and thick flesh walls often striated with thin brown lines. They are the most common hot chile in the U.S. Their heat is medium hot to hot, and they hail from Veracruz state in Mexico. Most fresh jalapeños are sold green, though occasionally red ripe ones may be found. When smoke-dried, red jalapeños are called "chipotles."

New Mexico peppers are fairly mild. They are long and tapered in shape and may be brown, green, red, orange, or yellow. When fresh they are often stuffed; when dried they are used for chili powder.

Pasillas are mild dried Mexican chiles that are often used to make Mexican *mole* sauces. They are called *chilaca* chiles in Mexico when used fresh. However, in California the term "pasilla" is incorrectly attributed to poblanos. Since most poblanos are distributed from

California, this mislabeling carries over into supermarkets nationwide, causing much confusion.

Poblanos, called "pasillas" in California, originated in the Puebla region, south of Mexico City. A large chile shaped like a long, pointed heart, the poblano is deep green in color and is moderately hot. It is often stuffed for chiles rellenos. When smoke-dried, it is called an ancho chile.

Rocotillo peppers originated in the Caribbean and are often found in Caribbean markets. They resemble tiny pattypan squash and can be green, red, or gold. They are usually used fresh in hot sauces and salsas, and they are mild enough to use raw.

Serranos have small bullet-shaped pods and are named for the mountain ridges in Mexico where they originated. Mainly eaten green, serranos are popular in Mexico and commonly used in salsa and guacamole. Serranos are normally about twice as hot as jalapeños.

Thai hot peppers, or **Thai dragons**, are small, thin, bright red chiles that are extremely hot.

Season:

Different kinds of chiles are found at the market year-round, with the most variety in hot summer months and in areas with a large Hispanic population.

Purchase: Choose firm, plump chiles with shiny skin and a fresh smell. For the most flesh, get the heaviest ones.

Avoid: Undesirable chiles are wrinkled or soft. Avoid chiles with any mushiness toward the stem end or soft, brown, spoiled spots.

Storage: Refrigerate fresh chiles in a plastic bag for up to 1 week.

Preparation: **Note: Handle chiles with care. Protect your hands because the capsaicin can make the skin burn. Wear rubber gloves, or coat your hands with oil, which native cooks have done for centuries. Once your hands or gloves have been in contact with chiles, do not touch your lips, eyes, face, or delicate body parts. To prevent burning those sensitive areas later, scrub your hands and arms vigorously with plenty of hot soapy water. Don't rinse chiles in water because this removes the oils, which hold much of the chile's flavor. Preparation will depend on the desired heat.**

For a More Mild, Smoky Flavor:

1.   **Hold the chile with tongs over high, direct heat, either from a gas burner or a backyard grill. Alternatively, place on a baking sheet under the broiler. They are done when brown-black and blistered.**

2.   **Remove from heat and place in a heat-resistant, heavy plastic bag. Let sit until the chiles are cool enough to handle.**

3. **Peel by rubbing the skins off with your fingers, or scrape with a knife.**

4. **Trim off the stems. The inner fibers and seeds may be kept or discarded.**

 *For a Fresh, Hot Flavor:*

1. **Slice the stem end off the raw chile.**

2. **If a mild flavor is desired, slice the chile open and cut out the seeds and white ribs. If intense heat is desired, do not discard the seeds.**

3. **Chop the pepper.**

Serving Suggestions:
Stuff poblanos with picadillo (a mixture of ground beef, raisins, almonds, and green olives) or Monterey Jack cheese to make chiles rellenos. • Combine thinly sliced serrano or jalapeño peppers to chopped tomatoes and onions to make fresh *pico de gallo*. • Add diced red and green chiles to a black bean salad. • Make a Thai curry with shrimp or chicken, coconut milk, fish sauce, and thinly sliced hot chiles.

Flavor Affinities:
Latin American foods: cilantro, lime, mole sauce, pinto beans, pumpkin seeds, tomatillo sauce, tomatoes. **Asian foods:** coconut milk, fermented black beans, fish sauce, ginger, kaffir lime, peanuts, sesame oil, soy sauce.

93a–d.

PEPPER, SWEET BELL

General
Description:

Sweet bell peppers (Capiscum annuum) *are in the same genus as hot chile peppers, though these peppers are blocky in shape with thick flesh walls and sweet flavor.* Peppers originated in Mexico and were eventually spread, probably by birds, over South and Central America. Sweet bell peppers come in many colors—green (or unripe), red, yellow, orange, purple, white, and even brown. (Unfortunately, the purple and white colors tend to disappear with cooking.) The color depends on the variety and the stage of ripeness. Almost all peppers start out green—a few start yellow—and ripen to another color.

The most common bell peppers are green, which are fully developed but not ripe. Red, orange, and yellow peppers are riper, sweeter, and pricier than green peppers. **Suntan** peppers are harvested when red or another color just starts to develop, leaving most of the pepper green. Many peppers on the market come from hothouses in Holland, Israel, and Canada. These peppers are evenly sized and have thick, juicy flesh and sweet flavor. Their calyxes are noticeably fleshy and firm. **Sweet mini** peppers were bred from bell peppers and hot peppers to develop a small, crunchy, sweet pepper with relatively few seeds.

Season:

Sweet bell peppers are in season year-round with peak season from May through August. At different times of year there may be domestic or imported hothouse peppers on the market. Hothouse peppers sell for a higher price but also have greater yield.

Purchase: Choose fresh, firm peppers that are bright in appearance and thick fleshed with a firm green calyx and stem. The peppers should feel heavy for their size.

Avoid: Immature green peppers are usually soft, pliable, thin-fleshed, and pale green in color. Avoid peppers with wrinkled skins or any brown or soft spots.

Storage: Sweet peppers will keep in the refrigerator for 3 to 4 days. Since red peppers are riper than green ones, they will spoil faster. Mini peppers will keep up to 2 weeks. Don't wash peppers until you're ready to use them.

Preparation:

1. **Cut around the stem to remove it and discard.**

2. **Pull out the spongy membrane encasing the seeds and shake the pepper to remove the seeds.**

3. **Rinse peppers in cold water to remove the remaining seeds.**

Serving Suggestions: Cut peppers into rings or strips and eat them plain or with dip. • Roast peppers tossed with fresh herbs, garlic, salt, pepper, and olive oil at 425°F (220°C) for about 15 minutes or until the peppers have softened and are brown at the edges. • Brown hot and sweet Italian sausage with strips of peppers, onions, and garlic, then toss with hot pasta and grated Romano cheese.

Flavor
Affinities:

Beef, cheese, eggplant, eggs, garlic, hot chile pepper, onions, pork, poultry, sausage, tomato, zucchini.

94a–e.

POTATO

General
Description:

The potato (Solanum tuberosum) *is a tuber in the nightshade family that comes in a variety of shapes, colors, and sizes with flesh that is starchy.* Potatoes were cultivated as long as 2,000 years ago at high altitudes in Peru. These early potatoes were small, knobby tubers of many colors whose bitterness could only be made palatable by special, complicated techniques used by Native Americans since antiquity. Wild potatoes continue to be eaten in the Andes and are known as *papas criollas* (native potatoes). The Spanish brought the potato to the Old World in the 1550s, and it spread to much of the world. Potatoes became the basic food of the Irish until they were wiped out by a fungus in the late 1830s.

There are innumerable varieties of potato, falling into several general categories. New potatoes are freshly dug potatoes that have not reached maturity and have never been kept in storage. They have thin skin and fine-textured flesh. Starchy or mealy potatoes, such as russets, are high in starch. The potato cells in starchy potatoes separate easily upon cooking. When cooked, they have a glistening appearance and a dry, fluffy texture, making them suitable for baking or mashing. They also have a low sugar content so that they will not brown excessively if deep-fried. Waxy potatoes, such as red-skinned potatoes, are low in starch. They are smooth, creamy, and moist when cooked. The cells in these potatoes have a greater tendency to adhere, helping them to hold their shape well. This quality makes them ideal for boiling and steaming.

All Red potatoes have brilliant red skin and pink red flesh. They are very popular in potato pizzas and make for pink mashed potatoes. **B** potatoes are small all-purpose white or red potatoes ranging in size from 1¹/₂ to 2 inches (3.8–5 cm) in diameter.

Blue and **purple** potatoes originated in South America and until recently have not been widely cultivated elsewhere. They have a subtle nutty flavor and flesh that ranges in hue from dark blue or lavender to white.

Creamers are also called **baby** potatoes. These marble-sized potatoes are less than 1¹/₂ inches (3.8 cm) in diameter. **Fingerlings** are small, thin-skinned potatoes resembling a fat finger. Most have yellow flesh with a rich, buttery texture. Fingerling potatoes are excellent for baking, roasting, grilling, and steaming. The most popular fingerling variety is the **Russian Banana**.

German Butterball, a medium-sized round to oblong potato from Germany, has smooth golden skin with flesh more yellow than butter. **Long whites** are grown primarily in California and have thin, light tan skin and a firm, creamy texture when cooked. They have a tendency to turn green when exposed to light.

Round reds are often referred to as **new** potatoes, **red bliss**, or **boiling** potatoes. They have rosy-red skin with dense, waxy white flesh. **Round whites** are grown and used most often in the eastern U.S. Medium in starch level, they have smooth, light tan skin with white flesh. Regarded as an all-purpose potato, they are creamy in texture and hold their shape well after cooking.

Russet potatoes are the most widely used potato in the U.S. Note that "Idaho Potato" is a registered trademark; the same potato grown outside Idaho must be called a russet. They have thick, netted brown skin and white flesh. Their low moisture and high starch content make them light and fluffy when cooked. They are excellent for baking, French fries, and mashing. European chefs often return home with a bag of russets, because they are unlike any European potatoes.

Yukon gold, **Yellow Finn**, or **yellow-flesh** potatoes are all golden-fleshed boiling potatoes with dense creamy texture and a naturally buttery flavor that makes them excellent for mashed potatoes. They are very popular in Europe and increasingly popular in the U.S.

Season: All Red is harvested by late August or early September. Blue and purple potatoes are most available in the fall. Fingerlings are available October through April. Russian Banana is harvested by late August or early September.

German Butterball is harvested by late August or early September. Long whites are available spring through summer. New potatoes are sold from late winter or early spring through midsummer. Round red potatoes are available mostly in late summer and early fall. Russet potatoes are available year-round. Yellow-flesh potatoes are available in late summer and early fall.

Purchase: Choose potatoes that are firm, smooth, and fairly clean with few eyes and good color. All potatoes should be blemish-free. For russets look for net-textured skin, oval shape, and brown color.

Avoid: Potatoes with irregular shapes will produce more waste in peeling, and it is more economical to buy more uniform sizes. Avoid potatoes with wrinkled or wilted skin, cut surfaces, soft dark areas, or a green appearance. Potatoes should not be sprouting.

Storage: Store potatoes in a cool, dark, well-ventilated place for up to 2 weeks. Prolonged exposure to light can cause potatoes to turn green. When green, the potatoes may contain an alkaloid called solanine, which has a bitter flavor and can be toxic if eaten in quantity. Cut the green portion off and use the rest; it will be safe. Low temperatures (below 40°F, or 4°C) can cause the potatoes to have a sweet taste. Warmer temperatures and prolonged storage encourage sprouting and shriveling. Always trim off sprouts before using potatoes.

Preparation:

1. **Gently scrub potatoes with a vegetable brush or cellulose sponge under running water to clean.**

2. **Peeling is optional. When peeling potatoes, use a vegetable parer to keep peelings thin and maintain nutrients close to the skin. New potatoes or potatoes with thin, colorful skins are generally not peeled.**

Note: Uncooked potatoes can become discolored once pared or cut, first appearing pinkish in color, then brownish, and finally dark gray. The speed and intensity of discoloration vary with each potato. These discolored potatoes are safe to eat. The color usually disappears when the potato is cooked. To prevent cut potatoes from discoloring, immerse them in cold water until ready to use, for up to 2 hours. Some types of potatoes blacken when cooked. This discoloration appears as a blue-black area as the cooked potato cools. Any discoloration can be cut away. Some potatoes are more susceptible to this discoloration depending on the soil and climate in which the potatoes were grown.

Serving Suggestions: Bake gold or russet potatoes and serve with butter, yogurt, *labneh*, or sour cream and fresh chives. • Make German-style potato salad with warm bacon dressing and chopped eggs, French-style potato salad with vinaigrette and fresh herbs, or American-style potato salad with mayonnaise and chopped celery. • Make potato gratin, layering thinly sliced potatoes with cream, or rich stock and onions, shallots, or chopped garlic, and bake.

Flavor
Affinities:

Butter, chicken, herbs, mayonnaise, olive oil, onions, pork, salads, shallots, vinaigrette.

95.   **RADICCHIO**

General
Description:

Radicchio (Cichorium intybus) *belongs to the chicory family.* Radicchio started out as a form of wild chicory on the plains of Venice, still the largest production area. Radicchio looks like a small red lettuce. It's more fibrous than its cousins escarole and endive. Modern radicchio, with its rich wine-red leaves with white ribs, was developed in the 1860s by applying complex techniques similar to those used to force Belgian endive (see page 176).

Radicchio has a distinctive, bitter flavor due to intybin, which stimulates the appetite and digestive system. Americans mostly know radicchio as the red leaves in their salad mix. Italians know that radicchio is superb cooked, whether grilled or simmered in risotto—although the gorgeous color turns to rich brown in the cooking process. There are five main varieties of radicchio, each named for its growing region in Italy.

Radicchio rosso di Chioggia is by far the most common. It resembles a compact though lightweight head of cabbage with dark red leaves and white ribs, pronounced bitterness, and fibrous texture. **Radicchio rosso di Treviso** comes in two varieties: *precoce* (early) and *tardivo* (late). **Precoce**, which is known simply as **Treviso** when grown in the U.S., has narrow, pointed, fleshy leaves and forms a compact bunch shaped like a tapered head of romaine. **Tardivo** has much more pronounced pearly ribs, thin splayed leaves that resemble exotic feathers, and deep red color on the edges. Tardivo is flavorful, with strong bitter accents.

Radicchio variegato di Castelfranco resembles a head of butter lettuce with deep wine-red speckles on an eggshell background. Also known as the edible flower, it's a cross between radicchio and round-headed endive and is mild in flavor and tender in texture. **Radicchio di Verona**, which is uncommon in the U.S., has burgundy red leaves with white ribs. It grows in a small, loose head resembling an elongated butterhead lettuce with tender but firm leaves with a slightly bitter flavor.

Season: 	Italian radicchio appears in the markets in late November, remaining throughout the winter. It is at its best after the frost. In California, radicchio is a year-round crop, with a peak season from midwinter to early spring.
Purchase:	Choose heads that have crisp, full-colored leaves. Buy radicchio from a market that sells it quickly. Radicchio is generally fairly expensive, but a little goes a long way if used in a salad.

Avoid:	Avoid radicchio with brown or wilted leaves.
Storage:	Store radicchio in a plastic bag in the crisper of your refrigerator. It will keep for a couple of days.

Preparation:

1. **Trim off the bottom stem and prepare as you would lettuce. Cut out the core in a cone.**

2. **If the radicchio has a root, trim it off, but don't discard. Use it as you would a radish or other root vegetable.**

3. **If the leaves look wilted, soak them in a bowl of cold water to revive. Otherwise, radicchio generally does not need washing.**

Serving Suggestions:	Use whole large outer leaves as a shell to hold chicken, tuna, or seafood salad. • Cut into wedges, toss with olive oil, top with cheese (such as smoked mozzarella) and broil till the red turns reddish brown. • Combine fresh, cooked cranberry beans, preferably while warm, with red wine vinegar, olive oil, chopped oil-cured black olives, and shredded radicchio. • Make a radicchio risotto, adding shredded leaves near the end of cooking.
Flavor Affinities:	Butter, fresh shell beans, Italian cheeses, lemon, olive oil, prosciutto, red onions, salami, vinegar.

96a–c. 📷

RADISH

General
Description:

Radishes (Raphanus sativus) *are root vegetables in the Brassica family.* The sharp, biting flavor of radishes ranges from the juicy crispness of red globe radishes to the pungency of turnip-shaped black radishes. They were first cultivated thousands of years ago in China, then in Egypt and Greece. In the U.S., radishes are usually eaten raw; however, they can also be briefly steamed, sautéed, or stir-fried. Their green tops are edible and lend a peppery taste to salads. Growers classify radishes by shape—round, oval, oblong, and long—while markets frequently label them by color.

Black radishes are turniplike in size and shape, with dull black or dark brown skin. When peeled, their flesh is white, pungent, and drier than other radishes. **Daikon** radishes are native to Asia and are cucumber-shaped. Their white flesh is juicy and hotter than red radishes but milder than black ones. **French breakfast** radishes are shaped like small carrots with red skin tapering to white at the root end and white flesh. They are mild tasting and juicy.

Korean radishes are large, jade green, squat radishes that are juicy with sweet-tasting flesh that ranges from green to white. **Red globes** are the familiar small round or oval "button" radishes and have solid, crisp flesh. Red globe bunch radishes are sold complete with their greens. Bagged radishes have had their tops removed and keep better but aren't as fresh.

Watermelon radishes are about the size and shape of black radishes with green outer skin and pink to red color radiating out from the center. They are sweet and crunchy. **White icicle** radishes are long and tapered with white flesh that is milder than red radishes.

Season:

Red and white radishes are sold year-round with peak season during the spring. Black radishes, which have a long shelf life, are at their peak in winter and early spring. Daikons are most flavorful in fall and winter, though they are available all year.

Purchase:

Look for fresh, bright radishes that are firm, well formed, tender, and crisp with a smooth, unblemished surface. If the tops are attached, they should be fresh and perky. Choose radishes that feel firm when gently squeezed. Check bagged radishes to make sure they are free of mold and excessive cracking.

Black radishes (often sold in Russian or Polish neighborhoods) should be solid, heavy, and free of cracks. Daikon and Korean radishes should be evenly shaped and firm, with a glossy, almost translucent sheen.

Avoid:

Pass up radishes with growth, cracks, cuts, pithiness, or yellowing. If the radish gives to pressure, the interior will likely be pithy instead of crisp.

Storage:

If you've bought radishes with their leaves attached, remove the tops unless you'll be serving them the same day. Radishes will not keep as well with their tops left on. Place radishes in a plastic bag if they are not already packaged. Red radishes and daikons will keep for up to 2 weeks in the refrigerator. Black radishes can be stored for months if they remain dry; store them in a perforated plastic bag in the refrigerator.

Preparation:

1. **Wash radishes in cool water.**

2. **Trim off the stem end and tip.**

3. **Peel, if desired. The skin contains most of the enzymes that give radishes their mustardy tang. Daikons have a very thin skin that can be removed with a vegetable peeler, if you wish.**

Serving Suggestions:

Steam shredded daikon alone or with shredded carrots, then dress with vinaigrette made with rice wine vinegar, sesame oil, and chopped cilantro. • Stir-fry sliced radishes or matchsticks of daikon, being careful not to overcook so that they retain most of their crispness. • Cook black radishes as turnips—the heat will tame their rather harsh flavor. • Serve fresh young radishes, preferably French breakfast, with sweet butter and salt. • If the leaves are fresh and green, cook them like other greens or use in soups—they have a peppery taste similar to arugula.

Flavor Affinities:

Chicken livers, chives, lettuce, mild fish, mint, scallions, scallops, smoked salmon, sweet butter, vinaigrette.

97. 📷   **RAMP**

Other Names: Wild leek.

General
Description: *Ramps* (Allium tricoccum) *are wild leeks that have*
small white bulbs, rose pink stalks, and broad green
leaves. The odor of ramps is akin to that of garlic and
onion, but is distinguished by its persistence and occasionally musty character. Native to eastern North
America, its Appalachian name is derived from "ramson,"
the name of a similar wild plant of the British Isles.
English settlers of Appalachia called the plant by its
English folk name, which was later shortened to ramp.

Though more delicate than other wild onions or
garlic, ramps are bold and lingering in flavor. In late
winter or very early spring, each bulb sends up two or
three broad, smooth, oval leaves, similar to those of lily
of the valley. Eventually growing 8 to 12 inches (20–30
cm) tall, these leaves show deep maroon streaking at the
base and up along the parallel veins.

Season: Ramps may appear occasionally in the market anywhere
from March through July.

Purchase: Choose ramps that are firm and springy with intact roots.
The leaves should be bright green with rosy pink centers.

Avoid: Slimy, wilted, or overly dirty ramps are past their prime.

Storage:

Store the ramps without washing. Wrap damp paper towels around the roots and place in a double layer of plastic bags to prevent the odor from permeating everything in the refrigerator. Store for up to 1 week.

Preparation:

1. **Trim off the roots.**

2. **Rinse well.**

3. **Peel off the first layer of skin from the bulbs.**

4. **Remove any yellowed or wilted leaves.**

5. **Rinse again in a bowl of cold water, swishing vigorously to dislodge any dirt.**

Serving Suggestions:

Fry ramps and potatoes in bacon fat and serve with bacon in traditional Appalachian ramps 'n' taters. • Sauté chicken breasts and top with chopped ramps several minutes before serving. • Dress blanched ramp greens (rinse in cold water to set color after blanching) with vinaigrette. • Beat together blanched ramps with cream cheese, sour cream, salt, and pepper, fold in some chopped raw ramps, and use as a spread on crackers.

Flavor Affinities:

Asparagus, butter, cream, hollandaise sauce, new carrots, new potatoes, peas, salmon, vinaigrette.

98. **RHUBARB**

General Description:
Rhubarb (Rheum rhabarbarum) *is a perennial spring plant with thick, red, fleshy stalks topped by inedible wide leaves.* Rhubarb comes originally from Asia and although it is often used as a fruit, it is a vegetable. Rhubarb was used as a medicinal tonic until the 19th century. Note that only the stalks are edible; the leaves are toxic if eaten in quantity because of large amounts of oxalic acid. The leaves are normally cut off before sale.

There are two basic types of rhubarb: hothouse (or strawberry rhubarb) and field-grown (or cherry rhubarb). Hothouse rhubarb tends to have smoother flesh, more delicate texture, and less acidity than field-grown. Field-grown rhubarb has deeper color, more juice, and bolder acidity. Green rhubarb is also available. Rhubarb is versatile; it can be used in savory dishes and desserts.

Season:

Rhubarb is in season in spring and summer. Hothouse rhubarb is available mid-January through mid-April.

Purchase:
Choose rhubarb with stalks of the brightest color that are firm and crisp.

Avoid:
Check both ends of the stalks for pithiness or decay. Avoid rhubarb with bruises or blemishes.

Storage:

Refrigerate in a plastic bag for up to 1 week.

Preparation:	**Note: Rhubarb should be cooked only in nonaluminum pots because it will react with the metal.**

1. **For stringier field-grown rhubarb, pare the stalks or pull off the strings. Hothouse rhubarb generally does not need peeling.**

2. **Cut off any greens and discard them.**

3. **Cut rhubarb into slices, on the diagonal if desired, against the grain of the stalk.**

Serving Suggestions:	Make strudel with phyllo dough and a filling of sweet apples and rhubarb. • Sauté rhubarb with Chinese five-spice powder and serve with salmon fillets. • Make rhubarb crumb bars with pastry on the bottom, rhubarb in the middle, and a topping of oatmeal-walnut streusel.
Flavor Affinities:	Blackberries, brown sugar, duck, ginger, goose, honey, maple syrup, oily fish, orange, raspberries, strawberries.

99a–b.

SALSIFY AND SCORZONERA

Other Names:	*Barba di becco* (Italy), black oyster plant, black salsify, mock oyster, Oyster plant, *salsifis* (France), viper's grass.
General Description:	*Salsify* (Tragopogon porrifolius) *and scorzonera* (Scorzonera hispanica) *are two closely related plants in*

the Compositae family. Salsify is a hardy perennial native to the Mediterranean region with long, edible white roots. Scorzonera is a close cousin with long, edible, black roots and artichoke-like flavor and texture. Both salsify and scorzonera are rare in American markets nowadays, although in Thomas Jefferson's time, salsify was common. In the U.S., scorzonera is imported from Belgium, which is the world's largest producer of this black root.

White salsify has pale tan skin, resembling thin parsnips with thin, often forked roots covered with scraggly rootlets. Salsify can be found growing wild in both North America and the Mediterranean. **Scorzonera** is a perennial popular in central Europe with black-skinned roots resembling a long muddy brown stick that may be somewhat slimy with a creamy-colored interior. Its name comes from the Spanish for a venomous toad or lizard, and it was also known as viper's grass for its supposed ability to fight venom.

Season:	Salsify is available in the fall and winter. Scorzonera is available in the winter and spring.
Purchase:	Choose firm, full roots. Scorzonera roots are naturally sticky, or even slimy.
Avoid:	Pass up limp roots.

Storage:

Store the roots wrapped in plastic for up to 2 weeks in the refrigerator.

Preparation:

Note: If your hands get discolored from working with the roots, clean with vinegar and salt.

1.   **Scrub scorzonera under running water with a brush. Salsify will likely only need to be lightly scrubbed.**

2.   **Cut off and discard tops and the portion of the tail that is thin and fibrous.**

3.   **Peel using a vegetable peeler.**

4.   **Place in a bowl of water with lemon juice to prevent darkening. Scorzonera exudes a sticky substance that is removed when washed.**

Note: Both roots go quickly from tender to mushy, so cook gently by poaching or steaming rather than boiling.

Serving Suggestions:

Roast cut, peeled lengths of either root tossed with olive oil and fresh herbs in a 400°F (200°C) oven for about 20 minutes, or until somewhat shriveled but tender. • Braise chicken with scorzonera along with onion, mushroom, and stock and finish with a little lemon juice. • Sprinkle cooked roots with Parmesan cheese, roll in thinly sliced prosciutto, and briefly bake in a hot oven till the prosciutto crisps.

Flavor
Affinities:
Bay leaf, butter, cream, hollandaise sauce, lemon, mushrooms, nutmeg, orange, prosciutto.

100.   **SAMPHIRE**

Other Names:
Chicken claws, *criste marine* or *pousse-pied* (France), glasswort, Marsh Samphire, *Meerfenchel* (Germany), pickle plant, rock samphire, salicornia, sea bean, sea pickle.

General
Description:
Samphire refers to two similar salty plants, Salicornia europaea *and* Crithmum maritimum, *that grow along seacoasts.* In the U.S., **salicornia**, which belongs to the Chenopodiaceae (goosefoot) family, is abundant along both the Pacific and Atlantic coasts. Its spiky green leaves and its stem are crisp, aromatic, and taste of the salty sea. Sea bean is a recent name used in marketing this plant, which is not seaweed but rather a succulent salt-tolerant plant that grows wild in North America, Europe, Asia, and Australia.

Rock samphire is a member of the Umbelliferae family that grows along the coasts of Great Britain and northwestern Europe. It is a succulent, smooth, many-branched vegetable, woody at the base. Its bright green fleshy leaves have a thick, translucent coat and are full of salty, aromatic juice. Rock samphire commonly inhabits inaccessible ledges of sea cliffs, and at one time collecting it was a hazardous and sometimes lethal trade.

Season:

Wild samphire is sold mainly in the summer. By fall, when it may turn reddish, it develops a tough, fibrous central filament but can still be used as a bed for cooking. Cultivated sea bean is sometimes available.

Purchase:

Choose crisp, brightly colored, small sprigs of samphire that are firm.

Avoid:

Pass up samphire that is flabby, darkening, or slimy.

Storage:

Store samphire in the refrigerator for up to 1 week. Refrigerate tightly wrapped in plastic for up to 2 weeks—though the sooner it is used the better the flavor.

Preparation:

Note: Samphire is best used raw in salads or as a garnish. When cooked, salicornia can taste salty and fishy unless pickled.

1. **Soak in ice water to revive any limp leaves after storage.**

2. **Trim off any rootlets and discard.**

3. **Cut away the base and cut into pieces.**

Serving
Suggestions:

Fill the cavity of a sea bass with sprigs of fennel and bake, then serve on a bed of steamed samphire that has been tossed in butter and seasoned with freshly ground black pepper. • Briefly boil samphire leaves, then cover with vinegar and spices to pickle. • Steam sea beans with mussels, chicken stock, wild onions, lemon, and butter to maximize their seashore flavors.

Flavor
Affinities:

Aioli, butter, crab, fish, lemon, mussels, olive oil, sweet onions, vinegar.

101.

SHALLOT

General
Description:

The shallot (Allium ascalonicum *or* Allium cepa, Aggregatum group) *is a small member of the onion family.* Shallots probably originated in Asia, traveling from there to India and the eastern Mediterranean. The name "shallot" comes from Ashkelon, a city of ancient Israel, where people in classical Greek times believed shallots originated.

Shallots are formed like garlic with a head composed of multiple cloves. Their skin color can vary from golden brown to gray to rose red, and their off-white flesh is usually tinged with green or magenta. Shallots are much favored by chefs because of their firm texture and sweet, aromatic, yet pungent, flavor.

The two main types are the large **Jersey** shallot (from the Isle of Jersey) and the more subtly flavored "**true**" or **gray French** shallot. Jersey shallots of either the long or half-long type are the most common in American markets. ***Cuisse de poulet*** are French shallots shaped like a chicken thigh with deep gold skins. **Dutch** shallots are more rounded with either yellow or coppery red skin. Asian markets usually carry plentiful stocks of relatively inexpensive shallots that are smaller and stronger than European types. In France, Belgium, and the Netherlands, markets overflow with all colors and sizes of shallots. More shallots are grown in Southeast Asia than anywhere else in the world.

Season:	Fresh green shallots are sometimes available in the spring, but dry shallots are available year-round.
Purchase:	Choose large, plump, firm, well-shaped shallots that are not sprouting.
Avoid:	Shallots that are wrinkled or sprouting or that show any signs of black mold should not be purchased.
Storage:	Store shallots in a cool, dry, well-ventilated place for up to 1 month.
Preparation:	**Note: Shallots are usually diced into small pieces for use as an aromatic in various dishes.**

I. **Peel the skin with a paring knife, leaving the root end attached.**

2. **Cut in half, then set the shallot, cut side down, on a work surface.**

3. **Make horizontal cuts toward the root.**

4. **Cut crosswise into pieces of desired fineness.**

Serving Suggestions:

Slice shallots thinly and brown in butter with a little chopped thyme till deeply caramelized, then serve as a topping for grilled chicken, calf's liver, or hamburgers. • Use as the base for gravy. • Make creamy shallot vinaigrette by blending chopped shallots with olive oil, red wine or sherry vinegar, and a little mustard.

Flavor Affinities:

Beef, beets, Brussels sprouts, butter, chervil, chicken, chives, cream, duck, fish, lentils, potatoes, tarragon, thyme, turkey, veal, white beans, wine.

102a–b.

SPINACH

General Description:

Spinach (Spinacia oleracea) *is a deep green leaf vegetable in the Chenopodiaceae family with mild flavor and soft texture.* The Persians cultivated spinach as early as the 4th century. From Persia (now Iran), spinach was exported eastward to China where it is still known as "Persian vegetable." The Arabs call it "the prince of vegetables." In French haute cuisine, any dish *"à la Florentine"* includes spinach, due to Caterina de

Medici's Florentine cooks who brought their sophisticated methods of cooking this Italian favorite to France.

There are two main types of spinach: **flat-leafed** and **curly** (or **savoy**), although there is also **semi-savoy**, which is somewhere in between. Flat-leafed spinach is more tender and milder in flavor, especially the baby variety. The bouncing, firm, dark leaves of savoy spinach, usually sold in bunches, have a stronger "iron" flavor with a very slight bitter aftertaste and a crunchy texture.

Season: Spinach is in season year-round.

Purchase: Look for spinach with deeply colored, crisp, perky leaves that are unbroken.

Avoid: Do not purchase spinach with yellowed leaves. Spinach is tender and will spoil quickly. If it's questionable, sniff it; you will quickly detect any unpleasant odor. Inspect the contents of bagged spinach; because it has been pre-washed, it deteriorates quickly.

Storage: Store bunch spinach in a plastic bag in the refrigerator for 2 to 3 days. To keep keep spinach a few days longer, steam it, chill it, and bag it.

Preparation: **Note: A lot of spinach goes but a little way; when cooked, spinach shrinks by about 90 percent.**

1. **Pull off the leaves and discard the stems (in**

Italy the stems are often cooked separately like
Swiss chard stalks).

2. **Fill a large bowl with cold water and swish the
   leaves in it. Scoop the spinach from the water. If
   you see a lot of sand on the bottom, wash the
   spinach again. Flat-leafed spinach is easier to
   clean, while savoy spinach must be washed two
   or even three times if especially sandy.**

Serving
Suggestions:
Cook spinach in water till just wilted, drain, squeeze
out excess water, and reheat with garlic and olive oil or
shallots and butter. • Make a classic spinach salad with
bacon, mushrooms, and hard-boiled egg quarters with a
warm mustard and bacon fat dressing. • Top spinach
salad with grilled portobello mushroom strips and
spice-marinated grilled chicken. • Make spinach dip for
pita bread Persian-style by combining cooked spinach
with browned onions, yogurt, salt, and pepper.

Flavor
Affinities:
Aged cheeses, chicken, cream cheese, egg noodles, garlic,
mushrooms, nutmeg, onions, shallots, sour cream.

103a–b.

SPROUTS

General
Description:
*Sprout seeds of various vegetables, grains, and legumes
have just begun to germinate.* Sprouts can grow from
the seeds of vegetables such as broccoli and radishes,

from grains such as alfalfa and buckwheat, and from beans such as lentils and soybeans. Sprouts vary in texture and taste. Some are spicy (radish and onion sprouts), some are hardy, standing up to brief cooking (mung bean and soybean), others are more delicate (alfalfa and pea) and are used in salads and sandwiches to add texture and moistness. The flavors range from a garden-fresh sweet pea to a mild radish. There are also many kinds of packaged mixed sprouts that combine different colors, flavors, and textures.

Alfalfa sprouts are thread-thin and white with tiny green tops and have a subtle nutty flavor and crisp texture. They are the most common sprouts found in grocery stores. Other sprouts exist, however, and each takes on the flavor of its host seed. **Clover**, **dill**, **lentil**, **onion**, **pea**, **pumpkin**, **radish**, **soybean**, **sunflower**, and **wheat** sprouts are all occasionally available.

Mung bean sprouts are about 2 inches (5 cm) long, have small, light yellow leaves and a silvery white shoot. They have a subtle nutty flavor and high water content

Season:	Sprouts are in season year-round.
Purchase:	Choose crisp sprouts with firm, moist, white roots.
Avoid:	Do not buy musty-smelling, dark, or slimy sprouts.
Storage:	Store sprouts in the vegetable for crisper up to 3 days and use as soon as possible. More delicate sprouts such

as alfalfa should be refrigerated in the ventilated plastic container in which they're sold for no more than 2 days.

Preparation: **Sprouts need little preparation. Rinsing daily under cold water can extend their life.**

Note: You need not remove the yellow head of soybean sprouts before using. In China the root end of mung bean sprouts is removed, and for special events the yellowish head end is also removed. These full-trimmed sprouts are called "silver sprouts."

Serving Suggestions: Add any raw sprouts to salads, sandwiches, burgers, or tacos. • Stir-fry mung and soybean sprouts, but cook no longer than 30 seconds to avoid wilting.

---

104. 📷 **SUNCHOKE**

Other Names: Jerusalem artichoke, sunroot.

General Description: *The sunchoke* (Helianthus tuberosus) *is a gnarled tan tuber of a perennial flower in the Compositae family.* Sunchokes originated in North America where they were a common food for Native Americans. In Italy, they are known as *girasole articiocco*, "sunflower artichoke." This may actually be the source of their other name, Jerusalem artichoke, not the city in Israel, as people misheard the word *girasole*. The French term, *topinambour*, comes from a South American tribe, the Topinambas, members of which visited France around the same time the tubers were introduced to Europe in the 16th century. The French are credited with improving the tubers and cultivating sunchokes on a large scale.

Sunchokes have ivory-colored flesh that is crispy when raw. Their delicate flavor is slightly sweet and nutty, reminiscent of jicama, water chestnuts, and even artichoke. They can be smooth but are often bumpy with crackly skin. Sunchokes can cause flatulence, so eat in small portions till you know your own tolerance.

Season: Although available year-round, they are at their best in fall and winter.

Purchase: Choose smooth, clean, unblemished, firm tubers with a minimum of bumps.

Avoid: Pass up sunchokes with wrinkled skins, soft spots, blotched green areas, or sprouts.

Storage: Handle sunchokes with care as they bruise easily. Store in a cool, dry, well-ventilated area away from light. Or, wrap in paper towels and place in a plastic bag in the refrigerator crisper for up to 1 week.

Preparation: **Note: Avoid aluminum or iron pans as these metals will cause the sunchokes to turn an unappealing grayish color. Even after cooking, iron content may**

cause them to turn gray. Add a little lemon juice or
vinegar to the cooking water to prevent this.

1. **Scrub thoroughly with a vegetable brush.**

2. **Slice off the small, bumpy areas and then peel.**

3. **Drop peeled pieces into a bowl of water with
   lemon juice to prevent darkening. Or, cook
   whole and then peel.**

Serving
Suggestions:

Shred, slice, or julienne, then soak briefly in acidulated
water, drain, and add to salads or slaws. • Deep-fry thin
slices to make nutty sunchoke chips. • Make savory
pancakes by shredding and combining with flour, egg,
and shredded onion. • Roast whole sunchokes tossed
with oil, or add to the roasting pan with chicken, turkey,
lamb, or pork during the last half hour of cooking.

Flavor
Affinities:

Butter, cinnamon, cloves, cream, mint, mustard, nut
oils, nutmeg, onion, roasted meats, vinaigrette.

105a–b. **SWEET POTATO**

Other Names:　Yam.

General
Description:

Sweet potatoes (Ipomoea batatas) *are sweet-fleshed,
pointy-ended tubers in the Convolvulaceae family.*

Native to the New World, sweet potatoes traveled to the Old World before the potato. Columbus introduced them to Europe with the name *batata*, later potato. When the tuber we now call potato (see page 237) came on the scene, it was given the same name, and the sweet varieties began to be distinguished from them, rather than vice versa. The sweet potato is botanically unrelated to the potato or the African yam. The word "yam" is an English adaptation of *nyami*, the Senegalese word for the large starchy African tuber from the *Dioscorea* family. African yams are rather bland and dry, so they're often served with spicy sauces. They are imported to the U.S. from the Caribbean.

In the 1930s, Louisiana farmers chose the word "yam" to set their product apart from the dry, pale sweet potato grown in the North. In American markets today, "yams" are sweet potatoes with vivid orange color, and, when cooked, are sweet and moist. The most popular yam is the **Beauregard**, which is uniform in size and shape with smooth skin and deep orange flesh. Other varieties include **Garnets**, which have garnet-colored skin, orange yellow flesh, and excellent flavor. They are popular with organic growers. **Jewels** have more orangey skin and deep orange flesh.

Dry-fleshed yellow or white sweet potatoes are grown in the northern part of the U.S. These have pale white-to yellow flesh and beige skin. They appear occasionally at local markets with names such as **Nancy Hall** and **Jersey Yellow** sweet potato.

Boniatos are starchy reddish-skinned sweet potatoes whose white flesh is dry and fluffy with delicate, mildly sweet flavor similar to chestnuts. Boniatos are popular in Latin American and Asian markets and are a staple in countries from Mexico to Vietnam. There is a Hawaiian sweet potato called **Okinawa**—*poni* in Hawaiian—that cooks to a lilac color and has rich, sweet flesh.

Asian sweet potatoes are various rose-skinned, ivory-fleshed cultivars. They fall between the drier boniato types and the moist-flesh whites. More than 90 percent of the world's sweet potatoes are grown in Asia.

Season:

Year-round, with the greatest selection in the winter.

Purchase:

Choose firm sweet potatoes with smooth, unbruised skins without cracks.

Avoid:

Do not buy wrinkled, sticky, or sprouting sweet potatoes.

Storage:

Because of their high sugar content, sweet potatoes don't keep very well, so store them in a cool, dark place—but not the refrigerator—and don't plan to keep them more than 1 or 2 weeks.

Preparation:

Note: Sweet potatoes may be peeled before or after they are cooked.

If peeling before cooking, use a vegetable peeler or sharp knife to remove the skin and discard.

If peeling after cooking, cut the sweet potato open and scoop out the flesh.

Serving
Suggestions:

Bake whole sweet potatoes in their skins and serve with butter. • Make a sweet potato pie by baking or steaming orange-fleshed yams, then beating the mashed flesh together with brown sugar, egg, and cream and baking in a pastry shell. • Mash boiled sweet potatoes and potatoes together (for extra smoothness), adding grated fresh ginger and a little ground cardamom. • Fry boniato sticks like French fries.

Flavor
Affinities:

Bourbon, brown sugar, butter, ginger, honey, orange, pecans, rosemary, rum, spices.

106a–c.

SWISS CHARD

Other Names:

Chard, leaf beet, seakale beet, spinach beet.

General
Description:

Swiss chard (Beta vulgaris, Cicla group) is a close relative of the beet root (see page 132) grown for its large green leaves and thick edible stalks. Chard has been traced back to the famed hanging gardens of Babylon. The name derives from the Latin for "thistle" and came to refer to two plants grown for their stalks—cardoon and chard. In the 19th century, seed catalogs started adding the word "Swiss" to distinguish chard from the look-alike but unrelated cardoon. Swiss chard's leaves are similar to beet greens but larger, wider, and flatter, with mild flavor and full-bodied texture similar to spinach.

The stalks of Swiss chard are completely edible; in fact, in Europe they are considered the best part of the plant and the leaves are often thrown away. There are thin-stemmed and thick-stemmed chard varieties. **Ruby** chard has brilliant red stalks and leaf veins and is usually thin-stemmed. **Rainbow** chard has stems colored yellow, ruby red, and white.

Season:

Swiss chard is widely available April through November.

Purchase:
Look for fresh green leaves that are moist, crisp, and unwilted. Check that the stems are also juicy and crisp.

Avoid:
Yellowed or browned leaves are subpar; leaves with tiny holes indicate insect damage.

Storage:
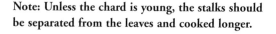
Wrap unwashed Swiss chard in damp paper towels, then place in a plastic bag; store in the refrigerator crisper for 3 to 5 days.

Preparation:

Note: Unless the chard is young, the stalks should be separated from the leaves and cooked longer.

1. **Separate the leaves from the stems.**

2. **Swirl the leaves in a large bowl of cool water.**

3. **Lift out, letting the sand and grit settle; repeat if necessary.**

4. **Wash stems separately under cool running water.**

Note: Don't cook Swiss chard in an aluminum pot; the chard contains oxalic acid, which will discolor the pot.

| Serving Suggestions: | Wrap seasoned fish fillets in blanched Swiss chard leaves and then bake. • Sauté blanched Swiss chard in olive oil with sliced garlic, then add currants or golden raisins and toasted pine nuts. • Substitute Swiss chard leaves for spinach when making ravioli, manicotti, or cannelloni. |
| Flavor Affinities: | Anchovies, capers, cured meats, cured olives, garlic, hot chile pepper, lemon, olive oil, onions, orange and lemon zest, raisins and currants, sweet spices, vinegar. |

107a–b.

TARO AND YAUTIA

| Other Names: | **Taro:** cocoyam, colocasia, dasheen. **Yautia:** malanga, malanga blanca, new cocoyam, ocomo, tannia. |
| General Description: | *Taro (Colocasia esculenta) is a starchy tuber that has brown, fibrous skin and gray-white (sometimes purple) flesh and comes from Asia. Yautia (Xanthosoma sagitti-folium) is a similar plant from the American tropics.* |

Taro is a wild tropical plant native to Asia that was first cultivated in India 7,000 years ago. From there it spread through Asia, South America, and the South Pacific islands that today are its largest consumers. In Hawaii, taro cultivation is tied to cultural and religious beliefs. The famous poi is made from steamed, mashed taro. The word "lu'au" refers to the leafy tops of young taro plants cooked in coconut milk (a dish at a traditional feast).

Taro ranges in shape from fat oval to oblong. Its flesh, which can vary from white to yellow to pink, turns mauve-gray or violet when cooked and is often speckled with purplish red or brown markings. Its flavor and texture fall somewhere between potato and coconut. The main tuber of the taro plant is about the size of a turnip and covered with shaggy brown skin circled with distinct rings. Along the roots that spread deeper into the soil are smaller tubers called "eddo." The large edible taro leaves (called "callaloo" in the Caribbean) are cooked in soup.

Yautia, a Hispanic staple, is a New World plant similar to taro. From America, the yautia reached West Africa, which is now the major producer. It has shaggy, scaly skin that does not quite cover the flesh, and it is elongated, tapered, and bumpy. **Yautia blanca**, which is the most common type in the U.S., can be earthy and waxy to mild and smooth. **Yautia lila** has gray-lavender flesh and a heavier texture. **Yautia amarilla** is barrel-shaped, ridged, and dense. Cooked, it is sweet, nutty, deep gold in color, and so dry and dense that it is often used for making dough.

Season:	Taro is available year-round especially in Asian markets. Yautia is available year-round especially in Latin American markets.

Purchase: Taro roots should be firm to the touch at both ends, with hairy roots. Freshly dug taro will be pinkish or whitish green at the stem end. For a rich and creamy consistency, choose medium to large taro with a dark muddy look and clear, reddish veining on white flesh. Choose firm, light-colored yautia tubers. Prick with your fingernail: The flesh should be juicy and crisp.

Avoid: Pass up taro or yautia with any soft spots, traces of mold, sprouts, or shriveling at either end.

Storage: Store taro in a well-ventilated area, such as a hanging basket, and do not refrigerate, for this will prolong the cooking time. Store yautia in a cool, moist place.

Preparation: **Note: Never eat raw taro, as the sap may irritate the throat. This compound is quickly transformed by cooking. If you have sensitive skin, wear gloves when peeling and cutting taro.**

1. **Wash in cool running water.**

2. **Slice the ends off the roots.**

3. **Pare away the hairy skin and trim until you get to firm, white flesh. Place in cold water at once.**

Serving
Suggestions:

Layer sliced taro and sweet potatoes in a baking dish, dot with butter, brown sugar, raisins, salt, and pepper, and bake till soft, then top with a flour, macadamia nut, butter, and coconut milk streusel and bake till brown. • Steam cubed taro with rice. • Make taro or yautia chips, fries, or fritters. • Simmer half-inch cubes of taro in coconut milk sweetened with sugar and a small amount of salt till soft and thick.

Flavor
Affinities:

Almonds, capers, coconut milk, ginger, green olives, hot chile peppers, lime, nuts, onion, queso blanco.

TOMATILLO AND GROUND CHERRY

Other Names:

Tomatillo: husk tomato, jamberry, Mexican green tomato, strawberry tomato, *tomate verde* (Spain);
Ground cherry: dwarf cape gooseberry, husk tomato, physalis, strawberry tomato.

General
Description:

Tomatillos (Physalis ixocarpa *and* Physalis philadelphica) *and ground cherries* (Physalis peruviana *and* Physalis pruinosa) *belong to the same family as the tomato.* The **tomatillo** is a native of Mexico with shiny, flattened fruits that are greenish yellow in color and average 1 to 2 inches (2.5–5 cm) in diameter encased in papery husks. The husks split, but don't fall off, and take on a purplish hue as the fruits mature. Their tart flavor hints of lemon, apple, and herbs, and is the primary feature of *salsa verde*. Although tomatillos can ripen to yellow, they are generally used while still green and quite firm.

The **ground cherry**, commonly called the **cape gooseberry**, is rare in the U.S. except for Pennsylvania Dutch country and parts of the Midwest. These small fruits are $1/2$ to $3/4$ inch (1.3–2 cm) in diameter and are encased in a loose, papery husk shaded with purple. When they are ripe, they resemble yellow cherry tomatoes. They are smaller and sweeter than tomatillos and can be eaten raw or used in preserves. The dwarf cape gooseberry is the most popularly grown variety. Its tight-fitting husk curls back to expose the ripe fruits.

Season: Tomatillos are available year-round and can be found

sporadically in specialty stores. Latin American markets carry them regularly. Ground cherries can occasionally be found at farmers' markets or specialty stores.

Purchase: Look for shiny, firm, dry tomatillos that fit snugly into their husks. Make sure that each tomatillo husk is dry to the touch. Inside the husk, the fruit should be green, which indicates that the tomatillo is not totally ripe, the preferred state.

Avoid: Avoid sticky or yellow tomatillos.

Storage:	Store tomatillos in their husks in a paper bag in the

Store tomatillos in their husks in a paper bag in the refrigerator for up to 1 month.

Preparation:

1. **Remove the outer husk by pulling it off.**

2. **Wash thoroughly before using.**

Serving Suggestions:

Simmer or roast whole tomatillos, onion, garlic, and jalapeños till soft, then blend to make a delicious green enchilada sauce. • Add chopped tomatillos to guacamole. • Dip ground cherries in chocolate, fondant, or caramel using the pulled-back husk as a handle.

Flavor Affinities:

Cilantro, cucumber, green chile peppers, grilled foods, lime, pumpkin seeds, tequila, tomatoes, onion.

109a–e.

TOMATO

General Description:

The tomato (Lycopersicon lycopersicum) *is a member of the nightshade family.* The tomato is native to the Americas and was cultivated by the Aztecs and Incas as early as A.D. 700. Tomatoes were unknown outside of the New World until the Spanish brought them back to Europe in the 16th century. The English word "tomato" comes from the original Aztec name, *tomatl.* Tomatoes once enjoyed a reputation as a powerful aphrodisiac, especially in France, while people in other countries believed them to be deadly poisonous.

Tomatoes come in all sizes, shapes, and colors. Many famed local tomato varieties (like Jersey tomatoes) require tender loving care. Because of their thin skins and plentiful juices, they are prone to splitting and bruising. Sometimes you'll notice "cat-facing," dark streaks radiating from the stem end of the tomato, a result of cold mornings.

Tomatoes were the first genetically engineered food approved by the U.S. Food and Drug Administration. Scientists have altered the ripening gene in tomato seeds named "Flavr Savrs." These tomatoes ripen on the vine longer and remain firm enough to ship cross-country.

Old-fashioned (or heirloom) tomatoes are open-pollinated varieties that self-fertilize. If you save seeds of an open-pollinated variety, the plants you get will vary, but they'll all be basically similar. These old varieties are the product of natural and human selection.

Some heirloom tomatoes to look for are brilliant yellow **Taxi** tomatoes, **green grape** tomatoes, fuzzy, pink-blushed **peach** tomatoes, red and orange–streaked **pineapple** or **tigerella** tomatoes, green and red–striped **Mr. Stripy's**, and the green-skinned, green-fleshed **Evergreen** tomato. The **White Queen** reigns as the best white tomato while the **Black Krim**, actually a brownish purple, is an old variety from Crimea. **Pink Brandywine**, **red Brandywine**, and **Amish paste** tomato are old Pennsylvania varieties. **Sicilian plums** have dense flesh, ideal for homemade tomato paste. **Red** and **yellow currant** tomatoes are tiny and ruby or golden, and make cherry tomatoes look big. **Sweet 100s** are a **cherry** tomato that grows in cascading clusters of sweet fruit. **Yellow** tomatoes are lower in acid than red, making them more digestible for people with acid intolerance.

Modern tomato varieties, such as the **Burpee Big Boy**, came about through controlled laboratory experimentation and manipulation of plant genetics. These plant hybrids won't self-fertilize. (If you save and plant their seeds, you'll get a mixed bag of results.) **Beefsteak** tomatoes are large and oblate, and weigh more than 1 pound (.45 kg) so that one can cut big, thick, juicy slices the size and color of a steak.

Hothouse tomatoes now represent nearly one-fourth of the retail fresh tomato market in the U.S. Canada has led the development of the hothouse tomato industry. Israel and the Netherlands are also major exporters of hothouse tomatoes, often sold in bunches still on the vine.

Season: Tomatoes are available year-round. However, locally grown vine-ripened tomatoes are in season from July until October.

Purchase: Look for firm, fully colored, plump tomatoes.

Avoid: Pale, unripe, spotted, or refrigerator-chilled tomatoes will be unpalatable.

Storage: Tomatoes are vulnerable and must be treated gently.

Ripen tomatoes by sitting them stem-side down. Because this is the last part of the tomato to ripen, it can best support the weight of a ripe tomato without collapsing. Don't refrigerate tomatoes.

Preparation:

1. **Gently wash the tomato in cool water.**

2. **Remove the core when dicing or slicing.**

Note: You do not have to do much to prepare a tomato. You don't have to peel thin-skinned round tomatoes, but plum tomatoes have thick skins that can be unpleasant unless peeled. To peel, drop them whole into a large pot of boiling water. Check after two minutes. The tomatoes are ready when the skin slides easily over their flesh. Remove the tomatoes from the pot, drop into a large bowl of ice water to stop the cooking, and then slip off their skins. The riper the tomato, the easier it is to peel.

Serving Suggestions:

Oven-roast plum tomatoes by splitting them lengthwise, combining with olive oil, garlic, oregano, basil, thyme, kosher salt, and black pepper, then baking at 225°F (110°C) for 4 to 5 hours or until shriveled and semidry, and add to pasta, sandwiches, and eggs. • Add sliced tomatoes to sandwiches or hamburgers. • Add tomato wedges to vegetable salads. • Cook tomatoes into tomato sauces or tomato jam.

Flavor Affinities:	Basil, blue cheese, cucumbers, feta, fish, garlic, leeks, mint, mozzarella, onion, oregano, pasta, poultry, ricotta, shellfish, stir-fries, veal.

110a–b.

TURNIP AND RUTABAGA

Other Names:	**Rutabaga:** Swede, Swedish cabbage, Swedish turnip, Yellow turnip.
General Description:	*Turnips* (Brassica rapa, Rapifera *group) and rutabagas* (Brassica napus, Napobrassica *group), both members of the Brassica family, are round, firm root vegetables with a biting flavor akin to cabbage and mustard.* Turnips have been cultivated since ancient times; many distinct kinds were known to the Romans and Greeks. In Rome turnips were known as both *rapa* and *napus*. In Middle English the latter term became *nepe*, which combined with the word "turn" (as in "make round") and became the word "turnip." Rutabaga gets its name from the Swedish *rotabagge*, suggesting a Scandinavian origin. Both white- and yellow-fleshed rutabaga varieties have been known in Europe for more than 300 years.

Although closely related, turnips and rutabagas are different. Most turnips are white-fleshed and most rutabagas are yellow-fleshed, but there are also white-fleshed rutabagas and yellow-fleshed turnips. Turnips and rutabagas have a different number of chromosomes. Botanical studies indicate that a rare hybridization between a cabbage (18 chromosomes) and turnip (20 chromosomes) resulted in the rutabaga (38 chromosomes), which was probably first found in Europe in the late Middle Ages.

Turnips are smooth and have several circles of ridges at the base of their leaves with white flesh and purple-tinged white skin. Small young turnips are delicate and slightly sweet; as they age, their taste becomes stronger and their texture woody. **Rutabagas** are larger, rounder, denser, and sweeter than turnips.

Season: Turnips are available year-round with peak season October through March. Young turnips are sold in spring. Rutabagas are in season from September through June.

Purchase: Look for small turnips that feel heavy for their size. They should be smooth and firm with unblemished skin and have fresh, green leaves. Look for firm, smooth-skinned rutabagas that feel heavy for their size.

Avoid: Pass up turnips larger than 3 inches (7.5 cm) in diameter because they are apt to be woody. Avoid bruised or cut rutabagas as these will have been in storage too long.

Storage: Refrigerate turnips in a plastic bag for up to 1 week. Refrigerate rutabagas in a plastic bag for up to 2 weeks.

Preparation: 1. **Wash in cool water.**

2. **Trim the top and bottom of the vegetable.**

3. **Peel, if necessary, using a vegetable peeler.
    Young turnips need not be peeled; old turnips
    will have tough skin that should be removed.
    Rutabagas are generally waxed to prevent
    moisture loss and must be peeled before eating.**

Serving
Suggestions:

Dress shredded raw turnips, cabbage, and carrots with
sharp mustard vinaigrette and poppy seeds to make a
slaw. • Add diced turnips and/or rutabagas to chicken
potpie. • Serve slices of raw young turnips with
Kalamata olives and cherry tomatoes to make a simple
appetizer.

Flavor
Affinities:

Cream, curry, duck, lamb, lemon, marjoram, onions,
pork, potatoes, thyme, vinegar.

111.   **WASABI**

Other Names: Japanese horseradish.

General
Description:

Wasabi (Eutrema wasabi *or* Wasabia japonica) *is a
fleshy rhizome, resembling but not related to horseradish.*
A perennial herb native to Japan, wasabi grows wild in
or alongside mountain streams and is cultivated in
flooded mountain terraces. Since the 16th century,
wasabi has been cultivated in Japan, where it is an
important part of the cuisine. Wasabi roots are grated
to make a fresh green paste that is the essential condi-

ment for Japanese sashimi and sushi. Few geographical areas are suited for growing wasabi, so the fresh root is somewhat rare. In Japan the roots are sold in pans of water.

Season:	Occasionally available in specialty markets.
Purchase:	Choose whole firm roots.
Avoid:	Do not buy slimy or deteriorating roots.
Storage:	Store in water in the refrigerator for a few days only.

Preparation:

1. **Scrub wasabi with a soft brush.**

2. **Carefully peel if desired.**

3. **Grate wasabi against a rough surface. Sushi chefs prefer a sharkskin grater because it gives grated wasabi a smooth, soft, and aromatic finish.**

Serving Suggestions: Use grated wasabi in dressings, dips, sauces, and marinades. • Spread wasabi paste on sushi. • Top tofu with soy sauce and wasabi paste. • Season Bloody Marys with grated wasabi. • Season mashed potatoes with grated wasabi.

Flavor Affinities: Crab, cucumber, green onions, miso, potatoes, raw fish, salmon, sesame oil, shrimp, soba noodles, tofu.

112a–b.   **WATER CHESTNUT**

Other Names: Buffalo-head fruit, bull nut, horn chestnut, Jesuits' nut, *ling ko* or *ma tai* (China), water caltrop, water nut.

General
Description: *Chinese water chestnuts* (Eleocharis dulcis) *and European water chestnuts* (Trapa natans) *are two unrelated water plants that carry the same name.* The **Chinese water chestnut** resembles a small muddy tulip bulb and is sweet and crunchy; the **European water chestnut** resembles a tiny horned bull's head and is quite starchy. Americans are most familiar with the Chinese water chestnut. Technically a corm—the swollen tip of an underground stem—Chinese water chestnuts grow underwater in mud, have brown or black scalelike leaves, and are round, though somewhat flattened. They are the roots of an aquatic plant that grows in freshwater ponds, marshes, lakes, and slow-moving rivers and streams in Japan, Taiwan, China, Thailand, and Australia. They are difficult to harvest, explaining their generally high price. Chinese water chestnuts have mildly sweet, crisp, white flesh.

The European water chestnut or water caltrop has seed capsules with four spikes and is named after the caltrop, a vicious medieval weapon with four iron points. This hard-shelled ebony black fruit has two prominent, downcurved horns resembling a bull's head and a woody, sculptured surface that looks like a face or a bat. It grows abundantly in Indonesia, Southeast Asia, southern

China, Japan, Italy, and tropical America. Its Chinese name, *ling ko*, means "spiritual horn." There is also a slate brown European caltrop that has been eaten in Europe since prehistoric times.

Season:

Fresh Chinese water chestnuts are sold primarily in Asian food markets. Though available year-round, they are most plentiful from early summer through late fall. Water caltrops are also sold in Asian food markets. In China, water caltrops are harvested and consumed during the mid-autumn festival to celebrate the overthrow of the Mongolians in ancient China.

Purchase:

Fresh water chestnuts should look muddy but smooth, except for a few leaf scales. They should be hard and completely free of soft spots. Water caltrops are hard-shelled and quite tough.

Avoid:

Water chestnuts spoil easily and should be selected carefully. Press each one to check for soft spots, an indication of decay. Choose the largest ones and get more than you think you'll need because of loss from spoilage and peeling.

Storage:

Store water chestnuts, unwashed and unpeeled, in a loosely closed paper or plastic bag in the refrigerator crisper for up to 2 weeks. Keep water caltrops in a cool, dry place.

Preparation:

Chinese Water Chestnut:

1. Wash water chestnuts thoroughly in cold water to remove the surface mud.

2. Peel using a sharp paring knife, cutting away any soft or greenish spots till only creamy white firm chestnut is left.

3. Place immediately in a bowl of cold water until ready to use.

European Water Chestnut:

Note: Caltrops can be toxic if eaten raw—always boil, steam, or roast them prior to consumption.

1. Using a sharp knife, cut open the hard shell.

2. Remove the flesh.

Serving Suggestions:

Add sliced or quartered Chinese water chestnuts to Asian stir-fries. • Add chopped, steamed Chinese water chestnuts to soups, salads, rice, and stuffing. • Wrap whole steamed Chinese water chestnuts with bacon and broil.

Flavor Affinities:

Bamboo shoots, cilantro, ginger, pasta, rice, rice noodles, sesame oil, snow peas.

113. **WATERCRESS**

Other Names: American cress, garden cress, Indian cress, nasturtium, pepper cress, Peruvian cress, winter cress, yellow rocket.

General Description:
Cress is a common name for more than a dozen sharp, pungent, small-leafed plants from various families of which watercress (Nasturtium officinale) *is the most well-known.* Watercress has been eaten since ancient times, but has only been cultivated since the 19th century. Its Latin name, *Nasturtium*, comes from *nasum tortus*, meaning "twisted nose," because of its sharp, peppery kick. Succulent watercress grows wild alongside slow-running waterways in Britain, Europe, Asia, and America.

Upland cress *(Barbarea verna)* grows on dry land and has a cloverlike leaf. Its flavor is close to watercress with a mild flavor, lingering sharpness, and delicate, peppery taste. It has an elegant look because of its tiny leaves and fragility. It is grown for market in micro and mini sizes for salads and decorative garnishes.

Garden cress *(Lepidium sativum)* is a large group of cresses of African origin, with a hot-sweet peppery bite like horseradish, including curly, golden, broadleaf, and common cress. These cresses are raised as tiny sprouts for use as a salad green or garnish.

Nasturtium *(Tropaeolum majus)* is grown both for its delicious gold to scarlet blossoms and its lily pad–shaped leaves. It originated in South America, was brought from Peru to Europe in the late 17th century, and now grows proliferously in the south of France.

Season:

Watercress is available year-round. Other cresses are occasionally available.

Purchase:

Purchase watercress with deep green whole leaves. Other cresses are generally hydroponically grown and sold with their root-balls attached. They should be perky and have a peppery aroma.

Avoid:

Sniff watercress and avoid any with an unpleasant smell.

Storage:

For watercress, remove the rubber band holding it together, stand the stems in water, cover with a plastic bag, and refrigerate. Or wash, spin dry, and refrigerate in a plastic bag for up to 3 to 4 days. Store hydroponically grown cresses complete with their root-balls in a plastic bag for up to 3 to 4 days.

Preparation:

1. **Soak in cold water to revive tired leaves.**

2. **Wash under cool running water.**

3. **Pat dry with paper towels or place in a salad spinner.**

4. **Trim small cresses away from their root-balls**

with scissors. For salad or quick cooking, trim watercress leaves and discard the larger tough stems. If making soup, retain the stems.

Serving
Suggestions:
Blend watercress, scallions, and yogurt or buttermilk and serve with salmon. • Serve watercress as a bed for roast beef or roast chicken so that it wilts and absorbs the juices. • Combine sprigs of watercress, orange or ruby grapefruit segments, and toasted almonds with shreds of Chinese barbecued duck meat or confit of duck, then dress with sherry vinegar and virgin olive oil.

Flavor
Affinities:
Buttermilk, cucumber, egg, goat cheese, mushrooms, potatoes, rice, roasted meats, tofu, tomatoes, yogurt.

114. 📷 **WINGED BEAN**

Other Names:
Asparagus pea, princess pea, four-angled bean, goa bean, Manila bean.

General
Description:
The winged bean (Psophocarpus tetragonolobus)*, a member of the legume family, has a pod which in cross-section looks like a rectangle with a fringed extension at each corner.* The winged bean is a tropical legume that originated in New Guinea or Indonesia. It grows quickly and is high in protein. Rapidly becoming a staple in the hot regions where it grows, it is extensively cultivated and consumed in Burma and India. All parts of this

legume vine are edible. The pods, which are green, purple, or red, are four-sided and flare into ruffled ridges or
wings. These beans have a flavor similar to a cranberry
bean with a hint of green bean, and their texture is like
a starchy green bean. The blossoms are used to color
foods blue.

Season: Winged beans may be found in specialty produce
markets and some supermarkets year-round.

Purchase: Choose small beans with no sign of discoloration.

Storage: Refrigerate, tightly wrapped in a plastic bag, for 3 days.

Preparation:

1. **Wash under cool running water.**

2. **Trim away bruised areas and tough stem ends.**

Serving
Suggestions: Fry winged beans in a tempura batter. • Add winged
beans to curry or stir-fry.

Flavor
Affinities: Cilantro, coconut milk, curry, green chiles, mustard
seeds, onion, turmeric.

WINTER SQUASH

General
Description: *Winter squash is the American name for numerous*
varieties of hard-skinned squash of Central and South

American origin in the genus Cucurbita. The word "squash" is derived from the Algonquian word *askutasquash*—something that is eaten green, or in an unripe state, like summer squash. When we say squash, we usually mean winter squash—such as butternut, acorn, or spaghetti squash—which have a hard, inedible peel. Summer squashes (see page 297) are entirely edible. The difference is also apparent in the seeds. Winter squashes have large, tough-skinned seeds that are edible only if roasted and shelled.

Some of the major winter squash species are *Cucurbita maxima*, which includes varieties such as Hubbard, blue and red kuri, and buttercup; *Cucurbita moschata*, which includes butternut, winter crookneck, some pumpkins, and calabaza; *Cucurbita pepo*, which includes acorn, spaghetti, and pumpkin; and *Cucurbita argyrosperma* (or *mixta*), which includes the golden striped and green striped cushaw.

Acorn squash, which may be buff-colored, orange, or dark green, is the most widely available small winter squash. It has smooth, sweet flesh that is rather stringy; buff varieties have the most concentrated flavor.

Buttercup squash are stocky in shape with a turban top that enlarges as the squash matures. Many people consider buttercup to be the best hard squash. When baked, the fine, dry flesh is smooth and tastes of roasted chestnuts and sweet potato.

Butternut squash is the most common all-purpose squash because of its abundant, firm flesh. It has a thick neck attached to a bulbous bottom and smooth buff skin. The meat of the butternut is a blazing orange and it has a creamy texture once cooked.

Calabaza is a general name for warm-climate pumpkins. In the U.S., calabaza has become the name for a round or pear-shaped large squash with mottled skin that may be deep green, orange, amber, or buff and speckled or striated, but always relatively smooth and hard-shelled when mature. Calabaza is often sold in large chunks. Unlike other pumpkins, it is grown primarily in warm climates and is available year-round.

Delicata is an old variety that has been revived. Petite to medium in size, this oblong squash has yellow-ivory skin with spruce green stripes inside the ridges. The light, sweet, yellow flesh is fine and moist. It will not keep for long because of its relatively thin skin.

Green striped cushaw is a longtime gardener's favorite and often shows up at farmers' markets. It has a bulbous bottom and thin neck with relatively thin skin and moist, rather coarse flesh.

Hubbard is a term for a group of large to huge squash that may be bluish, gray, orange, dark green, or light green and are mostly teardrop or top-shaped.

Jarrahdale pumpkin is an Australian cultivar that looks like a small "classic" pumpkin with heavily lobed sides but has celadon green skin. Its deep orange flesh is extremely smooth and creamy.

Kabocha is both a generic grouping and a marketing name in the U.S. applied to many strains of Japanese pumpkin and winter squash with fine flavor, rich sweetness, and dense, almost fiberless flesh. Varieties include Delicata and **green and orange Hokkaido** (with rough mottled skin). They all have deep flavor, honeyed sweetness, and fine-grained, extremely dense flesh. **Kuri**, or **orange Hokkaido**, are teardrop-shaped Japanese squash. They have smooth, deep red skin and deep yellow flesh and are similar to golden Hubbards.

Pumpkin is a term applied to nearly all hard-skinned squash. What is considered "pumpkin" changes from country to country and region to region. In the U.S. the term generally means a large rounded orange squash of the type used for jack-o'-lanterns. Miniature pumpkins are cream or orange in color with sweet, firm, flavorful flesh. Some may have edible skin.

Spaghetti squash is grown specifically for its prominent fibers. It is usually golden yellow in color with a lightly sweet, mild flavor and a thin hard shell. The larger the squash, the thicker the strands, which may be steamed and dressed like pasta.

Sweet Dumpling squash is a Japanese variety that is solid and plump. It is warm cream in color with ivy green stripes inside the ridges. The sweet, pale yellow flesh is fine and dry textured like a potato.

Season:

September and October are the best months for squash. Squash grown in colder areas will have more flavor and sweetness than quicker growing squash from warmer areas. Most squash is available year-round.

Purchase:	Choose rock-solid squash. Press as hard as you can to make sure there is no give. Look for firm, full, corklike, rather than skinny or green, stems. Choose squash with matte rather than shiny skin. Choose large butternuts with a relatively small bottom and a long neck. This neck portion contains solid meat without any seeds, making it easy to cut up.
Avoid:	Do not purchase squash with soft spots or bruises.
Storage:	Keep in a cool, dry place with good air circulation. Thick-skinned varieties can last for months. The soft, moist flesh surrounding the seedpod will deteriorate quickest. If that area is mushy, you've stored your squash too long. However, the "neck" area will probably still be firm and usable.
Preparation:	1. **Wash any winter squash in cool water.**
	2. **If the skin is thin, peel it using a vegetable peeler or a sharp paring knife prior to cutting into pieces or baking.**
	3. **If the squash has thick skin, it is generally cut in half and baked with the skin on. After cutting in half, scoop out the seeds with a spoon.**
Serving Suggestions:	Bake squash topped with brown sugar or maple syrup and a pat of butter in the empty seed cavity. ▪ Shred

squash and mix with an equal amount of standard pancake batter, then cook these savory pancakes on a griddle and top with salsa, tomato sauce, or sour cream. •
Fry cut, peeled raw hard squash in a tempura batter. •
Add cubes of squash to braised lamb shanks, beef stew, or chicken 15 minutes before the meat is done.

Flavor Affinities: Butter, couscous, garlic, honey, lamb, maple syrup, olive oil, onion, pasta, rosemary, sage, savory, thyme.

116.   **YARD-LONG BEAN**

Other Names: Asparagus bean, *bodi* or *boonchi* (West Indies), *dow gauk* (China), snake bean.

General Description: *Yard-long beans* (Vigna unguiculata) *are members of the legume family, closely related to black-eyed peas.* Yard-long beans are pencil thin with thin flexible pods that grow as much as 3 feet (1 m) long, though they are normally picked at 1½ feet (.5 m). Yard-long beans have been cultivated so long their origins are unknown, but Africa and Asia are most probable. They have been grown in China since prehistoric times and remain an important crop there. Yard-long beans are also grown in the Far East, Africa, the Mediterranean, and the Caribbean. They have a pronounced flavor with a dense, solid texture that is chewy when cooked.

Season:	Yard-long beans are available year-round, primarily in Asian markets.

Purchase:	Choose thin, relatively smooth, blemish-free beans without noticeable bulging.

Avoid:	Do not buy yard-long beans with overly developed seeds in bumpy pods or dry, limp, or rusty-looking beans.

Storage:	Store yard-long beans in plastic in the refrigerator for 2 to 3 days

Preparation:

1.   **Cut off both ends.**

2.   **Cut into suitable lengths, from 2 to 6 inches (5–15 cm) long.**

Serving Suggestions:	Deep-fry yard long beans, a popular Asian method of preparing them. • Add short lengths of yard-long beans to vegetable or meat stews and simmer together about 20 minutes. • Add short lengths of slow-cooked yard-long beans to fried rice. • Braise yard-long beans with strong flavored condiments such as Chinese fermented black beans, ginger, fish sauce, tamarind, or chili sauce.

Flavor Affinities:	Asian chili sauce, Chinese fermented black beans, coconut milk, curry, garlic, ginger, onion, sausage, soy sauce, tamarind.

117.   **YUCA**

Other Names: Cassava, mandioca, manioc.

General
Description:

Yuca (Manihot esculenta) *is a bland, brown-skinned starchy tuber that is native to Brazil.* In Brazil, this classic vegetable is known as *aipim* as a fresh vegetable and *mandioca* when processed for flour. Yuca was first domesticated by Amazon Indians thousands of years ago. Their name for manioc, *sekatsi*, meant "food." Yuca is widely used today throughout the Caribbean, Central America, South America, Indonesia, and Polynesia.

Amazonians bred two types of yuca: sweet and bitter. Both types contain two substances that react together to produce poisonous prussic acid as soon as the tubers are uprooted. Sweet yuca *(Manihot dulcis)*, the kind sold in U.S. markets, has a lower yield than bitter yuca but contains only a small amount of poison, which is concentrated in the skin. After peeling and cooking, sweet yuca may be safely eaten and will have a sweet, nutty flavor and creamy, rich texture. Bitter yuca is specially treated to form flakes, seeds, and pearls of tapioca. Note that yuca is not the same as yucca, though the two are often confused. Yucca is related to the agave plant from which tequila is distilled.

Season: Yuca is available year-round, especially at Asian and Hispanic markets.

Purchase:	Look for firm, evenly shaped cylindrical spears of yuca that are rock hard. Note that yuca is normally waxed.
Avoid:	There should be no streaks or darkening near the skin when the yuca is cut open. Avoid yuca with soft spots, blemishes, bald spots, mold, hairline cracks, or stickiness.
Storage:	Yuca can be stored at room temperature for up to 1 week. Store peeled yuca covered in water in the refrigerator for up to 3 days.
Preparation:	**Note: Never eat raw yuca as it contains small amounts of poisonous compounds.**

1. **Cut off and discard ¹/₂ inch (1.3 cm) off the tip and bottom of the yuca.**

2. **Pare the yuca of its outer brown skin and inner purple-colored layer until only white flesh remains, cutting away any dark areas.**

3. **Using a heavy knife, cut the yuca into lengthwise quarters, placing peeled yuca immediately in water.**

4. **There is a set of tough strings running down the center of large yuca roots. Cut away and discard the inner quarter of the yuca, which contains the strings.**

Serving Suggestions:	Boil yuca in water with a little vinegar and salt about 15 minutes or until tender and translucent, drain well, then fry in oil until golden brown and crisp, about 10 minutes, turning so the spears cook evenly, then sprinkle with a mixture of salt, chopped garlic, and pimentón (smoked Spanish paprika). • Press shredded yuca onto seasoned flounder fillets, then pan-fry and serve with chopped cilantro and a lime wedge.
Flavor Affinities:	Beef, cheese, chiles, cilantro, fish, garlic, lime, red onion, seafood, sour orange.

ZUCCHINI, SUMMER SQUASH, AND SQUASH BLOSSOMS

Other Names:	Courgette, vegetable marrow.
General Description:	*Summer (or tender) squash* (Cucurbita pepo *and others*) *are New World members of the Cucurbita family with tender skin and flesh, small edible seeds, and high moisture content.* There are many types of summer squash ranging in size from bite-sized to baseball bats. It was the Italians who first marketed summer squash in a small size and as immigrants they introduced this vegetable to the U.S. **Zucchini**, the Italian and American name for what the French and British call **courgette**, is the most common summer squash. It exists in many forms and colors, mostly commonly deep green. In Britain huge

zucchini known as **vegetable marrow** are grown and are suitable for stuffing. All types of summer squash may also be sold as baby squash, especially in farmers' markets and specialty stores.

Costata Romanesca has pale raised ribs in mottled green and is long and narrow with a slightly bulging bottom. This Roman variety may also be termed **cocozelle**, an old name for zucchini used when they were first introduced into the U.S. in the late 19th century. When solid and young, this squash is juicy and sweet but it quickly turns flabby and can be bland and bitter.

Golden zucchini has brilliant sunny yellow skin that retains its color when cooked. This squash starts out yellow rather than ripening from green. It has a bright, fresh flavor.

Middle Eastern zucchini are stocky, pale green, tapering cylinders with a thick, darker green stem. They have smooth, shiny skin that bruises easily and solid, crisp, moist, and flavorful flesh. They retain their firm texture when cooked.

Pattypan (or **cymling**) **squash** have a characteristic scalloped edge and may be flattened or bell-shaped. They may be cream, sunny yellow, celadon, pistachio, or ivy green in color, and they taste best when small. Smooth-fleshed, they are rather bland in flavor.

Round zucchini are dense and heavy for their size. They are nearly seedless with smooth-textured flesh. When cooked, the juicy, flavorful flesh has a green tint.

Squash blossoms are an extremely perishable,

edible delicacy that come from many types of squash, including winter squash varieties (see page 288). There are two types: male blossoms, which grow from the branches, and female blossoms, which bear fruit. Female blossoms have a soft, fleshy center that will spoil within 1 day. They should be picked in the morning when they open toward the sun and then sold that day. Male blossoms are hairier and not as fruity but will last longer. Squash blossoms can be found in specialty and farmers' markets, often attached to small fruits.

Tatume, which are common in Mexico, are shaped like a huge egg and weigh about 1 pound (.45 kg) each. They have dense, smooth flesh and are virtually seedless.

Yellow crooknecks have thick warty skin, heavily curved necks, sweet flavor, and crunchy texture. Newer varieties are straight with thin, soft skin, but bland flavor.

Zephyr is a hybrid of yellow crookneck and a cross between delicata and yellow acorn squash (both winter squash, see page 288). It has a sharply defined green bottom topped with yellow and resembles zucchini with a slightly bulbous bottom.

Season: Summer squash are available all year, but spring to summer is the best season for domestically grown squash.

Purchase: Choose small to medium squash with shiny, taut skin and solid flesh. Lightly scratched or slightly bruised squash are perfectly fine.

Avoid:	Overly large squash, squash with pitted skin, or those with flabby or spongy texture are all best avoided.

Storage:	Refrigerate squash in plastic for 2 to 3 days.

Preparation:

Squash:

1. **Scrub squash with a brush to remove any prickles or dirt.**

2. **Trim off the necks and bases.**

Blossoms:

1. **Open up squash blossoms and carefully inspect for insects.**

2. **Pull off and discard the dark green calyxes.**

Serving Suggestions:	Sauté thin half-moons of zucchini and yellow squash in olive oil and garlic, and serve as a side dish or toss with pasta. • Stuff squash blossoms with goat cheese and mozzarella, then briefly sauté in olive oil and serve with fresh tomato sauce.

Flavor Affinities:	Basil, chiles, corn, dill, eggplant, feta, fish, garlic, marjoram, mint, mozzarella, olive oil, goat cheese, onion, oregano, pasta, rice, thyme, tomatoes.

Sources

BOOKS

Davidson, Alan. *The Oxford Companion to Food*. Oxford: Oxford University Press, 1999.

Facciola, Stephen. *Cornucopia II: A Source Book of Edible Plants*. Vista, California: Kampong Publications, 1988.

Green, Aliza. *The Bean Bible: A Legumaniac's Guide to Lentils, Peas, and Every Edible Bean on the Planet!* Philadelphia: Running Press, 2000.

Grigson, Jane. *Jane Grigson's Fruit Book*. New York: Atheneum, 1982.

Grigson, Jane. *Jane Grigson's Vegetable Book*. Middlesex, England: Penguin Books, 1979.

Lang, Jennifer, ed. *Larousse Gastronomique*. New York: Crown Publishers, 1988.

Schneider, Elizabeth. *The Essential Reference: Vegetables from Amaranth to Zucchini*. New York: William Morrow, 2001.

Shaffer, Erica, ed. *The Guide: The Packer's 2001 Availability and Merchandising Guide*. Lenexa, Kansas: Vance Publishing Corp., 2001.

WEBSITES

Brookstropicals.com

Coosemans.com

Crfg.org/pubs/ff

Epicurious.com

Friedas.com

Fooddownunder.com

Melissas.com

Wegmans.com

Index

Numbers in **bold** (for example, **23**) are produce numbers, and can be used to locate produce in the photograph section. All other numbers are page numbers.

A

acorn squash, **115a**, 289
African horned cucumber. *See* kiwano
Agen plum, 88
aji. See pepper, chile
alfalfa sprouts, **103a**, 261, 262
All Red potato, 238, 239
alligator pear. *See* avocado
amaranth, **47a–b**, 111–13
Amarilla cactus pear, 18–19
American "cantaloupe," 29a, 61–62
American cress. *See* watercress
Amish paste tomato, 275
Anaheim pepper, **92a**, 230
Angelino plum, 88
anone. See cherimoya
apaz onion, 219, 220
apple, **1a–l**, 1–6
apple pear. *See* Asian pear
apricot, **2**, 6–8
Armenian cucumber, 169–70
artichoke and cardoon, **48a–b**, 52, 113–16, 229
arugula, **49**, 116–18
Asian chestnut, 158
Asian cucumber, 170
Asian eggplant, **70a**, 174
Asian pear, **3**, 8–10, 56
Asian sweet potato, 266
asparagus, **50a–b**, 119–21, 182, 249
asparagus bean. *See* yard-long bean
asparagus pea. *See* winged bean

Asparation, 139
atemoya, 21–22
atoca. See cranberry
avocado, **51a–b**, 121–23

B

B potato, 238
Babcock peach, **33a**, 75
baby corn, **66a**, 164
baby kiwifruit, 47
baby potato, 238
Baby Sugar Loaf pineapple, 85
Balegal pomegranate, 90
bamboo shoots, **52**, 124–26, 284
bamia. See okra
banana and plantain, **4a–d**, 10–13
Barbary pear. *See* cactus pear
Bartlett pear, **34b**, 78, 79, 80
Batavian endive, 176–77, 177–78
Batavian lettuce, 199
beans, green, **53**, 126–28
beans, shell, **54a–d**, 128–31, 244
bearberry. *See* cranberry
Beauregard yam, **105a**, 265
Beauty seedless grape, 39
beech mushroom, 207
beefsteak tomato, **109a**, 166, 276
beet, **55a–c**, 132–35
Beit Alpha cucumber, 169
Belgian endive. *See* chicory
Bermuda onion, 219
bhindi. *See* okra
Bibb lettuce, **81a**, 199, 201
Bi-Colored corn, **66b**, 163–64

bilberry, 17
Bing cherry, **9a**, 23
bitter greens, 110
Black Amber plum, **37a**, 88
Black Beauty eggplant, **70b**, 174
Black Krim tomato, 275
Black Mission fig, 37
black oyster plant. *See* salsify and scorzonera
black radish, **96a**, 245, 246
black raspberry, 96
Black Seeded Simpson lettuce, 199
black trumpet mushroom, 206–7, 210
blackberry, **5**, 13–16, 102, 251
black-eyed peas, **54d**, 129, 130
blanched celery, 152, 153
blanched curly endive, 176, 177, 179
blood orange, 66
blue potato, 238, 239
blueberry, **6a–b**, 16–18, 102
boiling onion, 219
boiling potato, 239, 240
bok choy, **56**, 136–38
bok choy sum, 136
boniato sweet potato, 266, 267
Bosc pear, **34c**, 78, 79, 80
Boston lettuce, **81b**, 199, 201
boysenberry, 14, 15
Braeburn apple, 1, **1a**
Braganza cabbage, 145
bramble. *See* blackberry
brandywine tomato, **109b**, 275
broccoflower, **57b**, 138
broccoli, **57a–c**, 138–41, 185
broccoli rabe, **57c**, 138–41,
broccoli romanesco, 138, 139, 141
broccolini, 139
brown Turkey fig, 37

Brussels sprouts, **59d**, 145, 146, 147
Buddha's hand citron, **10b**, 25
buffalo-head fruit. *See* water chestnut
bull nut. *See* water chestnut
Burbank plum, 88
burdock, **58**, 142–44
Burpee Big Boy tomato, 276
burro banana, **4a**, 11
bush greens. *See* amaranth
Butter and Sugar corn, 163–64
butter pear. *See* avocado
buttercup squash, **115b**, 289
butterhead lettuce, 199
butternut squash, **115c**, 289–90, 292

C
cabbage, **59a–d**, 144–47, 224
cactus leaves. *See* nopales
cactus paddles. *See* nopales
cactus pear, **7**, 18–20
calabaza squash, **115d**, 290
Calabrese broccoli, **57a**, 138
California red endive, 161, 162–63
calimyrna fig, 37
Calmeria grape, 39
candy cane beet, **55b**, 132
cantaloupe, **29a**, 61, 62, 63, 64
cape gooseberry. *See* tomatillo and ground cherry
Cara Cara orange, 66
carambola. *See* star fruit
Cardinal grape, 39
Cardona cactus pear, 18–19
cardoon. *See* artichoke and cardoon
"Caribbean" avocado, **51a**, 122
carrot, **60**, 144, 147–49, 249
casaba melon, **29b**, 62, 64
cassava. *See* yuca
Casselman plum, 88
Catalan chicory. *See* chicory

Catalonia. *See* chicory
cauliflower, **61**, 149–51
Cavaillon, 62
Cavendish banana, **4b**, 11
celeriac, **62b**, 152–53, 154–55
celery, 6, **62a–b**, 149, 152–55
celery root. *See* celeriac
celtuce, 199
cèpe, 205, 209, 210, 211
champion quince, 94
chanterelle mushroom, **84a**, 207, 210, 212
chard. *See* Swiss chard
Charentais melon, 61
chayote, **63**, 155–57
cherimoya, **8**, 20–22, 29
cherry, **9a–b**, 23–25, 77
cherry hot pepper, 230
cherry tomato, **109c**, 276
chestnut, **64**, 147, 157–59
chicory, **65a–c**, 160–63
chili pepper. *See* pepper, chile
Chinese apple. *See* pomegranate
Chinese artichokes. *See* crosnes
Chinese broccoli, 139, 140–41
Chinese celery, 153
Chinese gooseberry. *See* kiwifruit
Chinese water chestnut, **112a**, 282, 283, 284
Chioggia beet, **55b**, 132
chirimolla. See cherimoya
chocho. See chayote
chorogi. See crosnes
choy sum, 136
christophine. See chayote
cipollini onion, 219, 222
citron, **10**, 25–26
clementine, **45a**, 107, 108
Clingstone peach and nectarine, 74–75
clover sprouts, 261

cocktail avocado, 122
cococasia. *See* taro and yautia
coconut, **11**, 27–29
cocoyam. *See* taro and yautia
cozelle, 298
collard greens, **76a**, 187, 190
Comice pear, 78–79, 80
common American cucumber, **68a**, 168, 170
Concord grape, **17a**, 39, 40
cooking greens. *See* greens, cooking
corn, **66a–c**, 163–66
corn salad. *See* mâche
Cortland apple, 2, 4–5
cos lettuce, 200–201
Costata Romanesca, 298
courgette. *See* zucchini, summer squash, and squash blossoms
couve tronchuda, 145
crabapple, **1l**, 2, 4, 6
cranberry, **12**, 29–31, 49
cranberry bean, **54a**, 129, 130
creamer potato, 238
cremini mushroom, **84b**, 206, 207, 211
Crenshaw melon, **29c**, 62, 63, 64
crisphead lettuce, 199
Crispin apple, 2, 4–5
crosier. *See* fiddlehead fern
crosnes, **67**, 166–68
cubanelle pepper, **92b**, 230
cucumber, **68a–c**, 168–71
curly endive, **71a**, 176, 177–78
curly spinach, **102a**, 259, 260
currant, **13a–b**, 31–33, 269
custard apple. *See* cherimoya
custard marrow. *See* chayote
cymling squash, 298

D
daikon radish, **96b**, 245, 246, 247

Damson plum, 88
Dancy tangerine, **45c**, 107
dandelion greens, **76b**, 188, 190
dasheen. *See* taro and yautia
date, **14**, 33–34
date plum, 35, 81–84
David Sun peach, 74
Deglet Noor date, 34
Del Monte Gold pineapple, **36a**, 85
Delicata squash, 290, 291
dill sprouts, 261
donut peach, 75
Duke cherry, 23
Duncan grapefruit, **18a**, 41, 42
durian, **15**, 35–36
Dutch cucumber, **68b**, 168–69
Dutch parsley. *See* parsley root
Dutch shallot, 257
dwarf cape gooseberry. *See* tomatillo
    and ground cherry

E
Early Wonderful pomegranate, 90
edamame, **69**, 171–73
eggplant, **70a–d**, 173–76
El Dorado plum, 88
Elegant Lady peach, **33b**, 74
elephant garlic, **74a**, 183
Elephant Heart plum, 88
Emerald Beaut plum, 88
Emperor grape, 39
Empire apple, 2, 5
endive, **71a–b**, 176–78
English peas. *See* peas
enoki mushroom, 206, 207, 211
escarole, **71b**, 176–77, 177–78
etrog citron, 26
Eureka lemon, **23a**, 50
European blueberry, 17
European gooseberry. *See* currant

European water chestnut, 282–83, 284
evergreen blackberry, 14
Evergreen tomato, **109a**, 275

F
Fairchild tangerine, 107
Fairtime peach, 74
fava bean, **54b**, 129, 130, 131
Femminello Ovale lemon, 50
fennel, 52, 69, **72**, 178–81
fiddlehead fern, **73**, 181–82
field salad. *See* mâche
fig, **16**, 36–38
filet. *See* beans, green
"finger" avocado, 122
fingerling potato, **94a**, 238, 239
Fino lemon, 50
five-angled fruit. *See* star fruit
Flame seedless grape, **17b**, 39
flat peach, 75
flat-leafed spinach, **102b**, 259, 260
Flame seedless grape, **17b**, 39
Flavorcrest peach, 74
Fleshman pomegranate, 90
Florida avocado, **51a**, 122
flowering kale, 188
Forelle pear, 79, 80
four-angled bean. *See* winged bean
freestone peach and nectarine, **33c**, 74,
    75
French breakfast radish, 245, 247
French cornichon, 169
French endive. *See* chicory
Friar plum, 88
frisée, 176, 177, 179
Fuji apple, **1b**, 2
Fuyu persimmon, 81, 82, 83

G
Gala apple, **1c**, 2–3

Galia melon, **29d**, 61, 62, 64
Galician cabbage, 145
garden peas. *See* peas
garlic, **74a–b**, 182–85
Garnet yam, **105b**, 265
German Butterball potato, 238, 240
German parsley. See parsley root
gherkin, **68c**, 169
ginger, **75**, 185–87
glasswort. *See* samphire
gold kiwifruit, **21b**, 47
Goldcat apricot, 7
golden apple. *See* quince
golden beet, **55c**, 132
Golden corn, 164
Golden Delicious apple, **1d**, 3
Golden Nectar plum, 88
golden raspberry, **40a**, 96
golden zucchini, **118b**, 298
gombo. *See* okra
gooseberry. *See* currant
granadilla. *See* passion fruit
Granny Smith apple, **1e**, 3
grape, **17a–c**, 38–40, 84
grapefruit and pomelo, **18a–d**, 40–43
Gravenstein apple, 3
gray French shallot, 256–57
green beans. *See* beans, green
green garlic, 183
green globe artichoke, **48a**, 113
Green Globe pomegranate, 90
green grape tomato, 275
green Hokkaido, 291
green oak leaf lettuce, 199
green onion, **88a**, 219, 221
green striped cushaw, 290
Greengage plum, 88
greens, cooking, **76a–d**, 187–90
ground cherry. *See* tomatillo and
    ground cherry

guava, **19**, 43–45, 73
Guinea Verde banana, 11

H
habanero pepper, **92c**, 230–31
Hachiya persimmon, 81–82, 83
Hamburg parsley. *See* parsley root
hardneck garlic, 183
hardy kiwifruit, 47
Harglow apricot, 7
haricots verts. *See* beans, green
Hass avocado, **51b**, 122, 123
Hawaiian papaya, 69–70
hedged gourd. *See* kiwano
hedgehog mushroom, 207–8, 210
heung kunn, 153
highbush blueberry, 16
Honey Murcott tangor, 107
Honey tangor, 107
Honeybell tangelo, 107
honeydew melon, **29e**, 20, 62–63
hon-shimeji mushroom, 207
horn chestnut. *See* water chestnut
horned melon. *See* kiwano
horseradish, **77**, 135, 190–92, 224
hothouse tomato, 276
hubbard squash, **115e**, 290
huckleberry, **6b**, 16
Hungarian wax pepper, 231
husk tomato. *See* tomatillo and ground
    cherry

I
Ice Cream banana, 11
iceberg lettuce, **81c**, 199, 200–201
Idared apple, 3, 5
Indian date. *See* tamarind
Indian fig. *See* cactus pear
Indian mango, 58
Indian pear. *See* cactus pear

Italian eggplant, 174
Italian frying pepper, 230
Italian prune, 88
Italian red onion, **88b**, 219, 220, 221
ivory white eggplant, **70d**, 174

J
Jaffa orange, 66
jalapeño pepper, **92d**, 231, 234
jamberry. *See* tomatillo and ground cherry
Japanese artichokes. *See* crosnes
Japanese citrus. *See* yuzu
Japanese cucumber, 170
Japanese horseradish. *See* wasabi
Japanese medlar. *See* loquat
Japanese plum. *See* loquat
Jarrahdale pumpkin, 290
jelly melon. *See* kiwano
Jersey shallot, 256–57
Jersey Yellow sweet potato, 265
Jerusalem artichoke. *See* sunchoke
jewel yam, **105c**, 265
jicama, 54, 60, **78**, 192–94
Jonathan apple, 3, 4
Jonagold apple, **1f**, 3, 4–5
July Red nectarine, 74
juniper berry, 147

K
kabocha, 290–91
kadota fig, 37
kaffir lime, 234
kaki, 35, 81–84
kale, **76d**, 188, 190
Kandy Korn, 164
Kelsey plum, 88
Key lime, **24a**, 52, 53, 54
kintsai, 153
Kirby cucumber, 169

kiwano, **20**, 45–46
kiwifruit, **21a–b**, 46–48
knob celery, 152–53, 154–55
kohlrabi, **79**, 194–96
Kona Sugarloaf pineapple, 85
Korean radish, 245, 246
kuawa. *See* guava
kumquat, **22**, 48–49
kuri Hokkaido, 291

L
lady's finger. *See* okra
lamb's lettuce. *See* mâche
Laroda plum, 88
leaf celery, 152
leek, **80**, 196–98, 226, 278
lemon, **23a–b**, 48–52
lentil sprouts, 261
lettuce, **81a–e**, 198–201, 229, 247
lily root. *See* lotus root
lima bean, **54c**, 129, 130, 131
lime, **24a–b**, 52–54
limestone lettuce, 199, 201
ling ko. *See* water chestnut
lobster mushroom, **84c**, 208, 210, 212
loganberry, 14, 15
Lolla Rosa lettuce, 199
long white potato, 238–39, 240
looseleaf lettuce, **81b**, 199, 200
loquat, **25**, 54–56
lotus root, **82**, 201–3
lowbush blueberry, 16
Lunario lemon, 50
lychee, **26**, 54, 56–57

M
Macabu banana, 11
mâche, **83**, 204–5
Macoun apple, 3, 4
maitake mushroom, 208

maize. *See* corn
malanga. *See* taro and yautia
mamao. *See* papaya
Mandarin orange. *See* tangerine, tangelo, and tangor
mandioca. *See* yuca
mango, **27**, 58–60
manioc. *See* yuca
Manzano banana, 11
marionberry, 14–15
Mariposa plum, 88
marmelo. *See* quince
marrone chestnut, 158
Marsh grapefruit, 41, 42
Marsh Ruby grapefruit, 41, 42
matsutake mushroom, 110, 208, 210, 212
Maui onion, 220
May Glo nectarine, 74
Maycrest peach, 74
Mayfire nectarine, 74
McIntosh Red apple, **1g**, 2, 3–4
Medjool date, 34
medlar, **28**, 60–61
Meerfenchel. *See* samphire
Meiwa kumquat, 48
melon, **29a–f**, 61–65
Merveille des Quartre Saisons lettuce, 199
Mexican green tomato. *See* tomatillo and ground cherry
Mexican papaya, 69, 70, 71
Mexican water chestnut. *See* jicama
Meyer lemon, **23b**, 50–51, 52
Middle Eastern cucumber, 169
Middle Eastern zucchini, 298
Minneola tangelo, 107
Mirabelle plum, 88
mirliton. *See* chayote

monkey peach. *See* kiwifruit
Moongold apricot, 7
Moonpark apricot, 7
morel mushroom, **84d**, 182, 208, 210
Mr. Stripy's tomato, **109d**, 275
mung bean sprouts, **103b**, 261, 262
mushroom, **84a–i**, 205–12
muskmelon, 61–62, 63
mustard greens, **76c**, 188–89, 190

N
Nagami kumquat, 48
Nancy Hall sweet potato, 265
napa cabbage, **85**, 212–14
nasturtium. *See* watercress
Natal Queen pineapple, 85
navel orange, **30a**, 67
nectarine. *See* peach and nectarine
netted melon, 61–62, 63
New Mexico pepper, 231
new potato, 237, 239, 240, 241
Niño banana, 11, 13
nopal. *See* cactus pear
nopales, **86**, 214–16
Nubiana plum, 88–89
nut lettuce. *See* mâche

O
ocomo. *See* taro and yautia
O'Henry peach, 74
Okinawa sweet potato, 266
okra, **87**, 216–17
onion, **88a–e**, 218–22
onion, red, 69, 166, 194, 244, 297
onion, sweet, 104, 110, 147, 256
onion sprouts, 261
orange, **30a–b**, 65–69
orange Hokkaido, 291
Orlando tangelo, 107
Oro Blanco, 41, 42

Ortanique tangor, 107
ostrich fern. *See* fiddlehead fern
oxheart cherry, 23
oyster mushroom, **84e**, 209
oyster plant. *See* salsify and scorzonera

P

Packham pear, **34d**, 79
pak choi. *See* bok choy
papaya, 29, **31**, 48, 69–71, 73
parsley root, **89**, 222–24
parsnip, **90**, 224–26
Pascal green celery, 152, 153
pasilla pepper, 231–32
passion fruit, **32**, 71–73
pattypan squash, **118c**, 298
pea sprouts, 261
pea tendrils, 227, 228
peach and nectarine, **33a–c**, 71, 73–77, 97
peach tomato, 275
pear, **34a–d**, 40, 77–80, 97
pearl onion, **88c**, 219, 220, 221, 222
peas, **91a–c**, 226–29, 249
pepino melon, 63, 64
pepper, chile, **92a–g**, 229–34
pepper, sweet bell, **93a–d**, 235–37
perfumed quince, 94
Persian cucumber, 169
Persian lime, **24b**, 53, 54
Persian melon, 61–62, 63, 64
persimmon, **35**, 81–84
petit pois. *See* peas
Philippine mango, 58
Phoenicia pomegranate, 90
pickle plant. *See* samphire
pineapple, **36a–b**, 84–87
pineapple quince, 93–94
pineapple tomato, 275
pink Brandywine tomato, 275

Pink Lady apple, **1h**, 4–5
pink lotus. *See* lotus root
plantain. *See* banana and plantain
pleurotte mushroom, 209
plum, **37a–c**, 77, 87–89
poblano pepper, **92e**, 231–32, 234
pole bean. *See* beans, green
pomegranate, **38**, 84, 90–92
pomelo. *See* grapefruit and pomelo
porcini mushroom, **84f**, 205, 209, 210, 211
portobello mushroom, **84g**, 206, 209, 212
Portugal cabbage, 145
Portugal quince, 94
potato, **94a–e**, 237–42
potato bean. *See* jicama
precoce radicchio, 243
prickly pear. *See* cactus pear
princess pea. *See* winged bean
pumpkin, **115f**, 291
pumpkin sprouts, 261
puntarelle, 161
purple passion fruit, 73
purple potato, **94b**, 238, 239

Q

Quetsche plum, 88
quince, **39**, 93–95

R

radicchio, **95**, 242–44
radicchio di Verona, 243
radicchio rosso di Chioggia, 242–43
radicchio rosso di Treviso, 243
radicchio variegato di Castelfranco, 243
radish, **96a–c**, 245–47
radish sprouts, 261
rainbow chard, **106a**, 268
Rainier cherry, **9b**, 23, 24

ramp, **97**, 248–49
rapini, 138–39
raspberry, **40a–b**, 95–97
red banana, **4c**, 11
Red Beauty plum, **37b**, 89
Red Belgian endive, **65c**, 160
red bliss potato, 239, 240
red Brandywine tomato, 275
red cabbage, **59b**, 144–45, 146, 147
red corn, 164
red currant tomato, 275–76
Red Delicious apple, **1i**, 4
Red Diamond nectarine, 75
Red Globe grape, 39
red globe radish, **96c**, 245, 246
red micro amaranth, **47b**, 111
red oakleaf lettuce, 199
red raspberry, **40b**, 96
Red Sails lettuce, 199
Red Spanish pineapple, 85
Red Top peach, 74
Redhaven peach, 74
Redheart plum, 89
rhubarb, **98**, 250–51
riccia, 176, 177, 179
Rich Lady peach, 74
rocket salad. *See* arugula
rocotillo pepper, 232
romaine lettuce, **81e**, 200–201
Rome Beauty apple, 4, 5
round red potato, **94c**, 239, 240
round white potato, 239
round zucchini, 298
Royale cherry, 23
ruby chard, **106c**, 268
russet potato, **94d**, 237, 239, 240, 241
Russian Banana potato, 238, 239
rutabaga. *See* turnip and rutabaga
Ryan Sun peach, 74

S
sabra fruit. *See* cactus pear
salicornia. *See* samphire
salsify and scorzonera, **99a–b**, 251–54
samphire, **100**, 254–56
sand pear. *See* Asian pear
Santa Rosa plum, **37c**, 88
Satsuma plum, 88
Satsuma tangerine, **45d**, 107
Savoy cabbage, **59c**, 145, 146, 147
savoy spinach, **102a**, 259, 260
scallions. *See* green onion
scorzonera. *See* salsify and scorzonera
Scotch bonnet pepper, **92f**, 231
sea bean. *See* samphire
sea kale cabbage, 145
sea pickle. *See* samphire
seakale beet. *See* Swiss chard
Seckel pear, 79, 80
semi-freestone peach, 74
September Red nectarine, 74–75
serrano pepper, **92g**, 232, 235
Seville orange, 67
shallot, **101**, 256–58
Shanghai choy, 136
Sharon fruit (cactus pear). *See* cactus pear
Sharon fruit (persimmon), 82, 83
shell beans. *See* beans, shell
shiitake mushroom, **84h**, 206, 209, 211, 212
Sicilian eggplant, 174
Sicilian plum tomato, **109e**, 275, 277
Silver Queen corn, **66c**, 164
Simka plum, 89
Smooth Cayenne pineapple, 85
snake bean. *See* yard-long bean
snap bean. *See* beans, green
snow peas, **91b**, 227, 228–29, 284
softneck garlic, **74b**, 183

sour cherry, 23, 25
sour orange, 13, 297
soursop, 21, 22
South African Baby pineapple, **36b**, 85–86
soybean sprouts, 261, 262
spaghetti squash, **115g**, 291
Spanish onion, 219–20
sparrowgrass. *See* asparagus
spinach, **102a–b**, 135, 185, 258–60
Spring Lady peach, 74
spring onion, 220
Spring Red nectarine, 75
sprouts, **103a–b**, 260–62
squash blossoms. *See* zucchini, summer squash, and squash blossoms
star fruit, **41**, 46, 48, 60, 73, 97–99
Star Ruby grapefruit, **18b**, 41, 42
strawberry, **42**, 45, 56, 99–102, 251
strawberry tomato. *See* tomatillo and ground cherry
string bean. *See* beans, green
Sugar Giant peach, 75
sugar snap peas, **91c**, 227–29
Sugarone grape, 39
Summer Bright nectarine, 74
Summer Fire nectarine, 74–75
Summer Grand nectarine, 75
Summer Lady peach, 74
summer squash. *See* zucchini, summer squash, and squash blossoms
Sunburst tangerine, 107
sunchoke, **104**, 262–64
sunflower sprouts, 261
Sungold apricot, 7
sunroot. *See* sunchoke
suntan pepper, 235
sweet anise. *See* fennel
sweet bell pepper. *See* pepper, sweet bell
Sweet Dumpling squash, 291

sweet kumquat, 48
sweet lime, 53
sweet mini pepper, 235, 236
sweet potato, 69, 87, **105a–b**, 224, 264–67
Sweet Spineless pineapple, 85
Sweetie corn, 164
sweetsop, 21
Swiss chard, **106a–c**, 267–69

T
tamar hindi. See tamarind
tamarillo, **43**, 102–4
tamarind, **44**, 104–6, 294
tampala. *See* amaranth
tangerine, tangelo, and tangor, **45a–d**, 106–8
tannia. *See* taro and yautia
tardivo radicchio, 243
taro and yautia, **107a–b**, 269–72
tat soi, 136
tatume, 299
Taxi tomato, 275
tayberry, 15
Temple tangor, 107
Thai dragon, 232
Thai hot pepper, 232
Thompson seedless grape, **17c**, 39
Tientsin cabbage. *See* napa cabbage
tigerella tomato, 275
Tokay grape, 39
tomatillo and ground cherry, **108a–b**, 272–74
tomato, **109a–e**, 274–78
tree melon. *See* papaya
tree tomato. *See* tamarillo
Treviso, 243
Tropea onion, 220
trout pear, 79, 80
"true" shallot, 256–57

trumpet of death mushroom, 206–7, 210
tuna fig. *See* cactus pear
turnip and rutabaga, **110a–b**, 278–80
turnip greens, 188, 189
turnip-rooted celery, 152–53, 154–55
turnip-rooted parsley. *See* parsley root
Tuscan kale, 131, 188, 189, 190

U
Ugli (uniq), 41–42
upland cress, **113**, 285

V
Valencia orange, **30b**, 67
Valeria lettuce, 199
valerianella. *See* mâche
vegetable bamboo, 124
vegetable pear. *See* chayote
Vidalia onion, **88d**, 220–21
viper's grass. *See* salsify and scorzonera

W
Walla Walla onion, 220, 221
wasabi, **111**, 280–81
water caltrop. *See* water chestnut
water chestnut, 57, **112a–b**, 282–84
watercress, 43, **113**, 182, 285–87
watermelon, **29f**, 20, 63, 64
watermelon radish, 246
wax bean. *See* beans, green
West Indian gherkin, 169
wheat sprouts, 261
white beans, 147, 258
white beet, 132
white celery mustard. *See* bok choy
white icicle radish, 246
White Lady peach, 75
white mushroom, **84i**, 205, 206, 209–10, 212

white onion, **88e**, 220, 222
White Queen tomato, 275
white salsify, 252
white-fleshed peach and nectarine, 75, 76
whortleberry, 17
Wickson plum, 88
wild leeks. *See* ramps
Winesap apple, **1j**, 4–5
winged bean, **114**, 287–88
winter greens, 205
winter melon, 62
winter squash, 69, **115a–g**, 288–93
Wonderful pomegranate, 90

Y
yam. *See* sweet potato
yam bean root. *See* jicama
yard-long bean, **116**, 293–94
yautia. *See* taro and yautia
yautia amarilla, 270–71
yautia blanca, 270
yautia lila, 270
yellow bean. *See* beans, green
yellow crookneck, 299
yellow currant tomato, 275–76
yellow Finn potato, 239
yellow passion fruit, 73
yellow tomato, 276
yellow-flesh potato, 239, 240
York apple, **1k**, 4, 5
yuca, **117**, 295–97
Yukon gold potato, **94e**, 239, 241
yuzu, **46**, 109–10

Z
zephyr, 299
Zinfandel grape, 39
zucchini, summer squash, and squash blossoms, **118a–d**, 237, 297–300